Stanley Elkin

Twayne's United States Authors Series

Frank Day, Editor

Clemson University

TUSAS 568

STANLEY ELKIN.
Photo copyright © 1990 by David C. Dougherty. Used by permission.

Stanley Elkin

By David C. Dougherty

Loyola College in Maryland

Twayne Publishers
A Division of G. K. Hall & Co. • *Boston*

Stanley Elkin
David C. Dougherty

Copyright 1991 by G. K. Hall & Co.
All rights reserved.
Published by Twayne Publishers
A division of G. K. Hall & Co.
70 Lincoln Street
Boston, Massachusetts 02111

Copyediting supervised by Barbara Sutton.
Book production by Nancy Priest.
Book design by Barbara Anderson.
Typeset in 11 pt. Garamond
by Compositors Corporation, Cedar Rapids, Iowa.

First published 1990.
10 9 8 7 6 5 4 3 2 1

Library of Congress Cataloging-in-Publication Data
Dougherty, David C.
    Stanley Elkin / by David C. Dougherty.
       p.   cm. — (Twayne's United States authors series ; TUSAS 568)
    Includes bibliographical references.
    ISBN 0-8057-7616-8 (alk. paper)
    1. Elkin, Stanley, 1930–   —Criticism and interpretation.
I. Title. II. Series.
PS3555.L47Z64   1990
813'.54—dc20   90-39186
                                       CIP

Contents

About the Author

David C. Dougherty is professor of English at Loyola College in Maryland and adjunct professor of continuing studies at the Johns Hopkins University. He has taught briefly at Miami University and St. Johns College.

He earned his B.A. from West Liberty State College and did graduate work at Xavier University and Miami University. As a Woodrow Wilson dissertation fellow, he completed a dissertation on the narrative poetry of Robinson Jeffers.

His *James Wright* was published by Twayne in 1987. His essays appear in many professional journals and reference books. In addition to several studies of Wright and Jeffers, these include essays on John Updike, Saul Bellow, Walker Percy, John Gardner, Galway Kinnell, Raymond Chandler, Rex Stout, and Warren G. Harding. His contributions to regional newspapers treat literature as well as environmental and political issues.

Preface

While this project was in the planning phase, I expected to devote most of the study to the intense, funny rhetoric of this extraordinary wordsmith, to share my delight in his unusual and unexpected word combinations. As the work progressed, however, thematic clusters appeared. It quickly became evident that, Elkin's protests to the contrary notwithstanding, these novels exhibit a unified and challenging sense of our shared human experience. Although I hope delight in the richness of Elkin's language comes through to readers, I want to share as well my sense of the lasting importance of Stanley Elkin's work: his ability to invest in his extraordinary, often zany, characters a significant dimension of our shared human experience.

Like most other commentators on Elkin's fiction, I hope that this study communicates my enthusiasm for this talented but comparatively obscure writer and that readers will be challenged to read the novels and stories for themselves. These works should be savored and shared, for no commentary can hope to convey their richness and subtlety.

A surprising amount of good, provocative commentary on Elkin exists, and this study is indebted to the efforts of Peter Bailey, Doris Bargen, Robert Colbert, Tom LeClair, and Raymond Olderman. These and others listed in the Notes and Bibliography have taught me much, often by making me wonder about what they said, then consult the texts to confirm or revise my own interpretation. I hope this study has the same result for other readers. I have not always agreed with these writers, and I have noted appropriate differences in the text. Rather than engage in one-sided critical debate, I have noted our differences and presented my positions.

In this era of interviews, Elkin has been generous with interviewers, and his comments on his and others' work, while hyperbolic or deferential at times, indicate a trained literary scholar who knows exactly what effects he intends in each book. Authorial interviews are, however, a mixed blessing for critics. We get detailed information about the genesis and intention behind works, but this can inhibit our finding patterns of meaning the author may not be aware of in the texts. This raises the question of intention, which we thought was a "fallacy" when the new critics were new but which comes under renewed scrutiny from neohistoricists and neobiographers. I respect Elkin's authority over the texts he has invented, but when I see patterns he has not endorsed, as in *The Dick Gibson Show* and *The Magic Kingdom,* I quote his comments when possible and develop my own argument. Ideally each reader will decide who has the best textual authority and will come up with his or her own interpretation in doing so.

Many people helped in important ways with this project. My editors have been supportive, thoroughly professional, and, at appropriate times, challenging. My colleagues Dan McGuiness and Mark Osteen read and commented on selected chapters. Dan slipped many notes under my office door announcing new items by or about Elkin in the journals and second-hand bookstores offering relevant items. Mary Beverungen of the Loyola/Notre Dame Library worked cheerfully and efficiently to locate materials for me.

For two cold February days in 1989, Stanley and Joan Elkin extended their hospitality to me, and the information Stanley shared with me enriches the work. We chatted at length about his life and work, writers he likes and dislikes, movies, softball, life in general, and the intrigues of academic politics. He allowed me to shoot a roll of film, and the cover photograph comes from that session. The information he offered made the study better than it could otherwise have been, but Stanley's, Joan's, and their son Bernie's friendship is the best gift of all.

Inexpressible gratitude is due to Jill, Sam, and Carl, who remained enthusiastic about the project even on most of the days they could not play video games or listen to records in adjoining rooms because the sentences and paragraphs were not working. And Barbara, who knows.

David C. Dougherty

Loyola College in Maryland

Acknowledgments

Permission to quote from the following works is gratefully acknowledged here.

Boswell: A Modern Comedy © 1964 by Stanley Elkin; *A Bad Man* © 1965, 1967 by Stanley Elkin; *The Dick Gibson Show* © 1970, 1971 by Stanley Elkin; *The Living End* © 1977, 1978, 1979 by Stanley Elkin; *George Mills* © 1982 by Stanley Elkin; *The Magic Kingdom* © 1985 by Stanley Elkin; *Criers and Kibitzers, Kibitzers and Criers* © 1959, 1960, 1961, 1962, 1963, 1965 by Stanley Elkin. Reprinted by permission of Georges Borchardt, Inc., literary agency, for the author.

Searches and Seizures © 1973 by Stanley Elkin and *The Franchiser* © 1976 by Stanley Elkin. Reprinted by permission of David R. Godine, publisher.

The Rabbi of Lud © 1986, 1987 by Stanley Elkin. Reprinted by permission of Charles Scribner's Sons, an inprint of Macmillan Publishing Co.

"Appendix: An Interview with Stanley Elkin" by Doris Bargen, in *The Fiction of Stanley Elkin.* © 1980 by Verlag Peter D. Lang Gmbh. Reprinted by permission of Peter D. Lang, publisher.

"An Interview with Stanley Elkin" by Scott Sanders, *Contemporary Literature* 16 (1975). © 1975 by The Board of Regents of the University of Wisconsin System. "An Interview with Stanley Elkin" by Jay Clayton, *Contemporary Literature* 24 (1983). © 1983 by The Board of Regents of the University of Wisconsin System. Both reprinted by permission of the University of Wisconsin Press.

"Stanley Elkin: The Art of Fiction LXI" by Thomas LeClair, *Paris Review* 17 (Summer 1976). © 1976 by The Paris Review, Inc. Reprinted by permission of the *Paris Review.*

Chronology

1930   Stanley Lawrence Elkin born in New York 11 May, eldest son of Philip and Zelda Feldman Elkin.

1933   Family moves to Chicago.

1943   Bar mitzvah, 17 July, New York.

1948   Graduates from South Shore High School, Chicago.

1950   First story, "The Dying," appears in *Illini Writers,* September.

1952   B.A., University of Illinois.

1953   Marries Joan Marion Jacobson, an artist, 1 February; M.A., University of Illinois.

1955–1957   Military service, U.S. Army.

1957–1959   Doctoral student, University of Illinois; editorial staff, *Accent.*

1957   "A Sound of Distant Thunder" appears in *Epoch* (Winter).

1958   Son Philip Aaron born.

1960–1962   Instructor, Washington University, St. Louis, Missouri.

1961   Ph.D., University of Illinois.

1962   Longview Foundation Award for "In the Alley."

1963   *Paris Review* humor prize for "The Great Sandusky."

1962–1963   Travel in Italy and England, writing *Boswell.*

1964   *Boswell: A Modern Comedy.*

1964–1965   Visiting professor, Smith College.

1966   Son Bernard Edward born; *Criers and Kibitzers, Kibitzers and Criers.*

1966–1967   Guggenheim fellow.

1967   Daughter Molly Ann born; *A Bad Man*; visiting professor, University of California, Santa Barbara.

1968   Heart attack; "The Six-Year-Old Man" (filmscript).

1968–1969   Rockefeller Foundation grant.

1969   Professor, Washington University; visiting professor, University of Wisconsin–Milwaukee.

1971 *The Dick Gibson Show.*

1972 National Endowment for the Arts and Humanities grant; multiple sclerosis diagnosed; *The Making of Ashenden,* British edition.

1973 *Searches and Seizures.*

1974 American Academy of Arts and Letters Award; visiting professor, University of Iowa.

1975 Visiting professor, Yale University.

1976 *The Franchiser,* visiting professor, Boston University.

1979 *The Living End.*

1980 *Stanley Elkin's Greatest Hits;* Richard and Hilda Rosenthal Award for *The Living End;* edits *The Best American Short Stories 1980.*

1981 *Southern Review* prize for *Greatest Hits; The First George Mills.*

1982 *George Mills;* member, American Academy of Arts and Letters.

1983 Merle Kling Professor of Modern Letters, Washington University; National Book Critics Circle Award for *Mills.*

1985 *The Magic Kingdom;* bypass surgery; *Early Elkin.*

1987 *The Rabbi of Lud.*

Chapter One
Life and Literary Loyalties

For years, students in my contemporary fiction courses have been introduced to Stanley Elkin as one of America's best-kept literary secrets. Often at the semester's end a variety of students express admiration for Elkin's novels, determination to read more of his work, and regret that they had not heard about him before. Asked to identify those authors whose work most impressed them during the course, they frequently list Elkin along with Joseph Heller, Robert Coover, and Thomas Pynchon.

This is distinguished company for a novelist few had heard about before the course began. Over many years these students comprise a fairly representative sample. When my colleagues discuss Elkin, two groups form: those who know little about him and those who respect his work intensely. Those who know his work admire it for reasons similar to those of my students: his humor, his inventive fascination with language, his zany characters with their driving yet human obsessions, and his daring treatment of unusual themes.

Serious writers also often indicate admiration for Elkin's work. Frequently novelists and critics express their exasperation that this gifted novelist has not yet reached the audience he deserves. He has written seven novels; two collections of novellas; a short story collection from which selections like "A Poetics for Bullies," "I Look Out for Ed Wolfe," and "In the Alley" are often anthologized; a collection of previously published fiction, *Stanley Elkin's Greatest Hits,* which won the *Southern Review* prize for best collection of 1980; and a significant amount of occasional prose. Fellow writers and sophisticated critics are united in their mystification over the comparative lack of recognition this important author has enjoyed.

The breadth of Elkin's readership has probably been limited by his choosing to occupy a curious, unique position in postmodern American fiction. Novelists enjoying a wide readership form two camps, if we define the extremes of the spectrum as epistemological and mimetic. Writers like Saul Bellow, John Updike, and Philip Roth can be characterized as realists in that their novels are driven by the portrayal of characters who encounter problems one might typically face in contemporary society. Although these writers may experiment with literary technique, the primary emphasis in their fiction remains on the characters and the dilemmas they encounter. To the degree that these are novelists of ideas—Bellow certainly is—our contemplation of their themes depends on how we respond to the characters and the situations they encounter. On the other hand, writers like Pynchon, Coover, John Barth, and Vladimir Nabokov are concerned primarily with the fiction-making process itself. Their characters are frequently zany or extreme, and the situations they create are esoteric and occasionally bizarre. Often such fiction is concerned with the way everyone reconstructs reality by perceiving and narrating it. This does not, of course, rule out implicit or overt social commentary. In most cases, the ideas we encounter in such fictions derive from our preoccupation with literary technique rather than with character or situation.

Elkin occupies a middle ground on this spectrum. His novels are simultaneously epistemological, that is, preoccupied with technique and the logic of artifice, and mimetic, that is, concerned with the portrayal of characters in realistic social contexts.[1] His characters are intensely drawn; they are profoundly affected by their social environment, but their obsessive personalities place them in unusual relations with that milieu. Moreover, they become intensely preoccupied with their own processes of self-realization, and this leads them into flights of rhetoric. The novels themselves, while defining a precise sense of the context in which the characters operate—the splendid descriptions of Disney World in *The Magic Kingdom* and the energy crisis in *The Franchiser* are excellent examples—are marked by an abundance, perhaps an extravagance, in rhetoric that provides intellectual pleasure while calling our attention away from the characters or their situations. In effect Elkin offers us the pleasures of both the epistemological and the mimetic novelist. He thus carves a unique niche for himself in the canon of postmodern American fiction.

Two related reasons may explain Elkin's limited but devoted readership, but upon examination, each argues for Elkin's stature as an important American artist. First, he is a writer in love with the language and its possibilities. He consistently maintains that his primary loyalty is to the medium with which he works rather than to matters like plot, characterization, or theme. Replying to a question about the "pitchman's rhetoric" in his fiction, Elkin indicates not only his primary loyalty to the language but also his recognition that his concept of the fiction-making process features an element of artifice:

Rhetoric doesn't occur in life. It occurs in fiction. Fiction gives an opportunity for rhetoric to happen. It provides a stage where language can stand. It's what . . . I aspire to in my own fiction. I'd rather have a metaphor than a good cigar. . . . I *am* trying to upset the applecarts of expectation and ordinary grammar, and you can only do that with fierce language. You can do that only with aggression: the aggression of syntax and metaphor, the aggression, really, of actual, by God metered prose.[2]

In this statement Elkin concedes the artifice of fiction, thus minimizing realism or any of its derivatives as a primary intention in his work. The point of fiction, he implies, is not to portray situations we are likely to encounter in ordinary life but to construct a stage for verbal ingenuity. For some readers, this commitment may result in verbal excess, or "purple passages" in which the writer engages in linguistic experimentation at the expense of traditional concepts of plot or characterization.

Elkin can therefore be seen as more the poet than the novelist, committed more to the medium than to the matter. One characteristic of his fiction is that the hero, having a chance to make a speech, becomes so passionately involved in his own rhetoric that the action comes to a momentary standstill, and the reader's attention is focused primarily on the brilliance of the rhetoric: James Boswell in *Boswell: A Modern Comedy*, Leo Feldman in *A Bad Man*, and Ben Flesh in *The Franchiser* offer differing yet revealing examples. If Elkin is guilty of being more interested in the medium than in the material of his fiction, even of being more the poet than the novelist, he is in good company. Writers as diverse as James Joyce, William Faulkner (an important influence on Elkin), Nabokov (about whom he wrote a fictionalized reminiscence),[3] and Pynchon allow the rhetoric implicit in emotionally charged situations to take precedence over conventional matters like plot movement.

Second, Elkin's fiction is nearly unique in its treatment of the degree to which vocation shapes character. Most serious fiction writers implicitly recognize that vocation shapes character, and the personalities of Faulkner's V. K. Ratliff and Gavin Stevens owe much to their businesses as itinerant sewing-machine vendor and lawyer, respectively; that of Joyce's Leopold Bloom owes a great deal to his task as advertising canvasser, and Bloom is probably much more appealing than Stephen Dedalus because he believes in his business, whereas Dedalus condescends to his temporary vocation. Heller has explored with disturbing results the implications of vocation on character formation in *Something Happened*.

Elkin's treatment of the issue is, however, more functional than that of most other novelists. The inspiration for his novels is usually a meditation on a vocation, and the characters and situations, certainly the rhetoric, derive from the implications of the character's occupation. This process has thematic significance. His characters engage in fairly ordinary business ventures. Many are merchandisers, one is a radio personality, one is a bailbondsman, another is a rabbi. Unlike some writers whose characters have esoteric occupations —too often writers or professors—Elkin defines the potential poetry in ordinary business ventures and discovers, through his fiction, to what degree his characters' daily pursuits shape their ability to respond to ethical and personal crises. One central theme of this study is the unique sensibility Elkin's fiction brings to the hypothesis that what we do shapes who we are.

A Pitchman's Son

Stanley Lawrence Elkin was born in New York City on 11 May 1930. When he was three, the family moved to Chicago, where he spent most of his childhood, but the family vacationed in the summers at a bungalow they owned in northern New Jersey. In 1960 he took a position at Washington University in St. Louis. Because of his long residence there, his life and work are associated with the American Midwest, and many of his characters live in places like Cincinnati, Minneapolis, or St. Louis.

Each of his parents had a shaping influence on the writing career Elkin pursued. His father, Phil, was a traveling salesman whose territory included much of the Midwest. His product was costume jewelry, and Elkin recalls proudly Phil's ability to sell ("an absolutely supersalesman. He could sell you your watch"), his skill as a raconteur ("a great storyteller"), and his influence on Stanley's career as a writer ("he was a wonderful, wonderful man . . . and one of the things I regret is that he is not around to see what I have written, because he encouraged me"); introducing a short story collection, Elkin calls Phil "a snob with a heart of gold," a "geologist of the heart, . . . no alchemist but the true forty-niner, a panner of other people's instincts, an assay artist." A memoir associates Phil's love of language with "some golden age of the personal we shared through his stories, his actor's resonances, all those anecdotes of self-dramatizing exigency, of strut and shuffle and leap and roll. In those days it was his America."[4] Phil's absolute belief in his product and his joy in the adventure of persuading reluctant customers to buy his line certainly influence two of Elkin's most important character creations, Leo Feldman in *A Bad Man* and Ben Flesh in *The Franchiser*. Phil's commitment to the American economy and to the excitement of selling are felt throughout his son's fiction, and Elkin admires his characters' energy, commitment, and love of rhetoric—all qualities he saw in his father.

His mother, born Zelda Feldman, had a pragmatic influence on her son's career. Her maiden name figures prominently in his early fiction. Characters in many short stories, from the often-anthologized "In the Alley" to the recently collected "A Sound of Distant Thunder" and "The Party," are named

Feldman. Later Elkin punned on the name in *A Bad Man,* where Leo becomes a "felled man." He explains that the name seemed natural for him because in his childhood "we had a bungalow in New Jersey which we visited in the summers. Everybody in that small community was named Feldman and was either an aunt or a cousin of mine. . . . I hadn't read Joyce, I didn't know about Stephen Dedalus. But it didn't make any difference what story it was or what age the characters were. I named them all Stephen Feldman."[5]

Zelda Elkin gave her son more than a family name to play with. When he was a young writer, she gave him material encouragement he needed to launch his career. Having finished his Ph.D. thesis while teaching at Washington University and having sold several stories, Elkin was becoming frustrated because he could not find enough time to concentrate on his first novel. His mother generously offered to match his university salary for one year and to pay his travel expenses. The Elkins spent seven months in Italy and four in London; during that time he completed reading the newly published *Boswell's London Journals* and writing *Boswell.* Having a contract based on the first two chapters and the freedom to pursue his work , he completed the book. Years later, he said, "In effect, my mother changed my life by sending me."[6]

Although the family lived in Chicago, both parents were buried in New Jersey. Phil Elkin died on a business trip in 1958, and Zelda died in Miami in 1974. When selecting a coffin, Elkin discovered that Riverside Chapel is a franchise operation, a fact he included in *The Franchiser*; one of the few solvent franchises Flesh owns is a Riverside Chapel. The burial of family members in Lodi also provided inspiration for Elkin's most recent novel; he "set *The Rabbi of Lud* in New Jersey because my parents, and a lot of my family, are buried there, and chose Lodi—Lud in the novel—because when I went there for funerals, grief tunneled my vision, and left me with the impression that the town was all graveyard."[7]

Elkin took three degrees at the University of Illinois, completing his A.B. in 1952 and his M.A. in 1953. That year, he married Joan Marion Jacobson, a gifted artist. Except for frequent travel because of grants and honorific teaching appointments at various colleges and universities, the Elkins have remained in University City, Missouri, which "has always looked like what cities are supposed to look like," surrounded by close friends and excellent informal restaurants.[8] They have reared three children in St. Louis. Their sons, Philip and Bernard, were born in 1958 and 1966. Their daughter, Molly, was born in 1967.

Work toward Elkin's Ph.D. in American literature was interrupted by military service between 1955 and 1957. In the army he achieved the rank of specialist third class and intensified his interest in the jargon of radio, a knowledge that would pay rich dividends in his masterful exploration of the psychology of a radio personality, *The Dick Gibson Show,* which includes two extensive sections on the hero's military misadventures. While in the army, he wrote a manual on the operation of fork lifts.

Upon fulfilling his military obligation, Elkin returned to the University of Illinois to complete his Ph.D. in American literature, defending his dissertation, "Religious Themes and Symbolism in the Novels of William Faulkner," written under John T. Flanagan's supervision, in 1961. While writing the thesis, he joined the faculty at Washington University; since 1983 he has been Merle Kling Professor of Modern Letters, an endowed chair that permits him to teach two courses each fall semester and to devote his full attention to writing during the rest of the year. At Washington he has associated closely with a group of writers, particularly novelist and philosopher William H. Gass and poet Howard Nemerov.

While completing his graduate study, Elkin worked on the staff of *Accent* magazine, which published his "In the Alley" in 1959. "Among the Witnesses" appeared that year in *Chicago Review* and in 1962 won the Longview Foundation award. Two years later, "The Great Sandusky," later incorporated in *Boswell,* won the *Paris Review* humor prize. "I Look Out for Ed Wolfe," his first national publication, appeared in *Esquire* in September 1962 and was included in *The Best American Short Stories, 1963.* These awards began a distinguished series that has grown as the author continues to mature artistically. After publishing *Criers and Kibitzers, Kibitzers and Criers,* however, Elkin decided that his metier was the novel, and he has written only a few stories since. He discovered in the 1970s that he genuinely enjoys writing novellas (a form Henry James once called "blessed") and has written two collections, *Searches and Seizures* and *The Living End,* the latter written over three summers during the composition of the complex *George Mills.*

In the late 1960s Elkin's health became a major concern, but one he has faced heroically and with humor. He had a heart attack in 1968 and was diagnosed as having multiple sclerosis (MS) in 1972. He told me the first symptoms of this disease occurred in 1961, with a brief episode of partial blindness, but the formal diagnosis was not made until a decade later. Although characterized by periods of remission, this incurable disease involves progressive loss of walking ability (he has used canes for several years) and tactile sensation (he has limited use of his hands), as well as considerable discomfort. Despite his illness, Elkin has continued to teach, participate in workshops, and write. In fact much of his best writing comes from the period since the disease was identified. The condition was incorporated in *The Fran-*

chiser, in which Elkin decided, well into the writing, to have his hero suffer from MS and to make that disease the central metaphor of the book by associating Ben's physical condition with breakdowns in American economic and energy policies. His treatment of mortality, a major subject throughout his fiction, has changed since, and perhaps because of, his disease. Characters in *The Franchiser* and *The Magic Kingdom* are still obsessed by death, but they are concerned with the mortality of others and accept their own as a matter of course.

A final note of biographical interest is Elkin's appreciation for the technology of word processing. In an era when some writers disdain the computer as a devious instrument of an insidious technology, Elkin pioneered in doing serious writing with an invention that is more efficient than quill pens. He once hyperbolically responded to a question about the most important event of his career by saying, "June 6th, 1979, when my word processor was delivered. . . . Not even just a dedicated word processor, finally, but a devoted one as well."[9] This enthusiasm corresponds with Elkin's thematic interest in technology not as an inevitable enemy of human autonomy, but as a potential ally in our struggle to realize and express our humanity.

Elkin's Loyalties

Scholars and critics tend to think of writers as members of groups or movements because such categories enable us to treat individual or idiosyncratic authors in convenient historical and artistic paradigms. Writers themselves have understandably different views on their being categorized, and some regard this as detrimental to an appreciation of their individual efforts. Elkin has consistently denied affiliation with any movement, except for the group of writers who work together at Washington University, especially Nemerov and Gass. These are personal as well as artistic associations.

Elkin is often associated with four groups of contemporary writers and has denied affiliation with each. We shall briefly explore the claims, and Elkin's denials, of his affiliation with the satiric tradition, Jewish-American fiction, black humor, and metafiction.

Jewish-American Fiction   Like many other important postwar American novelists, including Bernard Malamud, Bellow, Roth, and Heller, Elkin comes from a Jewish family, but he is certainly not a Jewish-American writer in the sense that Malamud was or Roth is. His treatment of the cultural question differs in key ways from those of other major Jewish-American novelists. Whereas Malamud concentrated on accepting the Jewish tradition of suffering as the way to find fulfillment and Roth has satirized gentile clichés about family and upward mobility to the extent that some Jewish readers found *Portnoy's Complaint* and *My Life as a Man* offensive, Elkin's novels do not focus primarily on ethnic issues. Many of his stories feature Jewish characters, and Greenspahn, the hero of "Criers and Kibitzers, Kibitzers and Criers," is a shopkeeper who suffers in ways that remind us of Malamud. Feldman, in *A Bad Man*, learns to respond to his crazed father's private version of the diaspora. But ethnic identity has little to do with Feldman's role as a challenger to Warden Fisher's gospel—"life is ordinary"—though Fisher once associates his obsession to convert Feldman with Christian zeal. The family Ben Flesh, the gentile hero of *The Franchiser*, cares for is Jewish, but the issue of Gentile-Jewish relations is peripheral in that novel. Recently *The Rabbi of Lud* takes up the story of a rabbi whose family constitutes the entire Jewish population of a town in which Jews are buried. The ethnic issue is important here, for Rabbi Goldkorn's daughter claims to have visitations from the Blessed Virgin.

This list should indicate, however, that ethnic identity is not central to Elkin's novels. The heroes of *Boswell, The Dick Gibson Show, George Mills, The Magic Kingdom,* and *The Franchiser* are Gentiles, and religious affiliation or cultural heritage does not play an important role in these books. An accurate index to the distribution of Jewish-American themes can be found in the three novellas that constitute *Searches and Seizures*. The hero of "The Bailbondsman" is militantly a "Phoenician"; Ashenden in "The Making of Ashenden" is a privileged WASP; and Preminger (a name used in some early stories) of "The Condominium" is a Jew trying to come to terms with his father's assimilation. Elkin indicates that he does not see his work as central to the Jewish-American tradition—"I see myself as a writer who happens to be Jewish, happens to be American, and happens to be a writer"—and he makes careful distinctions among the types of Jewish-American writers that Bellow, Roth, Malamud, and Isaac Bashevis Singer are.[10] It would be misleading to consider Elkin a Jewish-American writer in the same sense one might approach Singer and Malamud, or Roth and Bellow, this way.

The Satiric Tradition   Early reviewers seized upon the term *satire* to describe the zany characters and situations Elkin's books treat. There are obvious reasons for this association. The situations are exaggerated and extravagant; the compulsive characters are inclined toward extreme variations from euphoria to depression, and they yield to any opportunity for rhetorical display; the funny dialogue is marked by allusions and non sequiturs; and the rhetoric operates at a constantly high level of intensity.

Although all these qualities characterize various satiric types, Elkin denies satiric intention more often than he rejects any affiliation except black humor. Two of his comments on satire, separated by thirteen years, illustrate his attitude. In 1975 he challenged a critic who reviewed *Searches and Seizures* as satire by saying, "Well, I wasn't satirizing a god damned thing in that book. . . . I'm not a satirist. I don't enjoy satire myself and certainly do not aspire to it." Recently he offered an even more definitive condemnation of this literary genre: "God, I hate satire, it's so self-righteous."[11]

It is understandable that readers find satiric effects in Elkin's works, for in addition to those conventions already listed, some books invite analysis as extended criticisms of certain foibles in our culture or our beliefs. *The Franchiser,* for example, could be read as satirizing the development of a fast food mentality in America and the evolving energy crisis of the 1970s. *A Bad Man* lends itself to examination as a critique of irrational objectives in the penal system. *The Dick Gibson Show* welcomes reading as a commentary on mass media culture, and *George Mills* can be seen as a satiric analysis of the tactics used by influential classes to reinforce a caste system. *The Rabbi of Lud* can be read as a satire on many levels, most obviously as a criticism of unconsidered religious belief (the hero was not intellectually adequate to read Hebrew and could not get into an American rabbinical academy, so he pursued his studies offshore). Fully aware of Elkin's attitude toward satire, one critic maintains that *The Living End* is "Menippean satire" aiming to show that "the message . . . seems to be that there is no message" and that the only positive value the triptych affirms is "the energy of creation" itself.[12]

Although such readings seem to be invited by the texts, these are the very premises on which Elkin denies any satiric intention. First, he feels that satire renders characters the embodiments of ideas rather than autonomous individuals. Thus characters in Swift and Shaw are first embodied ideas, then developed personalities. Because Elkin begins his works with a meditation on vocation, he finds the individual responses his characters make to the habits of mind their vocations encourage far more important than any idea they might embody. Yet the characters are uniformly obsessive, and obsessive behavior is characteristic of satiric intention.

More crucially Elkin denies any interest in writing satire because he feels that the genre is prescriptive; that is, he believes that satirists place themselves in a position of moral authority by claiming to know what is unworthy behavior. Elkin consistently maintains that an author has no right to prescribe behavior. Responding to an interviewer's question about the place of "social issues, politics, ideology" in fiction, he replied decisively, "They're off-limits, out of bounds. The writer doesn't have the moral authority to prescribe for

others. A novel's function is not sociological. A book doesn't have to sell people anything but language. Style, yes; lifestyle, no."[13] Elkin resists the label of
satirist because he believes that satirists claim the moral authority to legislate
right and wrong, an authority his fiction neither seeks nor claims.

If we accept this association between satire and prescriptive moral
authority on the writer's part, we can appreciate Elkin's efforts to disassoci-
ate himself from the satiric tradition. If the author says he intends no satire,
we should accept his statement of intention. This does not, however, mean
that we must deny that satiric elements exist in the texts. Many minor
characters—financier William Lome in *Boswell*, convict Ed Slipper in *A
Bad Man*, pharmacist Bernie Perk in *The Dick Gibson Show*, and others—
suggest satiric effects as manifestations of obsessions gone amok. Although
obsession is characteristic of Elkin's protagonists, the author explores fully
the implications of the obsessions among his heroes and raises them above
being mere embodiments of ideas. Minor characters, however, are often
deft strokes that suggest ways that uncritical responses to ideas, often derived from the culture in which the characters act, can create limitations on
our capacity to respond to our fellow human beings.

Black Humor   While many readers of Elkin's early novels responded to them as satires on ideas and institutions, others found them to exemplify the black humor of the 1960s. Even more vehemently than he denies
satiric intentions, the author insists that he does not write black humor. In
fact, Elkin says he does not know what the term means and often implies that
critics who use it do not either. His most scathing remark is, "Black humor is
a term invented by *Time* Magazine," and he said recently, "Black humor is
pointless cruelty for pointless cruelty's own sake."[14] He told me he resents this
more than any other label that has been attached to his work.

No one knows exactly where the term *black humor* originated—maybe it
was at *Time*—but it has come to suggest a bitter, usually morbid, response to
the absurdity perceived by many writers today. The common theme is that if
we cannot do anything about the absurdity of our condition, we may as well
laugh at it. This response, fairly frequent in the fiction and essays of Roth,
Bruce Jay Friedman, and others, leads to a cruel joke in which the individual's frailty and helplessness are exploited. This helplessness is suggested by a
grim, ironic, and often illogical consequence of a neutral or arbitrary cause.
Scenes from Elkin's most recent novels seem to have elements of black
humor. In *The Magic Kingdom,* a child selected to go on a dream holiday for
terminally ill children dies because he cannot wait for his parents to open the
letter announcing his selection. The pathology of his disease renders him vul-

nerable to cuts, but he is so excited when he sees the envelope containing his good news that he opens it, gets a tiny paper cut, and dies of complications. In *The Rabbi of Lud,* a friend of the hero's wife, and a nature lover, takes an autumn walk dressed in stylish muted tones for the season. She is killed by hunters who anticipate the legal hunting season, presumably mistaken for a deer because of her fall wardrobe.

These examples seem to suggest that Elkin does have an affinity with the black humorists, in that his fiction is full of grim and cruel jokes. The burden of black humor, however, is social commentary, something Elkin explicitly rejects as a fictional intention. Roth and Friedman define black humor as the writer's response to cultural events that rival in absurdity anything the writer's imagination could invent. Roth writes, "The American writer in the middle of the 20th century has his hands full in trying to understand, and then describe, and then make *credible* much of the American reality. It stupefies, it infuriates, and finally it is even a kind of embarrassment to one's own meager imagination." Friedman agrees that the absurdity of ordinary life challenges the novelist to strike out into unfamiliar territory and associates black humor with frustrated satiric intentions: "The novelist-satirist, with no real territory of his own to roam, has had to discover new land, invent a new currency, a new set of filters, has had to sail into darker waters somewhere out beyond satire and I think this is what is meant by black humor."[15]

Elkin's rejecting the black humor label makes sense on two counts. First, black humorists implicitly criticize social conventions, and Elkin sees this as an inappropriate goal. More importantly, black humorists see human life as absurd (the term is often associated with the absurdist tradition), and Elkin does not. We may be the victims of cruel turns of circumstance and fate; his fiction often challenges God to explain the human condition rationally, especially in the final sections of *The Living End* and *The Rabbi of Lud.* This does not, however, mean that we are victims of a cosmic, sick joke. Our responses do matter, for the way we conduct ourselves in the face of absurdity is the measure of our worth. This kind of thinking counters the principal trends of black humor fiction. Certainly Elkin's characteristic celebration of the richness of life contrasts with the bitterness often associated with black humor.

Metafiction   Critics have recently associated Elkin's work with the loosely defined school metafiction, and this is the only group of writers he has not denied association with. Until now, he has not been asked point-blank about this affiliation. When I put the question to him, he laughed energetically and asked, "What the hell is 'metafiction'? Fiction about writing fiction, right? . . . But fiction about the fiction-making process . . . seems so boring to me."

Several definitions of metafiction are proposed by writers and critics, and common denominators among those we shall explore are concern with the fiction-making process itself, interest in technical experimentation, and rejection of realism. Gass, Coover (who wrote an introduction for *Stanley Elkin's Greatest Hits*), Donald Barthelme, John Barth, and Ron Sukenick write metafiction.

In a theoretical essay Robert Scholes emphasizes the relation between criticism and metafiction, which "assimilates all the perspectives of criticism into the fictional process itself." Applying the concept to a work by Gass, Larry McCaffrey says the metafiction writer "had seen that only by creating a new form with its own referential language could he deal effectively with his original subject—fiction-making" and "the defining characteristic of metafiction . . . is its direct and immediate concern with fiction-making itself." Applying metafiction to Elkin's work, Doris Bargen defines it as "an epistemological interpretation of the nature of reality and a rejection of the Aristotelian concept of mimesis" and concludes, "Challenging the reader and frustrating his conventional expectations, the technical innovations of metafiction invite the reader to become increasingly aware of the artfulness of art and, by analogy, to ponder the possibly illusory nature of reality as it exists, or seems to exist, outside of fiction."[16]

I suspect that categorizing Elkin as a metafictionist clarifies fewer of his achievements than it obscures. As the definitions suggest, these theoretical discussions involve assumptions about the writer's self-conscious creation of analogies between the fiction-making process and the degree to which our thoughts and perceptions fictionalize a reality we cannot comprehend absolutely. Usually metafictions create complex structures in which the reader is challenged to determine what actually occurs, or what is a fact, much as we reconstruct reality when perceiving it. Coover's "The Babysitter" and *Gerald's Party* exemplify this procedure. Although Elkin's fictions involve complex movements in time and intricacies in plot, none compares with the kind of narrative complexity the metafictionists normally create.

This seems a good occasion to propose that Elkin's novels are not particularly "difficult," as too many reviewers persist in calling them. They are complex because of their interest in the dynamics of vocation and character and because of their intense rhetoric, but only inexperienced readers of modern or postmodern fiction will have trouble following most Elkin stories. Although a sense of mystery abounds in these texts, the mystery concerns not primarily the reality of plot and characterization but the wonder and excitement with which the protagonists embrace life in spite of its acknowledged potential for frustration and defeat.

At a more abstract level, the principal distinction between Elkin and the metafictionists is that his fictions, while accepting artifice rather than mimesis as a primary intention, are less concerned with the process of knowing than with the processes of doing and becoming. That is, the fictions do not treat primarily the inadequacy of human knowledge but the ways in which an obsessive personality enacts ideas and intuitions that may be imperfectly understood by the actor. This distinction is one of degree, but it is an important degree. Elkin's stories treat characters who struggle to embody concepts that give their lives focus. Dick Gibson, for example, works through a series of apprenticeships that have implications for personal identity as well as professional development. Elkin's fictions are character studies, not epistemological abstractions about the ways characters reconstruct reality. His characters are usually energetic, driven personalities caught up in the dynamics of their obsessions, but our interest in his fictions, despite the obvious delights of the medium—rhetoric, style, figurative language, and description—lies finally with the characters and their struggles to find themselves.

Summary   An original artist resists categories. Although labels like Jewish-American writer, satirist, black humorist, and metafictionist describe elements of Elkin's work, each limits our response to him as a writer. Elkin told me he wishes to be taken as an artist on his own terms rather than classified as a member of any group, and in a recent interview he insisted on the uniqueness of his art: "I can't define myself. I don't know who is doing what I am doing. I hope no one is. I hope *I'm* doing what I am doing."[17] Perhaps our best procedure is to suspend labels and examine the works themselves for the delights and mystery they offer. In the next chapters, we shall look at the novels in thematic rather than chronological groupings to discover some of the mystery and delight at the heart of Elkin's fiction.

Chapter Two

Boswell and *George Mills*:
A History of Uses and
Some Uses of History

Boswell: A Modern Comedy appeared in 1964. Like most other first novels, it received limited critical notice, but the reviews were often favorable. By contrast *George Mills* came out in 1982, when Elkin's reputation as an important innovative novelist was firmly established. It was extensively reviewed, often with enthusiastic appreciation, but some reviewers expressed reservations about what they perceived as self-indulgence on Elkin's part and his refusal to conform with traditional notions about the importance of plot in constructing a narrative.[1] Elkin himself usually expresses dissatisfaction with *Boswell* but consistently maintains that *George Mills* is the book of which he is most proud.[2]

These books complete a cycle in Elkin's work. *Boswell,* a picaresque account of a bodybuilder and professional wrestler modeled loosely on the career of Samuel Johnson's biographer, introduces many key Elkin motifs, whereas *George Mills,* the saga of sixty generations of men named George Mills doomed to blue-collar occupations and lives, synthesizes these motifs. Among these are playful historical reconstruction, a sense of entrapment in history, and a response to characters' being seen by others as second-rate or ordinary.

In both Elkin delights in reconstructing and reinterpreting history. In the eleventh century Greatest Grandfather Mills is credited with inventing or importing several useful arts to England, including picnics,[3] the Robin Hood legend (*GM,* 32), dressage (*GM,* 41), and psychiatry (*GM,* 26). The forty-third George Mills, conscripted by the Turkish Janissaries in the nineteenth century, precipitates a counterinsurgency by escaping that ends that group's reign of terror.[4] Adlai Stevenson tells James Boswell that his harassing both his and Eisenhower's presidential campaigns influenced the 1952 election because this made Stevenson lose confidence in his electability.[5]

A representative historical reconstruction involves the fictional Leo Herlitz in *Boswell*. Young James's mentor and first celebrity, Herlitz affected Western culture's evolution by encouraging Freud's ventures into psychology and Lindbergh's first transatlantic flight; his reorganizing the German army prolonged World War I; he counseled the French existentialists and advised history's foremost Harvard class; a fictional sociologist attributes the backwardness of Africa to Herlitz's death on a world tour before he arrived there.

By giving fictional characters such power to affect history without being public figures, Elkin introduces a theme that differs from those of other novelists who fictionalize historical characters and their impact, like Max Apple's *The Propheteers* (influenced by *The Financier* and *The Magic Kingdom*), Robert Coover's *The Public Burning*, and E. L. Doctorow's *The Book of Daniel* and *Ragtime*. Whereas these novels seem primarily concerned with debunking historical figures or demythologizing history, Elkin compels the reader to question the reliability of historical record and the ways being trapped in an unreliable oral tradition can affect our personal destiny. If a person is to some degree the product of personal and collective history and if history is a questionable record of events, how can individuals determine their relationship to the culture? In *George Mills* this issue is paramount, for the "Mills curse," a blue-collar mentality, is the product of a "hand-me-down history" (*GM*, 2) passed from one generation to another. This oral history determines the quality of every George Mills's life.

Another theme introduced in *Boswell* and brought to mature investigation in *Mills* is the notion of being second-rate and confronting the majority's concept of the ordinary. Since the eleventh century every Mills has labored under the Mills curse: "There are distinctions between men, humanity is dealt out like cards. There is a natural suzereignty. . . . Men have their place" (*GM*, 10), pronounced by Greatest Grandfather's master Guillalume, lost on the way to the first crusade:

Mills apologized silently to the sons he was yet to have . . . for the heritage he was yet to give them, grieved for the Millsness he was doomed to pass on, for the frayed, flawed genes—he thought blood—of the second-rate, back-seat, low-down life, foreseeing . . . a continuum of the less than average, of the small-time, poached Horseshit Man life, prophesying right there . . . all the consequences to others in the burdened bestiality of his blackballed loins. (*GM*, 10)

It is not the aristocrat's pronouncing this curse, but Mills's and his descendants' accepting its authority that gives it the power to determine the quality of Mills life for a millennium.[6] As each generation retells the family's history, each descendant, by acknowledging the tradition's authority, accepts limitations on the scope and effect of decisions individual Millses make.

This is the central subject of *George Mills*: sixty generations are condemned to being second-rate when the first Mills accepts Guillalume's curse. Although they are not stupid (the current Mills has a vision of DNA molecular structure), none has escaped being blue-collar. This current Mills, an apathetic furniture mover for a specialist in removing the possessions of evicted families, later becomes servant-companion to a dying heiress. None of his ancestors has escaped the curse, but in trying to break out of his family history, he will claim a limited victory.

Boswell too is cursed to a second-rate life. His fate was determined at age seventeen when Herlitz proclaimed, "You are Sancho Panza, Boswell. The second team. . . *Voyeur*, Eye, Ear, you will pull your chair beside the roaring fire. Boswell, Boswell, Go-between, Welcome Guest, Reliable Source, Persona Grata" (*B*, 18). Although James often questions this judgment, his reverence for celebrities and his desire to create a club for them originate in Herlitz's describing his character as second-rate. While mounting his first campaign to contact a celebrity, he sadly concludes that "Herlitz, that magician, was right again. I was . . . the world's sad fourth, who played other people's games by other people's rules. A reader of labels, of directions, a consumer on the most human of levels. Vampire. Sancho. Jerk" (*B*, 62). Elkin ironically synthesizes James's accepted identity with self-disgust as the symbol "vampire," which later describes Boswell's dependence on celebrities' attention, and the epithet "jerk" replace more witty metaphors like "fourth" and "consumer."

Dedicated to being an accessory to history by cultivating great men, James challenges the identity his history affords him. He divides humanity into "two kinds of men, the practitioner and the theoretician, and . . . it is the practitioner to whom the glamour attaches" (*B*, 337). His preferring practitioners, who receive public notice, over theoreticians, who may labor anonymously, explains his devoting his life to celebrity hunting: "I will not write my life off or cut my losses. . . . When the high tide of low death is in, *I must still have my history,* and it must, somehow, *matter!*" (*B*, 133). He attempts to create his personal history by cultivating the celebrities of his time.

The issue of being second-rate is important in Elkin's other novels. The heroes of *The Franchiser, A Bad Man,* and "The Bailbondsman" cultivate their uniqueness as a means of escaping the challenge of being nothing more than ordinary. In *Boswell* and *Mills,* however, this is a dominant concern. How does one who feels extraordinary respond when the world conspires to convince him he is nothing more than ordinary?

Boswell: A Modern Comedy

To a degree Elkin's is an allusive art. He delights in cultural and literary cross-reference, but his allusiveness differs from that of such predecessors as James Joyce, T. S. Eliot, and Ezra Pound. Whereas they used allusions to create resonances between their works and the literary tradition, Elkin alludes to literature and culture with ironic, often playful, effects. He delights in incongruously placing quotations from Shakespeare or Milton in the mouths of relatively unliterary characters. Dreaming about his club's first meeting, Boswell greets Robert Frost with "Provide, provide" (*B*, 371), the title of a Frost poem. When he asks a Nobel Laureate, "What is the proper study of mankind?" Morty Perlmutter completes the parody of an Alexander Pope line by answering, "It's man . . . at his worst" (*B*, 194). James later calls his forced entry into the Roman Colosseum "The Rape of the Lock" (*B*, 273).

The allusiveness of Elkin's fiction is nowhere as problematic as in this novel. Naming his protagonist and the novel after James Boswell encourages the assumption that the book satirizes or comments on modern society by alluding to Johnson's biographer.[7] Before drawing conclusions about this allusion's importance, we should examine the evidence connecting Elkin's with the historical Boswell. This includes the author's recollection of the novel's genesis, and the historical Boswell as compared with Elkin's James, but these clarify key meanings in *Boswell,* as well as the general issue of Elkin's allusiveness.

Elkin says a Boswell story inspired the novel. A colleague at Washington University, Phil London, told him about Boswell's presenting himself at Voltaire's door after a lengthy campaign to contact him by letter. The story, from Boswell's 1764 journal, vaguely resembles James's effort to meet the Great Sandusky. Elkin recalls that the anecdote "struck me as being so funny that I thought a modern Boswell, on the make for all the great men of his time, might be the source of an amusing novel." While writing the novel, he read the newly published *Journals* and discovered some similarities between the character he was developing and Boswell: each had an illegitimate child; each married a woman named Margaret (Elkin's is a Medici); and "I made him come from Saint Louis because Boswell came from Edinburgh and it seems to me that Saint Louis is to America what Edinburgh is to Great Britain."[8]

The novel contains two explicit references to the historical Boswell, one minor and the other major. Herlitz briefly considers biography as James's vocation but dismisses it to preserve "your splendid non-intervention" (*B*, 18). More important is this quotation from a letter in the *Life of Johnson*: "Life is not long, and too much of it must not pass in idle deliberation how it shall be spent; deliberation which those who begin it by prudence and continue it with subtlety [Johnson: "subtilty"] must, after long expense ["expence"] of thought, conclude by chance" (*B*, 133). Elkin employs the quotation ironically. James implicitly approves the content of Johnson's statement but devotes most of his life to "idle deliberation" about how to spend it.

Had Elkin actually patterned his character on Boswell, a quite different *Boswell* might have been written. The *Journals* are filled with self-revelations of a man consumed by sensual appetites while contending with powerful, religious scruples. Elkin probably transferred this personality split to Marty Penner, "an athlete of God like the old ascetics" (*B*, 54) with whom James lodges briefly, who struggles among the temptations of the flesh, the discipline of the bodybuilder, and an obsession with salvation through self-denying service to others. The biographer had little of the discipline, ethical or physical, of Elkin's hero. Although James at fifteen fathered a bastard, his life is relatively celibate until he meets the Principessa in his twenties.

James's favorite saying early in the novel, "Because my heart is pure" (*B*, 25, 35, 47), contrasts with the sensual and physically indolent traits of Boswell. Associating physical prowess with spiritual purity, James uses the phrase to motivate himself to exceptional achievements in weightlifting. Boswell practiced abstinence mainly after breaches, especially those resulting in inflammation (the London *Journal* records his affair with "Louisa," a story of temporary purity resulting from intemperance), and he shared Dr. Johnson's conviction that physical exercise is a necessary evil. Such indolence contrasts with the dedication to physical culture James undertakes to complete Herlitz's defining his vocation as a strong man, as well as his descriptions of gym and locker room camaraderie.

The most plausible conclusion is that Elkin got the nucleus for his situation from popular attitudes toward the biographer but that his James is a distinct literary creation relying little on parody or extended allusion. Both are obsessed with making celebrities notice them. Boswell campaigned to gain introductions to Johnson, Voltaire, and Rousseau and recorded Johnson's conversations for posterity. But this probably resulted from genuine respect for the great people of his time, a veneration shared by many other Londoners. Two biographers offer contrasting interpretations of his personality. Wyndham Lewis's Boswell was quite like James: "The celebrity-hunter had bagged other big fish than Johnson. . . . The connoisseur . . . had been on terms of friendship with . . . the most eminent Englishmen of his time." Frederick Pottle attributes Boswell's chronic melancholy to "frustration of his overweening ambition by any course of life which did not promise to make him a Great Man *soon*" and concludes that "he would always attach himself to great and good men; he would always sincerely seek their counsel. . . . He would always be a weak good man."[9] The *Life* and *Journals* persuade me that Pottle's judgment is closer to the truth than Lewis's. The key element generating Elkin's novel is a more popular than scholarly perception of the biographer, but the situation he developed from this perception is ideally suited to his artistic needs.

Reading Boswell was useful for Elkin. Minor characters in the novel probably originate in the *Life* and *Journals*. Lano, a revolutionary whom James courts, may be a Castro-influenced parody of Corsican hero General Paoli, whom Boswell admired; Nobel Laureate Perlmutter may be an anthropological send-up of historian Edward Gibbon, with whom Boswell and Johnson had a testy relationship. Nate Lace, James's patron who also appears in *The Franchiser,* could be based on actor-turned-bookseller Thomas Davies, who kept a fashionable meeting salon where Boswell met Johnson; conceivably Harold Flesh, the mysterious fixer whom Lace suspects of Mafia connections and who appears in *A Bad Man* and *The Dick Gibson Show,* owes something to John Wilkes, a rascal and member of parliament whom Boswell found irresistible and Johnson reluctantly found charming.

Two important elements of *Boswell* allude to the biographer's literary production. One involves Elkin's structure and the other his theme. This novel is arranged in three sections, the first and third (with one exception) being first-person central narrative and the second being James's "journal" entries recording his complicated campaigns to attract celebrities. In this section, Elkin is indebted to the *Journals,* in which Boswell is more candid about his intentions than in the *Life,* which was intended for publication, whereas the journals were not. James's journals, which he decides to resume after his final wrestling match, record the stunts by which he courts and tricks the great into intimacy.

The rest of *Boswell,* except the crucial eighth chapter of part 3, recording in journal from James's dream about opening the club, employs traditional first-person narration. The narrator is no less candid about his anxieties and motivations here than in the journals, but greater potential for irony exists because James is more subject to self-deception about his motives than in the journal entries. We should be cautious about pressing this comparison, for Boswell in the *Life* intends to tell the story of the great man of his time, whereas James respects no story but his own. This is the crucial difference between *Boswell* and Johnson's biographer: Boswell considered it his duty to tell a great man's story to posterity, whereas James is so self-absorbed that any story he tells is adjunct to his own.

A final influence casts light on Elkin's central theme, which concerns human mortality and how we may respond to recognizing that we are mortal. *Boswell* opens with this memorable quotation:

Everybody dies, everybody. Sure. . . . Everybody dies and that's that. But no one really believes it. They read the papers. They see the newsreels. They drive past the graveyards on the outskirts of town. Do you think that makes any difference? It does not! No one believes in death.

   Except me. Boswell. I believe in it. . . .

   I'm different. I remember I must die. It explains everything. (*B*, 3, 4)

The nucleus of James's obsession is that, recognizing his mortality, he attaches himself to celebrities in order to ignore it. An incident from the *Life* may provide the germ for the first paragraph and the theme of *Boswell*. Telling Johnson about watching executions at Tyburn, Boswell expressed surprise that many prisoners were cavalier about their impending doom. To his question, "Is not the fear of death natural to man?" Johnson answered with what could form a perfect epigraph for Elkin's novel, "So much so, Sir, that the whole of life is but keeping away the thoughts of it." [10] James is so anxious about his death that he devotes his life to finding ways to avoid facing it. Despite his claim in the opening paragraphs that he uniquely faces his death, he constantly seeks ways to avoid facing it.

Boswell, then, treats mortality and the strategies people create to avoid facing death. James's tactic is to cultivate great people. This is not simply transferring his anxieties by becoming affiliated with such people; it is substituting a process that requires full concentration of energy for one that cannot yield an acceptable solution. Many of James's celebrities die. He reads about financier William Lome's death and recalls it when he dreams about meeting Lome's son at the club; he cannot prevent the philosopher Lazaar's suicide; and he sends a ticket for a wrestling match to the Great Sandusky but learns Sandusky is dead (his surprise should be a clue to readers, for Sandusky lamented infirmity when James interviewed him). His celebrities often remind him of the universal defeat even if, as in Sandusky's case, Boswell ignores the evidence.

It is the process of courting celebrities, not the end, that provides a goal for Boswell's enormous energy. To capture a celebrity's attention, he must mount a campaign that demands total concentration and tests his creativity. He poses as a bellhop to get Lome's attention and follows him around Dallas until Lome becomes interested in him. He crashes a party to be introduced to Perlmutter, then insults the host to engage Perlmutter's interest. He runs up a ridiculously high bill in Lace's exclusive restaurant and tells Lace he cannot pay it.

This strategy for meeting celebrities is an end in itself. It places his creativity and ingenuity on the line, forces him to be resourceful, and offers him an effective challenge in his quest to ward off thinking about his death. He becomes a con man, another process more important than the end. He challenges himself to his limit by forcing himself on busy, influential people. Elkin confirms the notion that he courts the great to give himself an illusion of importance: "He doesn't give a damn for the great. He cares only that the great give a damn for him. . . . Boswell is not interested in other men's greatness. He is interested in his own. The idea is to get as many great men to say James Boswell, James Boswell, James Boswell as possible."[11] This preoccupation with strategies to ingratiate himself with celebrities is a challenge to his energy and ingenuity. While campaigning to impress Lome or Lano, he has little time to worry about dying.

An analysis of *Boswell*'s controlling metaphor supports this hypothesis. Elkin establishes a metaphor for aimlessness, itself a logical extension of personal mortality, and the consequent problem of finding alternatives to aimlessness. He discovered while writing the book that stairs and elevators became a motif,[12] but the dominant figure is James's disguise as "The Masked Playboy." It is first a literal, then a figurative, disguise that clarifies the motif of obsession as a means of not facing personal mortality.

James creates this identity to salvage his wrestling career and soon becomes a main rather than preliminary event fighter because the disguise is popular and matches are fixed to establish the Playboy as a contender. He enjoys creating fictions about this disguise when talking to the press. Obsessed with becoming great, he adopts some implications of this metaphor for his real self, but the metaphor is not his own. It was invented by the promoter, Bogolub, who discovered an opportunity to create a new contender while firing James for losing a fixed match. The wrestler designed the implementing concepts: "a whipper of Wops, a Spic scourger, Hebe hitter, Polack pounder—the White Hope of God Knows What. . . . The Capitalist's Friend, Free Enterprize's Prize. A Masked Playboy who didn't need the money but beat up guys to show he was regular" (*B*, 93). Pandering to prejudices among wrestling audiences, the disguise brings James success and provides relief from his concern with mortality because the constant challenge of inventing the Playboy focuses his creativity. He confronts the limits of this metaphor by wrestling John Sallow.

Sallow, whose epithet is the Grim Reaper, is an enigma to James. Rumor has it that, under a former alias, he killed a man in the ring. Although old, he is cunning and ruthlessly strong. James frantically attempts to communicate with Sallow; he leaves unanswered messages at every hotel in St. Louis. When he meets the Reaper before the match, Sallow refuses to communicate: "Upstairs [in the ring]. . . . Talk upstairs" (B, 111).

Whether or not Sallow believes in the identity his professional metaphor creates for him, James does. He believes Sallow really is the Reaper, so this is the confrontation he has feared. Battling death, James becomes a mythic hero: "Come on, Sallow, old enemy, Boswell the big goes against the Angel of Death to save the world. That the public would think me The Masked Playboy was fitting, too. Its heroes are never known to it, anyway. Masks beyond masks. No matter; I would save it anyway, anonymously, nom de plumely. In St. Louis I would whip death's old ass" (B, 99). The fight, which Boswell is slated to lose (an earlier match with Sallow was fixed in his favor), becomes an absurdly mythic confrontation for him; the Masked Playboy takes on the cares of mortal humanity. His life means something if he defeats humanity's universal enemy.

For James this is not a fixed match between professional wrestlers but a contest between metaphors: the pretender to wealth and commonness against the angel of death. Because he takes these metaphors literally, he enters the ring with a serious purpose quite unsuited to the wrestler's vocation.[13] Sallow beats him savagely and ends his wrestling career. Passing out and later awakening in a hospital, James thinks he has died.

Elkin skillfully varies this metaphor in later episodes, with incremental meaning. Each time James becomes a Masked Playboy, he attempts to define an identity that gives purpose to his life and is frustrated because he uncritically accepts his own metaphor.

His journal records his courting and marrying the last Medici, Principessa Margaret, whom the international set call "The Royal Welcome Wagon" and "the ignoblest Roman of them all" (B, 259, parodying Antony's verdict on Brutus, Julius Caesar 5.5.68). With the relief from poverty his marriage affords, James becomes a different Masked Playboy. Able to hobnob with the rich and famous and free from material cares, he and Margaret take up domestic life in New York and try to make their lives ordinary by subscribing to the Book-of-the-Month Club and taking group vacations, one of which turns out disastrously.

As this Masked Playboy, James becomes obsessed with his hereditary line. No longer needing access to the famous, he now seeks assurance that his genetic configuration will endure. This leads to three frustrations. First, he frets obsessively about Margaret's fidelity because he cannot tolerate uncertainty about an heir who may not be his own. Despite Margaret's assuring his acceptance by the famous and his respite from poverty, he introduces tension into their artificial domesticity by suspecting her of extramarital interests.

A second consequence of his accepting the metaphor as literal is his unwillingness to acknowledge his illegitimate son David. When Margaret cannot conceive, he learns in a zany scene that his sperm count is low. David, now a teenager, comes to live with him, but the boy is so deferential that James rejects him (he also rejected David before wrestling Sallow but did not then know who the boy was; the irony of his being so fixated on confronting death that he refused to recognize his son, a secular assurance of continuity, parallels the present rejection). By disinheriting David, James condemns himself to losing the posterity he wants.

Repudiating this definition of himself as the Masked Playboy, James undergoes a death-transformation ritual reminiscent of his confrontation with Sallow. Bored with his affluent life-style, he resumes his role as a con artist. He outfits himself in a pawnshop, seeking an image "not seedy so much as shabby, and not shabby so much as tasteless, and not tasteless so much as anonymous" (*B*, 327). Having rejected his image as the Masked Playboy, he resumes his plan for the club, but while preparing for this goal, he develops psychosomatic symptoms. Believing he is about to die, he cherishes his sickness "as a justification" (*B*, 355).

The Masked Playboy metaphor takes another form when James is near his goal. Having persuaded Nate Lace to fund his club, he dreams about the group's first meeting. In his dream (recorded in journal form), he appears in a host's cape and mingles with the guests but gives the host's mantle to Lace, to appear as one of the great, not merely the functionary who assembled them.

The Masked Playboy then delivers an impromptu speech. Like his earlier eulogy for Uncle Myles, the speech gets out of control and becomes an impassioned plea for the great to recognize James as a person. He encourages them to repeat his error, to think of one another as metaphors: "Since there isn't time for the other thing ["the proper study of mankind"—still quoting Pope], we're going to have to find a kind of shorthand for it, and it's occurred to me that one way we might do that is by looking upon each other as metaphors. . . . It would be like a morality play. You know. Only much more sophisticated. We'd be using metaphors to reveal ourselves to each other. . . . Every man his own anthropologist!" (*B*, 377). By defining one another metaphorically, the celebrities would replicate his experience. The dream ends when James, like the Blob of the movies, becomes gigantic and displaces all humanity, beginning with Perlmutter and expanding through the room, then the street, then the world. This suggests James's unconscious recognition that his error of self-metaphor can become epidemic. Elkin offers this interpretation of the "ultimate chapter": "the death of everybody in the world is what validates Boswell's life. He grows immense, becomes the ultimate body-builder, by destroying other bodies. Boswell is no sycophant. Boswell is a total egocentric."[14]

After this dream, he has his final epiphany. With the gala occasion imminent, a policeman denies him entrance to his club. All he must do to enter is identify himself, but he refuses. Instead he joins the proletarian sightseers and challenges their adulation of his gathering of the great by shouting, "*Down with the Club!*" (B, 387).

This scene may puzzle some readers, for James's life's work would culminate in this gathering of the powerful and influential. At his moment of triumph, he castigates his own principal achievement. Thematically this serves Elkin's needs by repudiating the premise on which James has created his life, but the scene also synthesizes other key meanings. The gesture is spontaneous; he has walked to the meeting in rain (he took mass transit in rain to wrestle Sallow), dressed formally (like a Masked Playboy), but an officer's refusal to allow him to cross the crowd-control barrier motivates this outburst. Its meaning, however, lies in Elkin's careful organization of the many disappointments of James's experiments in self-metaphor, in his boundless energy and love of challenge, and in his theatrical confrontation with the true enemy, his "death experiments" (B, 345).

Should he realize his dream, what goal could direct his passion and energy? When he married Margaret and became prominent enough that he need not scheme to attract celebrities, he became bored and adopted a counter-disguise to create freedom and pursue his dream. Now, with his objective in reach, James unconsciously realizes that the club's success would threaten his true purpose, by extension his identity. On the other hand, the club could fail. Although there are confused identifications of the Secretary of State (B, 384, 386), "the millionaire, whatsisname" (B, 384), and "some movie star" (B, 383), no celebrity makes a verified appearance. We should recall those guests who did not answer James's wedding invitation: Rockefeller, Faulkner, Bellow, Hemingway, Stevenson, Dr. Salk, Stravinsky, and fictional characters Lano, Perlmutter, Gordon Rail, and Sallow (B, 282). By condemning his club, James maintains rather than tests the illusion that he has influenced the great.

That he condemns the club to protect his life's purpose gains support when we consider his closest approximation to a confrontation with death, his "death experiments." Sending out invitations to join the club, James feels ill for the first time in his life. His symptoms teach him something about his nemesis. Death, he learns, is not an adversary but an inevitable element of one's personhood. It is not an abstraction one can personify as John Sallow: "That fatality was a chain reaction, death some ubiquitous thing on springs inside us, neither waiting nor ready to pounce, but set to go off at the merest untoward, uncircumspect jostle. I saw my body as something volatile as a bomb. Hypochondria was deep wisdom and ludicrous folly; there was nothing that we could do" (*B*, 344). The most important discovery James makes is that his enemy is not an abstraction, but himself. His bout with hypochondria, moreover, teaches him that "I have mislived my life" (*B*, 361), and in finally rejecting David, his guarantee against mortality, he paradoxically gathers strength to continue with his life. His epiphany occurs when, having learned that his death is not an enemy to be personified, he makes the spontaneous gesture of renouncing the club and, with it, the substitutions for accepting his mortality with which *Boswell* is concerned.

While convalescing, James adopts a maxim to replace "because my heart is pure." His new phrase, "fixing beyond fixing" (*B*, 356, 358, 362, 367), recognizes that some things are determined beyond human control. If the first echoed Horatio Alger, the latter sounds like something out of Emile Zola or Thomas Hardy. The second "fixing" refers to outcomes that can be controlled by human manipulation—fixing wrestling matches, scheming to make influential people take notice of James, or hustling grant agencies to fund his schemes. The first "fixing," however, suggests that certain events are beyond the control even of manipulative individuals, no matter how energetic or obsessed they may be.

Recognizing that death is the inevitable result of being, James embarks on a series of "death experiments." These are evasions, for six of the seven test the effect his death might have on others, not on himself. He simulates two suicide attempts, an appearance as a murder victim, two collapses on mass transit vehicles, and a heart attack in a cafeteria—the last a particularly sadistic one because it is designed to test its effect on a blind man. What these have in common is their theatricality. Each is staged to test others' reactions to James's death. Experimenting with the individuality assured by death—"I did not want to die, but the sense of rude power I experienced when I knew that I was dying was the most stimulating thing that had ever happened to me" (*B*, 345)—James still harbors the illusion that caused him to seek his purpose in celebrities. He defines the importance of his life and death in the value he can force others to attach to them.

Boswell is a remarkable first novel. It is very funny, but it is serious about the ingenuity with which people try to avoid existential confrontations. Elkin effectively alludes to Johnson's biographer without being dominated by that

text to create a character at whom we laugh but whose enthusiasm and appetite for self-expression we admire. We should recognize the existential errors
Boswell makes, but we marvel at his zest, energy, and inspired rhetoric.

George Mills

The Living End (1979) expanded Elkin's audience as the public became
aware of his comic genius. At that time, he was creating his most ambitious
fiction, a watershed in technique and scope. Although *George Mills* incorpo-
rates many concerns, technical and thematic, of his earlier books, Elkin is
more daring than ever in the limits to which he presses his innovative structure and style.

Mills is Elkin's most comprehensive exploration of the idea of entrapment
in oral history. The generating idea, that a family may be destined to be
second-rate, has long been implicit in his novels, but here it takes an unexpected turn. Unlike Boswell, the Millses do not seek alternatives to the threat
of being blue-collar. A central theme in this novel concerns the degree to
which the heirs accept the limitations on their options imposed by the oral
tradition they inherit.

Elkin's emphasis on oral history allows great flexibility in narrative technique and style. Concentrating on important stylistic devices will help us
understand the more complicated matter of how style and technique in
George Mills constitute Elkin's most explicit incorporation of William
Faulkner's methods into his own most ambitious work. Even more episodic
than Elkin's other books, it treats a millennium's response by the Mills family to Guillalume's curse. Elkin isolates four members of the Mills clan, and
the style adjusts to the temporal and cultural setting appropriate to each
character.[15]

Part I, the briefest section, narrates a failed crusade during which Greatest
Grandfather Mills accepts the curse and establishes the novel's controlling
metaphor, the "tapestry condition" (*GM*, 29). It parodies the quest romance
in which a knight and squire (here, a baron's fourth son and his "Horseshit
Man") set out to find adventure. These questers seek neither a chance to
prove themselves nor some Holy Grail, but alternatives to their duty.
Charged with joining the First Crusade, Guillalume deliberately allows Mills
to miss a crucial turn, so they end up as captive laborers in Wieliczka, a Polish
salt mine.[16] Guillalume missed the turn for self-serving reasons: if his elder
brothers die on crusades, he will inherit the family fortune. The parody of romance conventions culminates when Mills and Guillalume escape and confront Cossack barbarians. Mills delivers an impromptu sermon, telling the

Cossacks, "God hates hitters. . . . He told me to tell you you mustn't hit. If you have to hit you mustn't hit hard. And killing. Killing isn't nice. Neither shouldst thou maim   . . . Ain't gonna *study* war no more" (*GM*, 40), a series of anachronisms, Sunday school aphorisms, and clichés that have an unexpectedly desired effect. He takes this message through Eastern and Mediterranean Europe as the travelers find their way home, "and *that* was the First Crusade" (*GM*, 42).

The style of part I, a wonderful set-piece, blends anachronism, pun, cliché, and outrageous situation. Elkin parodies the conventions of romance by describing improbable adventures in modern ways. Examples include the fanciful descriptions of a large barbarian who steals their horses and sends them toward the salt mine (*GM*, 9) and a multilingual, complexly talismaned merchant (*GM*, 15). The culminating irony is that Mills, by delivering his pacifist's message, completes the crusade Guillalume tried to avoid, but his master's brothers have died on other crusades, so after inheriting he sends George, his companion and protector, back to the stables because "it would not do for one so high placed to have as a retainer a man who knew nothing of horses" (*GM*, 42).

The novel's controlling metaphor, the tapestry condition, is also introduced in part I. This figure, mentioned when Mills recalls a dream about visiting the castle, establishes that the Mills curse is not merely Guillalume's individual outburst, but assumptions wealthy and powerful people generally have about the serving class. When he saw how common folk were portrayed on the tapestry, Mills had a revelation: "It was how they saw us—see us. Shepherds and farmers. Millers, bakers, smithies. . . . Pastoral, safe, settled in the tapestry condition of their lives, woven into it as the images themselves. . . . We are a dour, luteless people" (*GM*, 29). This insight, which recurs when the forty-third Mills meets his king and again when the contemporary Mills meets Judith Glazer, defines the natural hierarchy Guillalume announces. The problem is that the Millses believe at least as much in the tapestry condition as the aristocrats do.

Much longer than part I, part IV treats the adventures of a descendant employed as the fall guy on a mission to the Turkish Sultan. His journey results in the family's removal to America, but like Greatest Grandfather, his figurative voyage is to adventure and disillusionment. This Mills delights in his story's legendary place in the family saga: "It was *all* adventure and he was an adventurer and an adventurer did not so much forget danger as acknowledge and then ignore it, that only then could he be vouchsafed immunity" (*GM*, 400). His meeting his king, being sent on a diplomatic mission, becoming a legend among the Janissaries and causing their downfall, and hiding out in the sultan's harem allow Elkin a stage upon which to diversify his style and to parody conventions of eighteenth-century diction and form.

The London episodes, in which Mills meets King George IV sneaking out of his "safe house," an anachronism for a home he shares with his mistress, introduce two Restoration and eighteenth-century conventions: the bawdy drawing room comedy of Restoration drama and the epistolary style. The king, setting up the safe house with Mrs. Fitzherbert,[17] has Josiah Wedgewood make their dinnerware, Dick Sheridan write comedies according to their outlines, and provincial novelist Jane Austen write novels to their liking.

After mistaking Mills for an assassin or spy, King George confides in this unfamiliar subject a narrative of bawdy intrigues and political complications in a style reminiscent of William Wycherly's plays. Some of the episode's humor derives from the king's diction, which recalls the sexual frankness of Restoration comedy. His advances to Mrs. Fitzherbert forty-one years before telling Mills the story suggest the kind of humor in Wycherly's *The Country Wife*: "When I leered your breasts, when I squinnied your nipples. . . . I'm Prince of Wales and I attentioned your tits. *You did not redden!*" (*GM*, 344). Because Mrs. Fitzherbert proves reluctant to commit adultery, the king makes his seduction an occasion for court theatrics, and his repartee becomes entertainment for the bystanders.

Having parodied some Restoration dramatic conventions in the story of the king's courtship, Elkin takes on the epistolary convention in the reference letter Mills shows the king. The personal letter was an eighteenth-century art form. Boswell's *Life of Johnson* features many letters to and from the great man, and Samuel Richardson used exchanges of letters as the mimetic principle in his pioneering novels. Elkin uses two variations on this motif in *Mills*, a long one in the Cassadaga section and this one. This letter serves the plot by providing the reason Mills is set up on the diplomatic mission (the addressee was the king's enemy) and, when he escapes the harem, is sent to America. Like many other elements of this novel, however, the letter offers the author an occasion for rhetorical diversity as well as a plot device.

Not only does Elkin parody the orotund, periodic style of the familiar letter, he points out in the text exactly what he is doing. The king thinks, "The damned thing's in code" (*GM*, 356), and he finishes the "prolix letter" wondering, "What pun? What word games?" (*GM*, 364). Ostensibly a character reference and testimony to Mills's deference, the letter actually calls attention to the writer at the expense of both reader and message.

Elkin continues to send up traditional forms throughout this section. In the Janissaries adventure, he adapts the American tall tale, then returns to eighteenth-century drawing room comedy in the harem episodes. Mills becomes a Janissary because of political intrigue, but his "Mills blood" enables him to adapt: "He understood the source of his fierce loyalties, could trace them back forty-two or so generations to a strange curse delivered by a pampered nobleman in a Polish wood. . . . He was proud to be a Janissary. Proud of hardship, humiliation, his hardcore elite corps humility. . . . A hero of hardship, a big shot of bane and outrage" (*GM*, 381). Despite his having been set up in a subtle political maneuver, the object of which is never clear to Mills or the reader, George accepts the ruthless Janissary discipline and becomes a legend in their folklore.

As Mills accepts this role, Elkin mixes first-person narration in a Cockney accent with omniscient narrative having the flavor of the tall tale. In an initiation battle, George sneezes his friend to death, uses his body as a shield, then disembowels him to find his "bribegold." This fierce resourcefulness, embodying the ruthlessness the Janissaries espouse, earns Mills a place in the order's oral tradition. He had none of this in mind when he acted; his sneeze was a reaction to horse dung stuffed into his nostrils, and the corpse mutilation was a desperate effort at self-preservation.

Similarly his escape from the Janissaries is the stuff of tall tales. Sent on a suicide mission by the Meat Cut, an officer whose request for a ritual bath pushes Mills as close "to harboring a pure revolutionary thought as anyone in the entire history of the world" (*GM*, 391), George senses that he and his friend are being condemned to death. Exploiting Mills's reputation for ferocity, they simulate an attack on the city. Elkin rearranges history to make this the occasion of the sultan's decision to end the Janissaries' power, but George thinks this may lift the curse: "They *were* grand. No Mills since the first George Mills had been grander, and even if his own had been a sidekick's grandeur—briefly he wondered if it were enough to lift the curse. . . . Bufesqueu couldn't have done it by himself. It had been his name, the living legend's, that had been passed on the street. George was satisfied" (*GM*, 404). Through the medium of oral tradition, the desperate effort of two frightened victims to escape their fate becomes a historical moment in which minor actions have heroic effects.

Elkin is not yet finished with parodies in the account of the forty-third Mills. Taking sanctuary in the sultan's harem, he again becomes a living legend. His manly voice causes curiosity among the concubines and slaves. Subjected to a humiliating examination, he becomes legendary as the only eunuch whose sex has regenerated. As he did in the garrison, Mills adapts, because of his "blue-collar habit of obedience," to the discipline of being a potent male in an environment designed to encourage prurience. He works with horses, a family tradition, and audits classes in court protocol to pass time.

The classes pay off; upon discovering the body of the sultan's mother, Mills exploits the protocol that a messenger cannot be detained and thereby escapes to the British embassy.

The most intriguing technique in the seraglio episodes is Elkin's parody of the conversational style of a fashionable eighteenth-century salon. The eunuchs, harem women, and servants frequently meet for enlightened conversation, engaging in "metaphysical discourse"—for example, whether female slaves are improved by servitude, whether eunuchs can rupture themselves, or "the metaphysical question of whether or not eunuchs could expose themselves" (*GM*, 427). Mills knows he must escape when he is again exposed to test this hypothesis.

Elkin successfully parodies the high style of polite conversation by designating trivial issues metaphysical. The speakers are more interested in scoring debate points than in communicating: "Bufesqueu was brilliant, locating his arguments scientifically but saving his great point to the end of the speech" (*GM*, 426). Playing to audiences for applause, the characters manifest a spiritual apathy comparable with the eunuchs' impotence. On a wider scale, Elkin implies that such empty, if polished, conversation for its own sake is a type of mental impotence.

Like the story of Greatest Grandfather's journey, part IV is a tour de force. Its many styles appropriately reflect conventions of eighteenth- and early nineteenth-century writing, and this constant reference, punctuated by anachronisms, reinforces the theme that history, especially oral history, is a trap that can limit individual or family horizons.

The rest of *George Mills,* treating the life of a contemporary St. Louis eviction specialist, features chronological complexity and abrupt shifts in narrative focus. Shifts from first- to third-person narration are effectively employed in chapter 6, part III, when Mills tells his employer how he met his wife. More explicitly than anywhere else in his fiction, Elkin creates a counterpoint between events recounted objectively (third person) and subjectively (first person). The narrator describes an event; immediately, in brackets, Mills's account of the same event follows. This contrast in points of view raises intriguing epistemological possibilities. Describing Mills's casual sexual encounters before he met Louise, the narrator advances the kind of vague suggestibility we often find in Faulkner: "As he believed, again vaguely, in virgins. Not—he was no prude—in their moral superiority. . . . Not, in fact, in anything petite or chaste or delicate, prudent, pure, virtuous, discreet or even modest. In virginity, in virginity itself, in its simple mechanical cause. He believed, that is, in the hymen" (*GM*, 261). This suggestibility, reinforced by repetition, recalls Quentin Compson's meditations on his sister's virginity in *The Sound and the Fury* or V. K. Ratliff's speculations on Eula Varner's sexuality in *The Hamlet*. By contrast, Mills's first-person account is practical and direct: "How could I deal with someone who did not mean to be dealt with? . . . If I did not think of them as incorruptible then I thought of them as indifferent, people outside my sphere of influence" (*GM*, 262).

Although sudden shifts between third- and first-person points of view are a trademark of Elkin's technique, nowhere else does he employ the method more subtly than here. The narrator consistently offers sophisticated but finally vague explanations of the fate that brought George and Louise together, but these are offset by Mills's no-nonsense explanations of his conduct.

Unlike the picaresque *Boswell*, the contemporary narrative blends three distinct story lines, each centered around a dominant character. These lines intersect as the characters interact and work together to counterpoint George's acceptance of being considered second rate and his curious notion of being saved.

Initially the narrative centers on Cornell Messenger, who habitually punctuates his conversation with a Conrad allusion, "the horror, the horror." It is tempting to see autobiographical references here: Messenger teaches at a St. Louis university, is a writer who has attracted little popular attention (his one well-known story is held on option by a movie producer; Elkin's "The Bailbondsman" was filmed as *Alex and the Gypsy* in 1976), and is the son of a charismatic traveling salesman. We should not press this comparison, for Messenger has accepted his failures and has serious problems with his children, especially dyslexic Harve, for whom his misguided efforts always backfire. Often "enhanced" by marijuana, Messenger cannot take on a serious obligation without the drug. With his habitual gossiping about university peers and officials, his failure as a writer and parent, his lapses into sentimentality about Jerry Lewis telethons, and his drug dependence, Messenger suggests an apathy intellectuals may acquire in the robust climate of American life. Structurally Messenger's sexual attraction to Louise Mills reinforces the idea that his apathy is an intellectual counterpart to George's acceptance of the Mills curse.

Messenger unifies the plot by linking Mills and another focal character, Judith Glazer. Messenger pays an obligatory visit to the dying woman, whose husband will soon be dean. He receives a task: to take over her Meals-on-Wheels route, a charity she has used to abuse her wealthy father by giving his unlisted telephone numbers to her clients. Among Cornell's clients is Louise's father.

In the book's most touching scene, Mr. Mead dies. He progressively loses interest in his being: "Denied psychology, he regards his Cheshire decline with what? With nothing. What should have been of interest, the most personal moment of his life, is now merely consciousness, knowledge, the mind's disinterested attention. He is like someone neither participant nor fan who hears a ball score" (*GM*, 208–9). Forced to attend this genuine instance of "the horror," Cornell forms a lasting friendship with Mills. When Mills loses his job as an eviction specialist, he mentions Judith's need for a companion to accompany her on a journey to a Mexican clinic.

A dying heiress with a history of mental disorder, Judith is a more complex character than Messenger, at once petty and heroic, suicidal and determined to live. Because of her vindictive, devious habits of humiliation, she is an unappealing character, filled with understandable malice toward those whose health promises continued life and bitter about the eleven years she lost to mental illness. In the asylum, she consistently attempted to undo other patients' therapeutic advances. Delivering her eulogy, her psychiatrist recalls letters she wrote to patients who received shock therapy, "reminding people whose own bad dreams has just been burned out of them . . . of everything they'd forgotten, rubbing their noses in their past" because "What happens if they get well?" (*GM*, 310). The question suggests selfishness and despair. If other patients recover, Judith's chronic madness is more unbearable.

Bitterly Judith lashes out at her father, husband, and friends. She promises not to take up quack cures and "other fast-food fixes of the hopeful doomed" (*GM*, 80). She claims she will face death squarely by placing her fate in God's hands but hires Mills to take her to a Juarez laetrile clinic. This broken promise motif clarifies Elkin's investing this unappealing character with remarkable courage and dignity without diminishing her pettiness or vindictiveness.[18] These episodes also serve as this Mills's journey and adventure, a chance to show what he is made of, to act on the human potential beneath his apathetic acceptance of generations of servitude.

Judith breaks her vow not to seek quack cures because her daughter, Mary, cannot cope with Judith's impending death. That she never believes in the cure explains most of her actions in Mexico. She knows she will die of cancer but hopes to buy time so her daughter can accept her fate. If she is doing this for Mary, however, her habitual self-destructiveness persists. In Juarez she forces Mills to take her on charity benders, in which they drive dark roads giving away money. She makes him cash her travelers' checks and leave currency lying around the motel room. George understands what is at stake; she is trying to commit ethical suicide by being killed in a robbery attempt, because "she believed in martyrdom. Saint Judith Glazer of Cancer. Because she needed holy bruises, some painful black-and-blue theology of confrontation. And that was when he realized she was dangerous" (*GM,* 246). She admits hoping "some bad man will take the bait, and God never notice that it was entrapment" (*GM,* 247).

In her final weeks, Judith becomes an emblem for the human condition, facing her death with other-directed courage yet self-centered enough to hope for a quick, beatific end to her suffering. These suicidal charity missions risk Mills's life too. This is a contemporary version of the tapestry condition. The rich, who "live unlisted lives" (*GM,* 319), are so indifferent to the concerns of the poor that it never occurs to Judith that her goal may bring harm, even death, to Mills.[19]

Although Judith's confrontation with her death parallels the stoic dignity with which Mr. Mead accepts his, her primary role is to allow Elkin an opportunity to explore the limited heroism of which Mills is capable. Judith is not an easy person to like, and the physical effects of disease make her an unpleasant presence. She is interested in Mills's stories about his ancestors but indifferent to the risks at which her suicide efforts place him.

Mills, who in accepting the job recognized the assumptions about his blue-collar tradition implicit in the offer ("he wanted this job, needed it. He had to make himself low" [*GM,* 228]), ministers to Judith's physical and psychological needs with self-effacement and almost heroic patience. In a touching scene similar to that in which Mead dies, Judith, having refused hospitalization despite intense pain, watches children playing Marco Polo in the motel pool. When she suffers an extremely severe episode, George desperately tries to administer pain killers. She cries out "Marco," and recognizing the allusion, he reassures her by saying "Polo" and "it seemed to soothe her heart that, blind and maddened as she was, she was not alone in the water" (*GM,* 252).[20]

The most technically complex part of this Mills's story, separately published in *Tri-Quarterly* as "The Cassadaga Section," chronicles the family's stay in a community of Florida spiritualists when George was twelve. Although the episode gives Elkin a chance to debunk spiritualists and psychics, he is tolerant. He treats them as one type of provider to the despair people feel when confronting death's finality. The episode immediately following the Cassadaga section offers compelling evidence that *George Mills* is Elkin's most explicit adaptation of certain styles and techniques of William Faulkner.

Elkin's doctoral thesis treats Faulkner's use of biblical themes and types, but frequent remarks, like this description of Faulkner's characterization, suggest the novelist's interest in the Yoknapatawpha County chronicler's

technique: "Faulkner's basic rhetorical staple is the hyperbole. He uses hyperbolic characters, superlative characters in the sense that their qualities represent the most extreme limits it is possible for those qualities to attain without
spilling over into parody."[21] Elkin is especially intrigued by the more epis-
temologically speculative among Faulkner's books, like *Light in August,
Absalom, Absalom!* and the Snopes trilogy, in which characters must reconstruct the actions and motives of others.

This speculative trend recurs throughout *George Mills* as a logical extension of the book's concern with oral history. Elkin's most explicit tribute to
Faulkner occurs when young Mills and Reverend Wickland, a spiritualist, reconstruct the story of George's parents' courtship and his sister's birth.

Unlike previous Millses, George does not know his immediate family history. He knows they moved from Milwaukee to Florida during the depression, and he watched his father panhandle a chain gang in a hilarious effort to
gauge the opposition in the blue-collar trade. Mills replaced the prisoners as
town flunky, and young George found his niche as messenger, confidant, and
medium for the spiritualists. He forms a personal bond with Wickland, who
shows him his sister and with him reconstructs recent family history.

This reconstruction is Elkin's most explicit debt to Faulkner, whose characters Quentin Compson and Shreve McLaughlin work together to reconstruct the intimate history of the Sutpen family in *Absalom, Absalom!* Like
Shreve and Quentin, George and Wickland move beyond fact into imagination to discover the secrets of a buried past. The most impressive feature of
this reconstruction is, as in *Absalom,* the degree to which it is the product of
distinct imaginations working in concert. Neither Mills nor Wickland can
discover the secret on his own. Taking clues from one another's insights, they
formulate a series of hypotheses about what must have happened, first specu-
lating on the origins of Cassadaga medium Jack Sunshine, then on George's
parents' courtship. Wickland, the "reverend of reality" (*GM,* 192), understands why the father hid in the basement of a Milwaukee apartment: "to
hide out for the fifty or so years I have left to live, to . . . accomplish by myself
in a single life-time what all my family hasn't been able to pull off in a thousand years—the extinction of my long, bland, lumpish line" (*GM,* 166).
This is a clue to how George will end the curse. But the line is not extinct, so
they must account for the failure of his father's plan.

This need leads them to reconstruct a plausible series of circumstances
about Mills's marriage to Nancy and their hope that any issue would be
female: "If you'd been a girl he thought he would still be able to dodge his
fate. He still believed in his fate, you see, saw himself in the myth victim's
delicious position" (*GM,* 175). Echoes of Faulkner's diction are inescapa-

ble, evidenced by the hypothetical construction, the belief in fate, and the controlling figure in which George's father sees himself as a "myth victim," a concept reinforced by several references to the Oedipus story (*GM*, 174, 185, 192).

As in Faulkner, one hypothesis creates a need for several related ones. If genetics denied Mills's escape from the family tradition when George was born male, he still had the option to withhold at least his consent by naming the boy anything but George. He could name him "Greg" to tease "what he thought he had for nemesis" and thus refuse to consent in fate's authority. So Wickland revises his conjecture: the father "wanted the character of a rebel without any of the expense" (*GM*, 176). After compiling conjectural evidence about George's sister, Wickland revises his estimate of the father's character again: "He still thinks there is a Corinth. He thinks it's Cassadaga. . . . Because he's no rebel. . . . Because telling you [the Mills saga] was *his* trump card, and playing it was the only way he had to avenge what I did and to stand by history" (*GM*, 192).

This Faulknerian reconstruction of recent Mills history introduces a new mystery. Wickland knows about Nancy's efforts in Milwaukee to escape being "the myth victim's victim" (*GM*, 176), including a plan to leave George and take her son and unborn daughter to New Jersey. Her method of raising funds for the escape, skimping on her own diet, results in the daughter's stillbirth (she visits the Cassadaga spiritualists to make contact with Janet) and her entrapment in Mills history. Yet she exacts a promise from her husband: "She was still in control of the ironies. She didn't want you ever to find out about the Millses. She made him promise" (*GM*, 190).

Like Judith's promise not to seek quack cures, this promise is broken. George knows, and is therefore trapped in, Mills history. Moreover, something Wickland did caused his father to feel justified in breaking his promise. We are never told exactly what the reverend of reality did, but it is consistent with the Faulknerian techniques of the Cassadaga section that he had an affair with Nancy that led to a pregnancy.[22]

This explains George's learning about the family history, as well as the process by which he revises his concept of salvation. When he "shows" George his sister, Wickland says, "She's going to have a baby" (*GM*, 192). The pronoun refers to Nancy. The grammar of the sentence could indicate the sister, but if the sister is a spirit, she would not be pregnant. So Nancy is pregnant, by Wickland, at whose home the Millses have stayed, and the husband broke his promise in order to get revenge for her infidelity.

This thread recurs at the end of *George Mills*. Having returned from Mexico, Mills tries to exploit his presence at the heiress's deathwatch to coerce contenders for her inheritance to provide for him and thus to escape the family curse. As his efforts fail (his fate is not to escape the curse but to end it), he sees a woman servicing vending machines and intuitively believes she is his lost half-sister. When she attends Reverend Coulé's church on the day Mills gives his sermon, he is convinced she is his sister and includes this in his sermon on miracles (*GM*, 507). His accepting that she is not his relative leads to a thematically important discovery: he "was convinced now that he had one, and that wherever she was she would be doing well" (*GM*, 508). As is often the case with Faulkner's characters, assumption is as good as certainty, and belief in a half-sister who is not a "myth victim" assures George that history can be escaped.[23] This concept clarifies Mills's sense of personal salvation and explains why, at novel's end, he feels "relieved of history as an amnesiac" (*GM*, 508).

A central motif, this state of grace means, first, an immunity George feels he has because of his family inheritance. It also implies his defeating the family curse. After the curse, the most frequent motif in the book is some variation on this description: "He is the man to whom everything has happened that is going to happen. This is his grace" (*GM*, 216). In a conversation with Gass, Elkin offers a similar gloss for George's salvation:

That's the essence of George's salvation; that's *his* state of grace, his notion that he has achieved it, not through any particular holiness of his own, but simply through the conviction that there's nothing, good or bad, that can happen to him any more. The certainty that George Mills reaches is the conviction that he is only George Mills—son of George Mills—who in turn was the son of still another George Mills, and so on. I mean, he's *shtupped* with his own history. And since none of these folks ever amounted to much, he finally cuts his losses and announces his salvation.[24]

If this is what Mills's salvation means—and it clearly does—his apathy results from this belief in grace. In the scene least flattering to his character, Mills demonstrates his grace to Coulé, a former televangelist desperate to see signs of grace in others. (Elkin's treatment of this character is as unexpectedly tolerant as that of the Cassadaga spiritualists.) His curiosity aroused by Louise's description of George's state of grace, Coulé visits Mills at the job to learn about it. He finds a bigoted expert in evicting black families, who hurls racial slurs indiscriminately. Mills has no religious conviction; he admits not believing in God or Christ, yet his eyes "glittered with certainty" such as Coulé has not seen since his electronic ministry collapsed. This certainty is evidenced by Mills's confidence that no matter how abusive he is to blacks, they will not harm him: "I parted them niggers like the Red Sea. They never touched me. You know how they do people in these projects? They didn't do *me*. They never will. Who *says* I ain't saved?" (*GM*, 65).

If this is all Mills's salvation means, the novel, despite its many technical merits, asks the reader to accept sympathetically the apathy and bigotry of a man whose excuse is a family curse. The theme is not significant enough to bear the burden of so ambitious a work of fiction. There is, however, evidence that Mills's grace is a renunciation by which he ends the family curse. If this evidence proves convincing, we may conclude that *George Mills* argues that human freedom, while limited by circumstance, has as much to do with what we make of our lives as destiny or fate.

The first thread of evidence is that Mills, delivering his sermon to Coulé's congregation, announces his salvation in his typical way (*GM*, 506) but discovers while recounting his family history and life's adventures to a confused audience that his grace was an illusion: " 'Hell, I ain't saved,' he said, *oddly cheered.* 'Being tired isn't saved, sucking up isn't grace.' " Ending the sermon, he stands "in *what grace he had,* relieved of history as an amnesiac" (*GM*, 508; my italics). He has seen in others, notably Father Merchant, the tout of Juarez, and Grant, the Claunch family's black servant with whom he felt instant enmity but whose death shocked him, images of the "blue-collar blood" he thought was a cause of his salvation. His journey to Mexico and the effort to capitalize on his attendance at Judith's death have meant something, and this meaning deals with the question of whether one's fate is one's character.

This issue is focused when, helping George reconstruct the family's recent history, Wickland concludes, "Our lives happen to us. We don't make them up" (*GM*, 179). Later Messenger, gossiping with Mills about the fates of acquaintances from the Glazer circle, concludes, "Things happen, that's all" (*GM*, 492). These exchanges of gossip incidentally resemble the Faulknerian technique of the Cassadaga section, for Messenger and Mills must conjecture about what happened and why.

The ironic, sentimental endings to the stories of minor characters lend some credibility to Wickland's and Messenger's positions. A Meals-on-Wheels recipient wins a magazine sweepstakes; after the Claunch family arranges his dismissal, Dean Glazer is reinstated because he has an affair with Dr. Losey's mistress; Mary Glazer, who drew pornographic pictures to compensate for frustration at Judith's death, is a promising artist; Messenger's son, Harve, proves not to be dyslexic but the victim of a remediable educational lacuna; the film producer exercises his option on Messenger's story; and so on.

These events have the aura of soap operas or situation comedies, a connection made explicit when Mills decides to listen to Messenger's gossip: "Because there were only reruns on television anyway and he was listening now. Listening despite himself. Salvation or no salvation. Because they could almost have been more Millses" (*GM*, 458). He becomes involved in the soap opera lives of the Glazer circle so much that he, better than Messenger, can reconstruct the events. He sees that others are less unlike the Millses than he thought, and this discovery leads him to attempt to remedy in his own life the Mills condition.

This attempt reduces George to a blackmailer, willing to trade what he knows or is willing to invent about Judith's last days for a job or an advantage. He hits Dean Glazer for a job at the university and Claunch for one operating an elevator. Both efforts fail, and one reason he reconstructs gossip with Messenger is, "*I want the goddamn goods on them!*" (*GM*, 454). The situation comedy endings of others' lives (Messenger calls his role in gossip reconstruction "*the epilogue man*" [*GM*, 499]) heighten the irony that, despite the duplicity involved in "Operation Bootstrap" (*GM*, 452), Mills cannot escape the curse, though others' lives work out well.

He does not escape it; he ends it. The remedy involves a lifelong act of renunciation. Mills's victory is his refusal to pass on his "flawed genes." He realizes this at the end of his sermon, and this realization leads him to reassess the Mills curse and his salvation: "The line's played out, watered" (GM, 507). His renunciation has been effective because he was not, like Millses before him, obsessed with procreation and passing on the oral history of the Millses.

Although Louise is comely enough that Messenger becomes infatuated with her, in no scene does George have procreative sex with her. Her virginity attracted her to him, and the scene in which he makes his commitment to her results in premature orgasm. In the only sexual scene he resists her advances and masturbates her. He rejects her explanation that his impotence is "psychological"; he offers "grace" to explain his lack of interest, and Elkin explicitly associates grace and abstinence: "He was saved, lifted from life. In a state of grace. Mills in weightlessness, desire, will and soul idling like a car at a stoplight. George Mills, yeomanized a thousand years, Blue Collar George like a priest at a time clock" (*GM*, 55). Greatest Grandfather lamented the curse's impact on his progeny, but the forty-third Mills provides the clearest contrast to George's salvation as his determination to defeat the curse by ending the line.

After escaping the Janissaries, Mills takes sanctuary in the sultan's harem, where he must pass as a eunuch or become one. His companion, Bufesqueu, finds the pleasures of seraglio life worth the price he must someday pay. For Mills, however, the need to escape is not just to preserve his manhood but to save his line and the oral tradition to which his adventures contribute an exciting chapter: "Mills dreaded another summons to the interdicted harem—he would be castrated. Then, even if he lived, there would be no son. His tale would go untold. And what a tale, he thought. . . . He had nothing to be ashamed of. Except his bachelorhood. Except his sonlessness" (*GM*, 419).

According to Wickland, the present Mills's father tried to escape history by hiding in a Milwaukee cellar, but destiny caught up with him. His son, who has been to Cassadaga and has seen his sister, can do what no other Mills has done. He has ended the curse. His efforts to end it for himself fail, but his grace is the knowledge that the Mills life is not exclusive to Millses and that one individual can make a difference by refusing to contribute to history. He ends his sermon by affirming brotherhood with his audience and discovering that "the meaning of life is to live long enough to find something out or to do something well" (*GM*, 508).

George Mills is Elkin's meditation on how history can entrap individuals but not without their consent. It is his most ambitious novel in both scope and technique. Technically fascinating, the book lacks the Elkin trademark: a central character driven by his design. Inevitably, because of the curse's impact, Mills is passive. Even his limited victory over the curse is what he does not do (procreate) rather than what he does (ameliorate). While we are fascinated by brilliant techniques, descriptions, and images, we never become completely engaged in Mills's struggles because he is not a battler. The world is full of passive people, but Elkin's fiction at its best is animated by an obsessive, driven character's fertile imagination. Such figures give vitality to the brilliant works discussed in the next chapters.

Chapter Three

A Bad Man and The Franchiser: Salesmanship and Obsession

Few writers succeed fully in treating daily concerns of American life like vocation and consumption. Although these issues are central to our lives, writers often ignore or treat these as beneath the notice of serious artists. Yet nothing is more American than asking what someone does for a living, and few activities take up as much energy as getting and spending. Elkin may be unique in the tolerance his fiction exhibits toward the attitudes of people who vend and consume products or services.

Many novelists of the postwar period, especially Philip Roth and Saul Bellow, focus on characters of wealth and intellectual refinement whose concern with production, distribution, or consumption is theoretical rather than direct. Bellow's Herzog and Charlie Citrine (*Humboldt's Gift*) have ideas about buying and vending, but their involvement is intellectual. Roth's characters, often writers or intellectuals, generally condescend to the concerns of producers and consumers. Other authors, notably Jack Kerouac and Norman Mailer, treat the problems of outsiders and ignore or condescend to the concerns of middle-class citizens. Among serious writers of the period, John Cheever and John Updike treat people's work and expenditures as worthy fictional subjects. Yet they differ from Elkin by treating primarily the ways in which work and material concerns impose limits on their characters' ability or willingness to confront spiritual questions.

Although Elkin is not primarily a realistic novelist, he is exceptional in the degree to which his fiction confronts the ways our work and patterns of consumption affect our conceptions of ourselves. It is a staple of Elkin criticism that his characters are driven by their vocations.[1] His heroes adopt the goals and means appropriate to their businesses with intense and original drive. Their vocations differ, moreover, from those of most other writers' characters; they are not artists, writers, or intellectuals but owners of franchises and stores, bailbondsmen, loan collectors, or radio personalities. They work within the American mainstream, and the vocations shaping their essential character are often the kind that affect the lives of many citizens in an industrialized society. A study of the businessman in American literature concludes that "Elkin has wrestled most directly with the problems of capitalism and the businessman."[2]

Elkin's emphasis on vocation has created controversy about both tone and meaning. Because characters like Leo Feldman and Ben Flesh embrace consumer culture wholeheartedly, critics differ about how sympathetically Elkin treats their obsessions. Is he, as one camp has it, a compassionate chronicler of our consumer culture, or, as another contends, an ironic or satiric commentator on ways a concern with merchandising limits individuals' meaningful response to life's higher opportunities? Should the author be believed when he says he is no satirist, that he admires his characters' energy and hopes readers will too?[3]

To answer these questions requires an examination of textual and biographical evidence, both of which clarify the tone and meaning of *A Bad Man* and *The Franchiser*. These, certainly among Elkin's best novels, are his most direct treatments of subjects like management, consumption, marketing, and the ways involvement in enterprise can affect one's sense of self. Ben Flesh and Leo Feldman are managers of, as well as respondents to, public taste; Feldman's finest pun is, "I am the master of all I purvey."[4] In their drive to satisfy consumers' needs, they become obsessed with the techniques and goals of their businesses.

Should we respond to their obsessions with admiration or disdain? In his store basement, Feldman provides illegal services, including abortion referrals, prostitutes, connections with drug dealers, and illegal arms for fanatics; at home, he mistreats his family shamefully. Flesh's goal cannot appeal to every reader: "A man of franchise, a true democrat who would make Bar Harbor, Maine, look like Chicago, who would quell distinction, obliterate difference, who would common-denominate until Americans recognize that it was America everywhere."[5] The Whitman dream, that popular American vision, celebrates our cultural diversity, but Flesh wants to obliterate every regional distinction, to make America itself as homogeneous as Howard Johnson's motels or minicinemas in shopping centers, a chain of which he owns.

For those who prefer that American culture preserve what pluralistic character it has left, Ben's goal seems lamentable, and Elkin's comments on this objective have been less than consistent. In a 1975 interview with Phyllis and Joseph Bernt he endorses Ben's statement that "it may be a franchiser, I think, who will save us. . . . Speaking some Esperanto of simple need, answering appetite with convenience foods" (*TF,* 258): "He makes a pretty good argument for the notion that [the world] won't be saved by a hero or a politician or a reformer. But the world will be saved by somebody who sup-

plies universal needs economically. Our salvation is in the franchise business."
The same year he told Scott Sanders, "He's the man who's responsible for
making America look like America, and to the degree that that's so, according to my lights, that makes him a hero." Eight years later he told Jay Clayton
he no longer shares Ben's enthusiasm for making America look like America
but now feels that he "manages . . . to rise above the kind of thing he is
doing."[6]

We are dealing with two distinct issues: how Elkin and his readers feel
about the object of Ben's commitment is one matter; how we and the author
respond to the intensity and significance of that commitment is another. On
this issue, Elkin is unambiguous in defining the relationship among vocation,
mystery, heroism, and obsession in his heroes: "I've gotten a bad rap for writing about losers. I don't regard any of my people . . . as losers. I regard them
as having a tremendous amount of integrity. I take them seriously. . . . They
are doing the best they can. They are really trying to understand the meta-
phorical implications of their own jobs. Every job has one, and every job is, in
its own way, a mystery."[7] It may be difficult to see how Feldman, ignoring
ethics and lying to make sales, or Flesh, hustling franchised goods and services to customers who may neither need nor want them, manifests "integrity."
Elkin suggests, however, that their integrity comes from the dedication with
which they pursue the ethos of the vocation they have chosen. Merchandising
as an art form is Elkin's central concern. Neither Feldman nor Flesh is terribly
interested in making money, but both are passionately committed to the art
of selling.

Like the financier William Lome, who gives Boswell a crash course in merchandising, these individuals commit themselves to a defined purpose in
order to have something by which to identify themselves. Flesh presents a
particularly revealing case. He did not choose the franchising business; the
vocation was thrust upon him. Summoned to Julius Finsberg's deathbed,
Ben inherited the ability to borrow at the prime interest rate. Then a graduate
student at Wharton, he did not know what to do with this opportunity until
Lotte Finsberg, after seeing several Howard Johnson's restaurants on a trip,
urged him to invest in a chain because, like the eighteen Finsberg children,
franchises in chains are identical.

The vocation upon which much of Ben's personality depends was chosen
for him when his character, both commercial and individual, was a blank
slate. A flashback recalls his high school anxiety because he was equally successful in academics, football, track, chorus, and the newspaper: "So he knew
he had no calling, no one thing among his talents that he did better than any
other one thing, and nothing at all that he did better than others" (*TF*, 48).

Buying franchises, with the Finsbergs creating both opportunity and goal, offers an alternative to this equilibrium in which he can do everything well but cannot be special: "He would discover which men's names were for sale and he would buy them and have that going for him. He would have them at the rate banks gave their favored customers and he would have *that* going for him, too. . . . He had never been so excited" (*TF,* 50). He compensates for his feared anonymity by franchising the names of successful entrepreneurs and paradoxically defines his identity by borrowing others' names.

Feldman also inherits his vocation. At no point does he actually choose to become a vendor, but he inherits the commitment of his crazed father who set the challenge of selling "the unsalable thing" (*ABM,* 55, 62, 63). Isidore Feldman, announcing the diaspora in Indiana, was obsessed with vending and acting out the Jewish peddler's role in a gentile society. He forced Leo to act that part, to say "regs, all close," instead of "rags, old clothes," to become "travelling Jews in the latest phase of the new Diaspora" (*ABM,* 48).

Like Lome in *Boswell,* Isidore relished the challenge of selling objects with no obvious commercial value. He felt contempt for selling items customers already wanted. Manipulating a customer created real excitement: "Where's the contest in sound merchandise? You sell a sound piece of merchandise, what's the big deal? Demand has nothing to do with good business, not *good* business. Need, who needs it?" (*ABM,* 49). The salesman's art was Isidore's creed: "Everything is vendible. It *must* be. That's religion. Your father is a deeply religious man. He believes in vendibility" (*ABM,* 53).

Leo's relationship with his father, and with Isidore's religion of merchandising, was ambivalent. He knew Isidore was crazy. Between his twelfth and fifteenth years, he often plotted to run away but remained. When Isidore died, Leo surpassed his business ethic by selling the unsalable thing, Isidore's body, to the county hospital. His obsession with artful merchandising, with selling unwanted items, is his inheritance. Working in the prison canteen, he puts this legacy into practice. He removes the vendible items—toothpaste, cigarettes, stamps—from the display and presses exotic postage stamps, shoetrees, and guava soda on the prisoners to experience the excitement of overcoming their sales resistance and manipulating their desires.

Elkin's principal aim in these novels is not merely to explore the business ethic from a tolerant perspective, although his technique of moving between third-person omniscient and first-person central points of view encourages sympathetic interpretation of the tactics and obsessions by which his characters wheel and deal. His main interest is in exploring, as he does in *The Dick Gibson Show,* ways in which commitment to a vocation is simultaneously a means of achieving identity and a substitute for an authentic one.

In one sense, Feldman and Flesh are men without real identities. Each depends on his vocation to give direction to his energy and to offer a challenge worthy of his creativity. This passionate concern with vending allows the protagonist to displace familial feelings, but Flesh cannot maintain this tension. In a central paradox of *The Franchiser,* his skill as a merchandiser becomes simultaneously a substitute for, an aspect of, and a competitor with his fanatical love for the Finsberg family. Feldman is less confused by love for his family—he begins to have tender feelings toward them only after he realizes he will not complete his prison sentence—but at one point his empathy with his fellow convicts conflicts with his inherited role as a merchant.

These novels are original because of Elkin's interest in the dynamics of trade and the commitment of vendors. *The Franchiser* particularly affords the author an opportunity to relate personal identity with general trends in the American economy. Their power, however, derives from the passion with which these characters throw themselves into their vocations, the flights of rhetoric these commitments inspire, and the treatment of a central Elkin theme: the complex ways in which an acquired identity can displace—and perhaps become—an authentic one.

A Bad Man

Although it treats the characteristic theme of obsession, Elkin's second novel differs significantly from *Boswell. A Bad Man,* dealing with incarceration and its effect on human character, is a much more polished work. This was a major fictional concern of the 1960s. Questions about the state's authority and methods in dealing with offenders against public values were raised in several influential books, especially Anthony Burgess's *A Clockwork Orange* (1962), Ken Kesey's *One Flew over the Cuckoo's Nest* (1962), and Bernard Malamud's *The Fixer* (1966), which Elkin reviewed unenthusiastically. Appearing in 1967, as the civil rights struggle and Vietnam protests called into question the state's authority to punish, *A Bad Man* contributes to the decade's literature of protest.

Fundamental differences, however, exist between *A Bad Man* and these other novels of incarceration, although it, like the others, probably was influenced by the "ur-text" of the decade's fiction, Franz Kafka's *The Trial.* The most striking difference is that the other books are essentially political, whereas *A Bad Man* has little political content. Yakov Bok in *The Fixer* is imprisoned for being a Jew unwilling to stay in the Russian shtetl, and his incarceration progresses toward political commitment; in his final dream he assassinates the czar. Alex, the antihero of *A Clockwork Orange,* is guilty of serious crimes, but in prison becomes a guinea pig in experiments with behavior modification, then a pawn in a struggle for political control based on methods of dealing with criminals. Nurse Ratched, the antagonist of *One Flew over the Cuckoo's Nest,* is a functionary in "the Combine," a national conspiracy to deal with those who differ in some way from popular public values, and her conflict with McMurphy becomes a contest between radical individuality and systems of repression.

Although comparisons between *Cuckoo's Nest* and *A Bad Man* are revealing[8], what sets Elkin's apart from the decade's other prison novels is that the conflict between Feldman and Warden Fisher is a matter of philosophy rather than politics. Both novels have allegorical overtones. Kesey's repeated references to Christ's trials (the shock therapy table is shaped like a cross, electrodes are called a crown of thorns, McMurphy leads twelve men toward the sea) suggest allegorical intentions, and one critic sees Feldman's final trial as a variation on Christ's Passion in that he has "released [the prisoners'] potential for passion" and is now "quite willing to pay the price," his own victimization.[9] Solid support for allegorical intentions in *A Bad Man* comes from the labyrinthine architecture of the prison, the Warden's omniscient authority, and the unique relationships he establishes with the prisoners.

A Bad Man and *Cuckoo's Nest* are, however, fundamentally different kinds of allegories. Kesey's is a study in officially sanctioned repression of rugged individualism. Nurse Ratched attempts to break McMurphy's spirit and to use his defeat as proof to other inmates that the system cannot be beaten. In death, McMurphy's values triumph; by defying the Nurse in the face of certain defeat, he liberates other inmates from their insecurities. By contrast, Feldman briefly experiments with the role of savior by becoming a confidant for the prisoners' confessions but quickly discards that role because the prisoners' stories are not extraordinary, and to be Feldman, he discovers in solitary confinement, means never to sacrifice his own interests for those of others.

Feldman's defeat, moreover, does not represent a triumph of principle within the prison. His final defense denies the very premise of "being Feldman," and there is no indication that anyone will be changed or saved by his defeat. The Warden reaps no obvious benefit from defeating him, for his power is never at issue; Feldman's trial is not a test of or challenge to Fisher's authority over the other prisoners. With one minor hesitation, they willingly cooperate in convicting Feldman.

Unlike the conflict between McMurphy and the Nurse in the *Cuckoo's Nest,* that between the Warden and Feldman is almost apolitical. It stems from opposing philosophies of life that prove, by the logic of paradox, to have much in common: Fisher advances his thesis that *"life is ordinary"* (*ABM*, 115, 117, 119) against Feldman's conviction that it need not be—although as a youth, he was disappointed at a county fair because the foods, exhibits, and games of chance persuaded him that there was "nothing strange *there*" (*ABM*, 55–57), and the prisoners prove to be similarly disappointing. They claim to be exceptional, but they are a pretty common lot. The same is true of the customers in Feldman's store basement. The conflict central to *A Bad Man* may be phrased this way: Fisher advocates that life is, and ought to be, ordinary, whereas Feldman's life as merchant, family man, and prisoner is a quest for the extraordinary—for what life should be.

Almost every commentator on *A Bad Man* has noted this conflict, but none has successfully traced its philosophical origins. One critic notes, but does not expand on,[10] the central issue of this conflict: Feldman's inspiration that Fisher is "one too. The warden. *He's a bad man, too!*" (*ABM*, 120). This discovery explains the Warden's obsession with Leo and Feldman's fascination with Fisher's essential character—an interest that goes far beyond that inherent in Fisher's authority over Feldman's prison life. It also clarifies the central metaphor of *A Bad Man* and some of the ambiguity Elkin invests in the title.

Literally "bad men" are a group the Warden segregates from other prison populations. They must wear unique prison clothes: Feldman wears a "clever parody" of the business suit he wore into prison, whereas Harold Flesh (perhaps the suspected Mafioso from *Boswell*) wears a cashmere version of the standard prison uniform. The guards, who virtually ignore other prisoners, watch bad men constantly. Their files are on open circulation in the prison library. Their features are models for gargoyles decorating walls used for Warden's Assembly (*ABM*, 201).

Figuratively a "bad man" is someone who cannot be rehabilitated. Without consultation or appeal, the Warden unilaterally determines which prisoners cannot be rehabilitated. It is no mistake that the suit for Feldman's release, made two weeks after he entered prison, is much too small. This suit is for a wasted, diminished Feldman—as he realizes, it is for his corpse. Because Leo is a bad man, he cannot leave the prison alive, and Fisher sadistically delays his "kangaroo court" (*ABM*, 336) and execution until shortly before his sentence ends. Bad men become objects of prison witch-hunts. In a Warden's Assembly, Fisher, launching a campaign against bad men, invokes God's help: "Teach us, O God, revulsion. . . . Grant these men [other prisoners] a holy arrogance and instill in them the courage to expose all bad men . . . and give them the memory to report *verbatim* whatever is spoken in anger behind my back or the backs of my guards" (*ABM*, 212).

At a more subtle level, the figure suggests that bad men are obsessive, passionate, and possessed. They are not criminals of impulse but men whose behavior reflects consistently compulsive character. Being a bad man has nothing to do with the crimes one commits (Feldman is not technically guilty of the crime for which he is convicted, but he is guilty of others); it is a matter of the kind of person one is. A criminal, however heinous his crime, who recognizes society's right to define what he did as wrong is not a bad man. But one, however trivial his offense, who sees it as his essence to have done what he did is a bad man. By the Warden's logic, any individualist is inevitably a bad man.

By most ethical standards, Feldman is literally a bad man. His obsession with selling renders him completely insensitive to others' needs and interests. He bullies his family and like Boswell denies his son in a nasty scene. Embarrassed by Billy's stupidity at a school open house, he professes to be the father of Oliver B., the brightest child in the class. He invents symptoms of Lilly's nonexistent illnesses to deceive Dr. Freedman into referring him to abortionists, whorehouses, and drug dealers so he can deliver these services to his basement clients. He parodies the claims of friendship with Dedman and tricks him into an unhappy marriage. He ruins Victman's promising career as a merchandiser by hiring him away from a progressive corporation, then bottling up his talents. He fires a salesgirl facing huge medical expenses for being lackadaisical about a sale. What is important, however, is not that he is a bad man by external ethical standards but that the Warden forces him into an arbitrary and unappealable category as a "bad man."

If Fisher consistently professes that "life is ordinary" and that bad men should be hounded to their deaths, can Feldman be right in believing he too is a bad man? He is, and therein lies a central meaning of the novel. It initially appears that Fisher is Feldman's opposite, professing the antithesis of Leo's interest in the extraordinary. He advocates the conventional, the commonplace. One of his letters advises Feldman to cultivate "*a good work ethic*" so that he "*will begin to understand how ordinary life is*" (*ABM,* 116), thus implicitly connecting his doctrine that life is unexceptional with the Puritan work ethic. This advice resembles what a hitchhiker, an ex-convict who must have done time in Fisher's prison, offers Ben Flesh: "Get a reality. . . . Get a normality. . . . Be bored and find happiness. . . . Cool it, cool it. The ordinary is all we can handle" (*TF,* 219, 220). Sending Feldman to solitary for looking at his file—among seven copies on library shelves, one has been checked out five times—Fisher reminds him, "I warned you and warned you! . . . 'Life is ordinary,' I told you. But you think you're an exception. . . .

You're up to here with passion. Up to *here* with it. But life is simple, Feldman. Now you'll see that" (*ABM,* 137).

Everything the Warden says suggests that he is Feldman's opposite, a man dedicated to his belief that nothing is, or should be, extraordinary. He disappoints Feldman by looking ordinary; his face "seemed conventional, not unintelligent so much as not intelligent. . . . Feldman had hoped, he realized now, for someone mysterious, a little magical" (*ABM,* 22). But the passion with which the Warden persecutes bad men, not to redeem them (that was ruled out when he designated them bad men) but to rub their faces in their status, convincingly indicates that Fisher, every bit as obsessive and eccentric as Feldman, is a bad man. In solitary, Leo wonders what being the Warden would be like and realizes, "The man was too much like himself. . . . He and the Warden had never dealt with equals" (*ABM,* 161).

Fisher's prison is a Kafkaesque extension of his obsession. With obscure rules and labyrinthine architecture, it is carefully designed so that no one can ever be sure exactly where he stands. He uses Warden's Assembly to announce policies, but these are never written down. A written document can be challenged, whereas an "oral tradition" (*ABM,* 210) retains a desired ambiguity and encourages the evolution of "penal Talmudists," a core of literate prisoners who debate the meanings of notes taken from his speeches. His announcement, off the record after one assembly has officially closed, of a pogrom against bad men is punctuated by religious zeal: "I am calling for the infusion of the sacerdotal spirit! I need inquisitors' hearts! You must be—you must be *malleus maleficarum,* hammerers of witches, punishers and pummelers in God's long cause. You must be Warden's familiars" (*ABM,* 213). His crusade works. Even bad men inform on one another; Feldman's cellmate, Bisch, tries to make Leo reveal secret thoughts of escape. Fisher's charisma makes his prison work. The inmates respond, chanting like delegates at a political convention, to the power of his personality, his rhetoric, and his zeal to destroy bad men. When the kangaroo court seems hesitant to convict Feldman, Fisher intervenes and charismatically restores the trial's purpose—to kill a fellow inmate.

His obsession with bad men leads to extraordinary, sadistic, tortures like fabricating a diagnosis of sugar diabetes to counter Feldman's offering candy to bribe Ed Slipper, a bad man obsessed with becoming America's oldest convict. Knowing Feldman's sexual drive was restored in solitary, Fisher arranges a party to celebrate his release. The party is designed not to confirm Feldman's learning anything from his stay in solitary but to exploit weaknesses the Warden learned about during that confinement. He arranges for Feldman to get drunk, then to encounter Fisher's wife, Mona, who is stimulated by reports in his file that prove him a bad man: the "terrible things" he did in the store basement (*ABM,* 185) and the cruel games he made Lilly play.[11] When Mona and Feldman return, they find the Warden carefully counting deposit bottles, hardly the response of an ordinary cuckold.

After the tryst, the Warden subjects Feldman to his most sadistic torture by locking him in a room with the electric chair and thereby introducing an important supporting metaphor for *A Bad Man.* His purpose is not to get revenge for Mona's infidelity but to explore Feldman's nature as a bad man by making him confront his death. The chair symbolizes the ultimate power authority has, but it suggests as well the force of imagination. Feldman's botched suicide attempt is an effort to recover control over himself, to counter the Warden's authority. At first terrified of the device and curious about whether this torture is merely a cuckold's revenge, he realizes that all he must do to save himself is refuse to sit in it. Then he comes to the startling discovery that to take his life in the chair is a way he can assert himself: "Feldman's death was Feldman's doing. His imagination was the murderer. . . . It was true: he wanted his death. He wanted his death because it was coming to him and he wanted everything that was coming to him" (*ABM,* 198). One way Leo can get control is to take his life, but he bungles the attempt. Probably his bungling was anticipated by the Warden, for he too wants to be sure Feldman gets "everything that was coming to him," including his full sentence—to see how far Feldman will pursue the logic of being a bad man.[12] This explains the odd directions for using the electric chair, initially written at a level appropriate for novices but becoming progressively menacing (treating the kindling temperature of human flesh), then highly technical and supported by schematic diagrams.

By accepting Feldman's discovery that the Warden is a bad man, we can understand Fisher's special fascination with Leo. Other bad men are in the prison, but Fisher concentrates on Leo as his special project. This happens because no other bad man is as involved in the process of self-discovery as Feldman. He is intelligent and sometimes introspective. In solitary or in the chair, he questions what it means to be Feldman. The Warden is obsessed not with the prospect of convincing him that life is ordinary—that was ruled out by designating him a bad man—but with learning how purposefully Feldman holds to the logic of his obsession. In short, he is obsessed with Feldman's obsession.

This explains a final similarity between them: both are gamblers. Feldman substituted games with Lilly and Billy for familial love, outsold his mad father, and built his store on the challenge of the venture. He gambled with Victman's business skill by ignoring his advice to expand into shopping centers, while hoping that competitors would heed Victman's advice and be-come victims of the "seven lean years" he expected (*ABM*, 249). When his family proved submissive, Victman proved weak, and his store succeeded too easily, Feldman expanded services in the basement to gamble on excitement. The basement originated in "serendipity" (*ABM*, 279), but its development was planned. Feldman wants a gamble, an ultimate test of his salesman's skill, and dealing with a conspirator who will not tell him what he wants, Feldman feels, "This is it. *This* is" (*ABM*, 305). Even his relative calm upon being arrested and sentenced for a crime he did not commit can be traced to his gambler's instinct. What challenges will prison life present?[13] His explo-rations of prison life, from goldbricking to listening to prisoners' confessions to making the canteen a replica of his ideal store, are not just strategies for survival; they are also gambles in which the risk is its own primary reward.

Obviously Feldman is a gambler, but the Warden is more subtly one. He plays with Feldman constantly; sending him to solitary, forcing him to con-front the electric chair, making him president of the Crime Club while requir-ing that he wrest power from other bad men who have also been named president, and allowing him to reorganize the prison canteen are all tests of Feldman's personality.

Fisher also enjoys gambling for its own sake. In the climactic scene, Feldman's trial, he exhibits the gambler's love of risk. Feldman, charged really with being himself, feels a slim hope that he may be able to sway his judges. He makes a speech to prove he is "*decent too*" (*ABM*, 354) and hopes to have convinced his judges that he is not extraordinary: "*This* is my charac-ter: I've been moved, roused. Lumps in the throat and the heart's hard-on" (*ABM*, 351). In a way Fisher's gamble pays off: defending his character by claiming to be ordinary, Feldman denies his essential nature, and this is what Fisher wants. But this victory may conceivably have swayed the judges, much as Leo was moved by his own rhetoric. Fisher intervenes and takes his most audacious gamble. It is not clear when he entered the trial arena. He was in his office arranging the cover-up that would explain the quarantine of the trial area, but after Feldman's speech, he tells the inmates, "He's *kidding*," "He made it all up," "He's selling you a bill of goods" (*ABM*, 354–55).

The Warden disqualifies all of the evidence accumulated against Feldman to let the verdict rest on a single issue, his treatment of Dedman: "I declare it a standoff and direct these men to ignore whatever they may have heard up to now. Feldman's innocent. I whitewash his history and make good all checks drawn on his character. He stands or falls on Dedman" (*ABM*, 355–56). The trial, however, has as its purpose convicting and executing Feldman one week before his sentence ends. Although the prisoners may have been swayed by

Feldman's argument that he is decent as well as innocent—Feldman is himself convinced—the evidence accumulated against his character up to this time is substantial. To allow the verdict to depend on one anecdote is a risk, one compounded by Feldman's recognition of this opportunity to turn his trial into a personal contest. When Fisher interrupts, Feldman says, "Take him. . . . *Take him!*" but "they hadn't understood. Only the warden knew what he had said" (*ABM,* 355). The challenge of a personal confrontation—the gambler's risk—motivates Fisher to let the entire issue rest on one throw of the dice.

The Warden is obsessive, charismatic, committed to expanding his ego and power over others. He is a bad man who can never leave the prison because it is an extension and definition of his essential self. The conflict central to the novel is not between an ordinary, reasonable philosophy and a dedication to the extraordinary; it is between two obsessions, one of these a paradoxically extraordinary obsession with the idea that life is ordinary. Elkin is not dealing with the essentially political issues of justice or punishment but with the more original problem of the forms obsessive preoccupation with one's vocation may take.

One final metaphor crucial to the meaning of *A Bad Man* is Leo's homunculus. Perhaps the most allegorical element in the book, the homunculus suggests the doppelgänger motif central to *A Bad Man* and *The Franchiser.* This fossilized antiself lying over Leo's heart has the capacity to destroy him. It also suggests the potential man Leo could have been had he not chosen to spend his life learning to be Feldman.

The homunculus affords Elkin the chance to deliver some of his finest puns. It is a "sit-in sibling" and Feldman is "O solo Leo" (*ABM,* 159) when ignoring it. It petitions the "greater frater," and the narrator calls it "stony, bony paradigm, scaled-down schema of waxing Feldman" (*ABM,* 157). As "paradigm" or "fossilized potential" (*ABM,* 159), it is the voice of conscience, something Feldman has been nearly able to eliminate from his life. While in solitary (and becoming paradoxically active sexually), the homunculus admonishes him, "I would have done things differently. I would have taken better care" (*ABM,* 157), echoing Lear's tragic recognition, "I have ta'en / Too little care of this" (*King Lear,* 3.4.32–33). It attributes Leo's "cynicism" to Isidore's influence (*ABM,* 159). After he has sex with Mona, it reasserts itself as the voice of conscience.[14] Once, talking with his doppelgänger, he reacts to his suppressed conscience by trying to sell it something (*ABM,* 160). Although it opposes Feldman's business methods, the homunculus contributed to his success as a merchant by exempting him from service during World

War II, when he laid the groundwork for his enterprise while most able-bodied men were in combat.

In addition to serving as Feldman's suppressed conscience, the homunculus is simultaneously a physical manifestation of Feldman's prized uniqueness and a threat to his existence. It physically represents Leo's obsession with being unique, and when Dr. Freedman warned him that this "early Feldmanic aggrandizement" (*ABM,* 14) may someday be fatal, Leo refused surgery because he chose to preserve his uniqueness. Betrayed by Feldman, Freedman informs a deputy, and by extension the penal community, that the homunculus will destroy Feldman if he is punched in the heart. A prison guard knows about it, and before the kangaroo court, a boxer has practiced blows that will take advantage of the homunculus. If Feldman has a victory over Fisher in his trial, it is that he forces him into rage so that he orders the men to beat Leo rather than waiting for the boxer to kill him. Feldman hopes they, inexpert in homunculus smashing, will not succeed in killing him, but that seems a vain hope. The Warden will find other means. Primarily the episode means that Fisher's system is thwarted, if only in detail, and he is a detail man.

A Bad Man is Elkin's most accessible novel and an ideal introduction to his themes and techniques. It blends offbeat humor with concern for serious philosophical issues. Typical of Elkin's fiction, it challenges the reader to identify with an obsessive character whose personal code of conduct resists sentimental empathy. By treating the conflict between the Warden and Feldman as conflicting aspects of the same personality trait, a charismatic obsession with a way of life, it accomplishes a goal of the best modern fiction by challenging the reader to question individually the price of, and possible alternatives to, a personality trait like obsession.

The Franchiser

If *A Bad Man* is Elkin's most accessible treatment of the relation between obsessive personality and commercialism, *The Franchiser* is his most comprehensive approach to that topic. Unlike *A Bad Man,* however, this is not an easily accessible text. For readers unfamiliar with Elkin's techniques, especially compound flashbacks, reluctance to employ linear plots, and the flights of rhetoric inspired in his characters by any chance to make a speech, *The Franchiser* can present challenges. The plot is episodic, but Doris Bargen shows that it is arranged around the itineraries for trips Ben makes to inspect his franchises in 1971, 1974, and 1975, with the largest portion of the novel treating the 1974 trip.[15]

This structure is thematic as well as organizational. Ben tells his Finsberg god-cousins, "I live along my itinerary" (*TF,* 249), but discovers in Oklahoma that all he has left is "his itinerary. Which was what he had left in lieu of a life. . . . Only that. His itinerary. He could have wept" (*TF,* 245). Although Elkin takes a sympathetic attitude toward this character, a distinctive concern in *The Franchiser* is the degree to which Ben's devotion to franchising America, with its demands on his energy, a diminishing resource, is a substitute for a full life of his own.

Thematically *The Franchiser* is a breakthrough for its author, although the techniques, while highly refined, are less spectacular than those of *The Dick Gibson Show.* It marks a dramatic shift in Elkin's characteristic subject, obsession. Like Feldman, Flesh is driven by a commitment to his business and is completely serious in his intention to democratize America by contributing to the proliferation of identical franchises. But that commitment, as the itinerary symbol suggests, competes with his desire for stability and his love for the Finsberg twins and triplets. Typical Elkin heroes like Boswell or Feldman seldom let familial feelings interfere with their self-directed passions. That Ben does contributes to his failure as a businessman. To compound his emotional stress, the Finsbergs reject him ("the man's a bore with his love and loyalty" [*TF,* 281]) and begin dying bizarre deaths.

Ben's irrational love for the Finsbergs is the first other-directed obsession among Elkin's characters, and this marks a major step in his development as a writer. Fascinating as the self-directed obsessions of Boswell or Feldman are, they lack the heroic potential of Ben's love for the freakish Finsbergs, which, when tested against his loyalty to his business, proves strong enough to make him a nearly tragic figure.

The Franchiser is remarkably efficient in clustering figures of speech. Most of Elkin's novels depend for central meanings on a key figure, like the Masked Playboy in *Boswell* and the tapestry condition in *George Mills.* *The Franchiser* subtly associates several such figures. At the center is an association between franchising and theatrical costumes, the industry in which his godfather Julius made his fortune and thereby earned Ben's legacy, the prime rate. Orbiting around these are related sets of figures: Ben's MS with symptoms like euphoria, sensory deprivation, and remission, which are associated with power failures, oil shortages, and other symptoms of the national energy crisis of the 1970s.[16] Although such associations can be reduced to social commentary, never an explicit intention in Elkin's work, *The Franchiser* is his most profoundly figurative work.

Although sympathetically drawn, Ben is not flawless. Like Elkin's other protagonists, his obsessive personality causes us both to admire and suspect him. He is driven by a dubious purpose: "his need to costume his country, to give it its visible props, . . . familiar neon signatures and logos, all its *things,* all its *crap,* the true American graffiti" (*TF,* 270). This quotation explicitly connects theatrical costumes with franchising, and his purpose makes him susceptible to both brilliant insights on the culture and flights of uncontrolled rhetoric.

His finest insight comes when he speculates on the packaged shapes of commercial products with Patty Finsberg, the "Insight Lady" modeled on a person from St. Louis,[17] and concludes, "We read shapes. The culture is pre-literate" (*TF,* 195). Situational irony functions here, for Patty has insights into everything—she bases her investment decisions on the handwriting of chief executive officers and is rich—but it is Ben who has this valuable insight into cultural preliteracy, and he, not Patty, can guess why Lotte Finsberg committed suicide (*TF,* 204–7). Although Ben's capacity for insight may depend on his intimacy with Patty and the unfamiliar terrain of the Colorado Rockies, Elkin attributes an ability to form profound intuitions to the merchant rather than to the insight specialist.

If Ben's obsessive personality enables him to form substantial insights, it also makes him prone to dangerous business ventures, unethical practices, and attacks of logorrhea, or uncontrolled verbosity. Two scenes, one related to opening and the other to closing franchises, are illustrative. Opening a Kentucky Fried Chicken operation in 1960, Ben has an attack of logorrhea that ends with partial blindness, his first symptom of MS. Perched absurdly in the franchise logo, a revolving bucket, he launches into "his address" (*TF,* 93), a story about a country hick that must seem to Ben's listeners totally irrelevant to the occasion. The story, the centerpiece of a journal publication,[18] anticipates a long letter from a spiritualist in *George Mills* in that its relevance to the plot is obscure, though the hick's discovery that "*existence has its spare parts, that the successful life is only a proper knowledge of accessory*" (*TF,* 101) corresponds with Ben's commitment to operating interchangeable franchises. Ben is himself unsure why he is telling this story but cannot stop: "He wondered what he was up to. Even as he'd told them his story, he'd wondered. . . . But why this logorrhea? He suspected his character. . . . And if he was so angry, then why was he so happy?" (*TF,* 102). Unwilling to surrender his podium in the bucket, he audaciously defines the spot as "hallowed American ground" and a "Gettysburg of the rhetorical" (*TF,* 103), then commits the franchiser's greatest sin by disclosing a recipe for Kentucky Fried Chicken. Obviously Ben's rhetoric is out of control, and he is under the spell of having an audience. The logorrhea is related to an initial phase of his MS, but verbal excess is not a symptom of the disease; it is a symptom of this obsessive character.

A similar clustering of disease imagery, wheeling and dealing, and logorrhea attends Ben's closing gala for his Fred Astaire Dance franchise. The studio, like many of his other operations, is in an unpromising location, a deteriorating Chicago neighborhood inhabited by elderly people afraid to go out at night, whose retirement homes provide dance instruction. It has degenerated into a brothel, for one client taking "private lessons" is taking liberties with instructor Clara, and Ben unwisely risks a racial confrontation with him. His antics in this scene stem from disappointment that the franchise is failing, but his mood is compounded by the studio's being located in the building his father's shop occupied after the Flesh-Finsberg partnership broke up. Throughout the scene he mentions his father's ghost as contributing to his emotional state (*TF,* 53, 71).

Seeing how badly the franchise is doing, Ben turns the planned celebration into a wake. He orders expensive refreshments, including liquor and marijuana, to replace the modest ones his managers provided: "He had not been this excited in a long while. . . . We're going *down* first class" (*TF,* 56). He recruits partygoers for the wake and, slightly high on marijuana, launches into his oration. The drug temporarily appeases an MS symptom and unleashes a tide of rhetoric: "The last tingling left his hand. He was suddenly caught up in a complex and true and magnificent idea" (*TF,* 60). To plunge big money into a dying operation and to invite legal vulnerability by giving away drugs are bad business decisions. But Flesh, excited by his father's ghost in the room, is more orator than entrepreneur.

And what a speech it is. As in the Fried Chicken opening, rhetoric takes control of Ben as his emotions run amok. He tells the dancers that dancing may itself be evil (*TF,* 68), but the burden of his message introduces a theme central to *The Franchiser*: that life, despite its inevitable disappointments, is to be treasured. Mildly stoned and in illusory remission (the tingling reappears before the speech ends), excited by his father's ghost and the franchise's failure, Ben proposes to "link the world for you. I am going to have it make sense," and he offers the unexpected theme that life "is better than you think and better even than it has to be" (*TF,* 62).

Is this merely chemically induced euphoria, as Elkin says Ben's euphoria at the end of the novel is?[19] It would be silly to deny that either euphoria episode is chemically generated, one by marijuana and the other by brain chemistry; but their frequency and iterative nature suggest that, like most other symbols, they have several, perhaps conflicting, meanings. If these episodes are symptoms of disease, their content nonetheless suggests Elkin's theme: a powerful affirmation of life in spite of setbacks and inevitable defeats. This conviction, more than the prime rate or the business manipulation that disbanded his father's partnership with Julius Finsberg, links Ben with his godfather.

Ben is animated by his father's ghost in the wake for the Fred Astaire Studio and in defeat feels that his achievement with the Travel Inn makes him "higher than my father, who, before he was a boss, had only been a partner" (*TF,* 319), but he is economically and philosophically Julius's godson. Although some studies[20] link Ben with the Elkin motif of the orphan, he was in the army when his parents died in an accident and was summoned from graduate school to take the place of the only Finsberg child who was a single birth, and died in infancy. His problem, then, is not, like Boswell's or Ed Wolfe's, compensating for the absence of parental influence, but choosing between conflicting paternal figures: his father, a modest businessman who took the safe route when his partner offered to buy him out during the depression; or Julius, a risk taker hoping to costume an emerging industry, willing to cheat his partner to take control of the business, eager to create a family, and firmly convinced on his deathbed that all life is a miracle.

When Ben accepts Julius's legacy—in part a reparation, for Finsberg conned the senior Flesh into selling the partnership—of perpetual ability to borrow from the Finsberg estate at the prime rate, he also inherits Julius's fanatical concern for his eighteen identical, freakish children. Julius warns him, "You're just godblood. I don't want you sticking my kids with a bankruptcy from some half-assed investment" (*TF,* 31), and Ben takes his caretaker role seriously. As the prime rate fluctuates crazily during the 1970s and the male Finsbergs begin to renege on Julius's promise of capital, Ben becomes erratic in his business dealings. In fact, his concern to protect the Finsberg inheritance is a major cause of his failure in venturing.

As a godson, he accepts Julius's love for his flawed children, becoming god-brother and surrogate father-provider for all eighteen, as well as lover to each of the nine daughters. All but the last were part of Julius's design when he provided for Ben but not for his sister. If guilt motivated Julius, he would have provided for both Flesh descendants, but he chose Ben out of fear that his children cannot take care of themselves. Ben explains his intimacy with the superficially identical daughters as an extension of his and Julius's dream: "Could he, then, have fallen in love with history, with modern times, the age's solutions to its anxieties? . . . Sexually evolving with them during the sexual revolution. . . . An archeology of sex, love, and memory" (*TF,* 180). Falling in love with the girls is an extension of his protective love for them. He tries to terrify Kitty in his autowash franchise into shock therapy for her unique ailment, bed-wetting, which, like most other Finsberg ailments, proves fatal.

That Ben inherits Julius's business ethic with this protective role is supported by Elkin's linking the metaphors of theatrical costumes with franchising or Ben's desire to "costume America." Both wheel and deal to exploit trends in American commercial life. If Julius's decade had musical theater as its growth industry, Ben's has franchises. But unlike Julius, he fails because his dream goes beyond exploiting economic trends. His love for the Finsbergs complicates his business decisions, and his disease compounds his efforts. National trends toward energy dependence work against him. And he is never content with being merely a franchiser; he wants to be somebody.

Although he has been successful franchising other people's names, Ben aspires to be an independent businessman. He wants to build an inn that will be "the capstone of my career" (*TF*, 232), a dream he is determined to complete despite the progress of his disease (*TF*, 275). His life has been spent on an itinerary, living in motels and Cadillacs, and he reluctantly realizes that his affiliation with the Finsbergs depends more than he would like on his business success. What will differentiate the inn from his franchises is that he will no longer be "Mr. Softee" (*TF*, 122, 127) or the "doppelgängster" (*TF*, 91; an epithet used by doppelgänger Roger Foster, who poses as a sophisticated Colonel Sanders) who hides behind franchised names; he will be "INNKEEPER: Benjamin Flesh" (*TF*, 309). By creating a location where there was never an identifying landmark ("it was not a place. As most of the earth is not a place" [*TF*, 309]) before he transformed it into "somewhere," Ben hopes to associate his name with those of visionaries and pioneers: Aeneas, Brigham Young, Theseus, Del Webb, Walt Disney, and "all those Founders, legendary and historic" (*TF*, 303).

To realize his dream of making his own name a symbol of achievement, Ben mortgages his successful franchises. With the Finsbergs dying and the survivors becoming nervous about the prime rate, he takes an entrepreneur's risk by allowing his operations to become "pledged, hostages to the success of the motel" (*TF*, 298). Only the One Hour Martinizing franchise, once operated by Irving Finsberg, is protected for "sentimental" (*TF*, 298) reasons, despite its being marginally successful. The minicinemas, his best operation, become collateral to protect the dry cleaners, and eventually he must risk both. These gambles represent a consolidation of Flesh's enterprises, and the inn provides him with a place, a focus, he has lacked and the Finsbergs have refused to grant him until he begs them to allow him to be buried in their family plot.

He builds the inn for personal reasons, but he also hopes to protect the

Finsberg estate against a new economic phenomenon of the 1970s, a rapidly fluctuating prime rate. The franchises he pawns, except the minicinemas and Riverside Funeral Parlors, are in trouble because of poor location, demographic changes, or economic shifts. One example is his Dunkin' Donuts franchise. "Conscious always of Finsbergs, . . . his deals dealt more for them than for himself" (*TF,* 272–73) to protect their investments, so he sells his interest in Evelyn Wood Reading Dynamics because reading is being displaced by electronic media and in H&R Block tax preparation service because of impending tax reform. He reasons that the doughnut franchise will prosper in coming hard times. These business decisions seem sound. He invests his equity in doughnuts, coffee, and supplies, but his costs for accessories like cream and sugar shoot "sky-high" (*TF,* 273). Sound business assumptions have been submarined by unpredictable economic fluctuations.

Similar circumstances trouble the inn. Profoundly concerned about investing in a sound business to protect the Finsberg estate and disturbed by worsening symptoms in his disease, Ben carefully calculates what growth industry will withstand the foreseeable economic woes of the 1970s. He decides that entertainment will withstand the recession and seeks a way to cash in on the opening of Florida's Disney World. Ben calculates driving time from major midwestern cities to Orlando and hires drivers to test his theories about the ideal overnight stop in a two-day drive from these places. He takes into account the driver's desire to cross a state line before stopping and decides on Ringgold, Georgia, as the perfect location for an inn. By contrast, many of his other franchises have been in poor locations (for example, the Radio Shack in a Kentucky town that gets poor FM reception). His business logic is sound, especially the acute insight into the psychology of the driver, and the calculations are correct. Delays, inevitable in any major construction project, slow the project just enough for disaster to strike.

Ben's calculations were based on the prevailing interstate speed limit: seventy miles per hour. An energy crisis forces the federal government to reduce the limit to fifty-five just before the inn opens. Although drivers will cheat (Ben figured on this in his original projections), the trip from major midwestern cities to Disney World now takes three days, and northern Georgia ceases to be a logical stopover. Before the inn opens, but after its debts are incurred, it is doomed to fail.

Ben's failure therefore originates in (1) his anxiety to create a stable investment for the remaining Finsberg children; (2) his desire to be a pioneer in commerce; (3) his ambition to achieve the American dream of owning a business and succeeding by hard work and shrewd calculation; (4) his deteriorating health, which adds urgency to completing his dream; and (5) economic factors outside his control, particularly the energy crisis. The last enables Elkin to synthesize two key symbols: Ben's illness and the deterioration of the American energy and economic situations.

This synthesis has been implicit throughout *The Franchiser,* particularly in Ben's journey from South Dakota to Colorado after his first hospitalization. In remission but not cured, he encounters electrical and petroleum shortages throughout the trip and takes the dangerous precaution of storing gallons of gasoline in his trunk, thus turning his Cadillac (his home, office, and source of mobility) into a bomb. The crisis finally ends—the country too experiences remission—and the bomb does not explode. But the association between Ben's disease and the national economic infrastructure has been set into motion. Elkin repeatedly highlights this association: "feeling chased by brown-outs and power-failed space, civilization's demyelination, slipping safely into temporary zones of remission" (*TF,* 140); "A high wall of the respectable around them [the Finsbergs] while his health failed daily, his own energy crisis unresolved, his body still demyelinating a mile a minute" (*TF,* 274); "There isn't enough energy to drive my body. How can there be enough to run Akron?" (*TF,* 258). Because of his disease, Ben, like his Cadillac, has a bomb within him.

This association allows Elkin astute economic and environmental commentary, for nature is, like Ben's body, subject to the second law of thermodynamics, from which the concept of entropy is derived. Like Pynchon and Heller, Elkin treats entropy frequently—most explicitly in *A Bad Man,* when Feldman tells Oliver B.'s father, "Your energy against my entropy. The universe is running down, Mr. Developer. . . . The smart money is in vaults" (*ABM,* 260; one of Flesh's solvent franchises is a funeral parlor). But Elkin is more interested in the inevitable deterioration of the human organism than in the conservation of resources. Ben, falling apart at an accelerated rate, must synthesize nature's message of progressive deterioration with his godfather's belief that life is a miracle.

Because of his disease and because his commercial interests habituate him to cities and highways, Ben is uncomfortable in nature. In the only scene in which he contemplates unspoiled beauty, when he vacations in the Rockies with Patty, he is terrified rather than consoled by nature's message. He has recently been hospitalized, and when they contemplate natural beauty, "It gives me the creeps this place. It makes me old and multiples my sclerosis" (*TF,* 191). He feels "out of his element, the franchiser disenfranchised" (*TF,* 199). This is not merely an inability to respond because of a commitment to business. For Ben, nature's message is entropic: "Vouchsafed to die of his disease, it was as if here, in nature, where everything was a disease, all growth a sickness, the mountains a sickness and the trees a sickness, too, with their symptomatic leaves and their pathological barks, the progress of his disease could leap exponentially, travel his bloodstream like the venom of poisonous snakes or the death-bites of killer spiders" (*TF,* 199). Nature is dying but more gradually than Ben, so its message is not hope but despair. The Finsbergs, whom he loves irrationally, are dying absurd deaths, conclusively proving they were never really identical. Each contains an anomaly that will kill him or her. Irving, a bigot who married a black woman and employed black workers at the dry cleaners to cure his prejudice, is killed in a race riot he starts in Detroit; Gertrude, who has heavy bones, dies taking a bath; and so on, until ten Finsbergs have died of the qualities that made them individual beneath their identical appearances. Ben recognizes that their deaths were "congenital," that "there are no ludicrous deaths" (*TF,* 290), only "ludicrous life, screwball existence, goofy being" (*TF,* 307). Contemplating his disease, the bizarre Finsberg deaths, nature's entropic message, and the failure of his grand design, he concludes, "Plague builds its nests in us" (*TF,* 331).

His disease forces Ben to establish the metaphor on which much of the meaning of *The Franchiser* ultimately depends: his remission. Medically remission means a temporary relaxation of the symptoms of a disease, and Elkin develops this figure through two distinct phases. In the Rockies with Patty, Ben's insights include, "*I want my remission back!*" (*TF,* 196), a cry that is much more than a jeremiad. He is afraid of dying and anxious that he will be unable to protect the Finsbergs against economic catastrophe. He has a right to be bitter about his malady, a bitterness that erupts in moments of anger. In the South Dakota hospital, he was cruel to Lieutenant Tanner of the Royal Air Force, suffering with lassa fever and an incurable tendency to speak like a character from a Hemingway novel; years later, Ben calls Tanner "the best friend I ever had" (*TF,* 337). He also feels sudden rage toward the grace of ice skaters and finds in their skill and his anger "the accusation of a wasted life" (*TF,* 190). Ben's insight is more than the cry of a bitter, dying man; wanting his remission back is a recognition of life's fragility. Ben cannot hope for a cure, and he does not merely wish he did not have this illness; all he wishes for is temporary relief from its symptoms and progress.

This insight is generalized by Ben's awareness that the Finsbergs' deaths are like the self-destruction he carries within his body, and like the gasoline bombs in the Cadillac or America's energy dependence, in that illness is a symptom of existence itself. In one remission stage, Ben tells one of the hitchhikers he picks up, "The truth is, we live mostly in remission" (*TF,* 214). Elkin has said, "If my books have a theme, it's the theme of self, the self and its diseases, and the disease as health."[21] This paradox—that health can be a result of disease—constitutes the central theme of *The Franchiser.* Ben recognizes that existence leads inevitably to disease and death, but he learns that how we face our disease defines our moral character. He faces his disease by accepting that all health is a form of remission and by recognizing that, in spite of this, life is itself a miracle.

When he accepted Julius's offer of borrowing power and the attendant responsibility, Ben also inherited his fundamental optimism. Dying, Finsberg orates about the odds against existence and consciousness and about the miracle of overcoming these odds. He tells Ben he could have been aborted, killed, or incarnated as a grain of sand, but "against all the odds in the universe you made happy landings! . . . Ain't that delightful? Wait, there's more. You not only have your existence but your edge, your advantage and privilege" (*TF,* 24). Ben's final euphoria attack, coming upon the failure of his inn and the onset of final MS symptoms, echoes Julius's faith:

He was broken, they would kill him. The Finsbergs were an endangered species and his Travel Inn a disaster. They would kill him. Within weeks he would be strapped to a wheelchair. And ah, he thought, euphorically, ecstatically, this privileged man who could have been a vegetable or mineral instead of an animal, and a lower animal instead of a higher, who could have been a pencil or a dot on a die, who could have been a stitch in a glove or change in someone's pocket, or a lost dollar nobody found, who could have been stillborn or less sentient than sand, or the chemical flash of somebody else's fear, ahh. *Ahh!* (*TF,* 342)

Although one critic[22] interprets "they" as the guests upon whom Ben has spied, Elkin intends the phrase in the businessman's idiom. There is no evidence that the guests know they have been spied upon and gossiped about on the Inn-Dex or that they care. Ben means his creditors, economic conditions, a paranoiac "they" (although his actual victimization rules out paranoia) that will ruin his business and, by extension, his life and dream. Everything he cares about is falling apart, yet Ben seems happy.

We must therefore return to the issue of euphoria and its impact on the meaning of *The Franchiser.* Ben's final ecstasy is clearly more than chemical or symptomatic: "His happiness was real, chemical, of course, but there, under his disease, under the chemicals" (*TF,* 342). Beneath the euphoria induced by MS is an ecstasy based on the miracle of existence itself. It is Julius's legacy and an earned vision based on Ben's experiences as entrepreneur, lover of the Finsberg children, and diseased human being. Like Julius, who created and loved his fatally flawed children as well as his vocation, Ben has had a meaningful life. He has succeeded in dubious enterprises and has failed in the quest after his grand design. He has loved the Finsberg family without full recompense. And he has participated in the evolution of his country. Because his experiences have been rich and intense, he has made the most of his franchise—life itself—and can justifiably look back on his experience as miraculous.

The Franchiser is Elkin's first truly affirmative book. Its affirmation is earned in the classic, tragic, sense, for Flesh does not win by any applicable material standard. He is, however, a winner by a much more important metaphysical standard; he responds to recognizing that life is a franchise and health is remission by living intensely and fully, realizing, as no Elkin character has before, that the best response to understanding the fragility of life is to make it count by loving others, without taking too careful an audit on their willingness to respond to the investment.

The book can be appreciated as social commentary. Although this is not Elkin's intention, *The Franchiser* yields many rewards in its account of the intricate connections between national cultural or economic trends and the art of business. It is to Elkin's credit that, unlike most other American writers, he explores the possibility that business is an art. It can also be approached as a study in the psychology of obsession, and the rich complexity of Ben's character and rhetoric offers rewards to its readers. It is, however, most rewarding when read in conjunction with *A Bad Man* as a study in the antithesis of Feldman's obsession, the decency and generosity of which a man of business can be capable when he realizes that the ultimate franchise anyone holds is life itself.

Chapter Four
The Dick Gibson Show: A Quest for Communication

After his critical success with *A Bad Man,* a thoroughly original study of obsessive personality in a prison setting, Elkin turned his attention to an even more startling technical problem: writing a novel about the communication process itself. This book, offering an opportunity to explore Elkin's preoccupation with obsession in new ways, became his most successful experiment in technique. By focusing on radio as a means of communicating, *The Dick Gibson Show* engages Elkin in a complex reflection on the implications of mass communication and on the effects a commitment to broadcasting can have on an unformed yet obsessive and paranoid personality.

The novel has its inspiration in Elkin's fascination with radio as a medium. He often mentions his delight in it, both as a gadget and as a means of communicating among lonely, alienated, or insomniac persons. He collects radios and listens to two-way talk shows because they offer alienated individuals an opportunity to share their unique interests with other listeners. *Dick Gibson* originated during Elkin's army years, when on the New Jersey Turnpike the author, fiddling with the tuner, happened on an announcer he assumed was broadcasting from a small town and who struck him as "very professional, very good, and there was something essentially so lonely. . . . But also the person who is listening to this stuff and all those other people in all those other cars who are listening to him must feel lonely. . . . His voice was a kind of link between all of us and it struck me that this was a strange, a very, very strange job."[1]

From these roots, nurtured over more than a decade, grew Elkin's most technically complex novel. Although *The Dick Gibson Show* is primarily a study in the process and possibility of communication, a matter of implicit concern to any writer, it also treats characteristic Elkin themes, especially the relationship between identity and vocation. As the hero seeks to perfect his voice and find his ideal format—in Gibson's language to "complete his apprenticeship"—he also defines his character.

More thoroughly than most of Elkin's other characters, this hero is formed by his professional aspirations. The first sentence of the novel rivals those of

Melville's *Moby-Dick* or Heller's *Something Happened* in suggestiveness: "When Dick Gibson was a little boy, he was not Dick Gibson."[2] We never learn his real name, even during two visits to his family in Pittsburgh; no family member, except his brother Arthur, is called by name. At times in his career, he uses many names, including Marshall Maine (he called himself Ellery Loyola at a Marshall, Maine, station), Tex Ellery, Ted Elson, Bill Barter, and briefly Doctor Torso. The name Dick Gibson came to him "from the air" (*DGS*, 16) when he had a chance to fill dead air space at a Montana station and, although convinced that this name defines his future identity, he uses it sparingly as he works through his apprenticeship. After establishing his format as a talk show host in Miami, and thereby, he believes, completing the apprenticeship, he legally changes his name to Dick Gibson and thus becomes the person his career has prepared him to be.

Entertainers commonly use names invented to project an image or to protect privacy, but in this novel the practice becomes a symbol for creating a personality that is simultaneously professional and private. From the first sentence to the final telephone call from Dick Nixon, Elkin suggests that Gibson has no identity other than that derived from his business. If Ben Flesh learns who he is by becoming a franchiser or if Leo Feldman studies the meaning of his personality by serving time in prison, Gibson presents a more extreme case of finding self through vocation. Nominally Flesh and Feldman had identities to build upon, whereas Gibson-Ellerby-Maine is pure potential, a tabula rasa. What he is, or will become, is dictated less by innate disposition than by the demands of his professional commitment and certain accidental associations, like a chance meeting with Miriam Desebour that results in his retreat to a New Jersey nursing home.

Gibson's quest for an identity transcends the personal, largely because of his business. He believes the identity he strives for has genuinely mythic proportions. The myth[3] he expects to participate in by becoming Dick Gibson synthesizes connection with, service to, and power over an anonymous, alienated American culture. Gibson's version of the myth is that he can become part of, as well as contribute to, the cultural dynamic. When he was a fledgling announcer, "even as he spoke the announcer's ritual words, he suspected the deeper ritual that lay beneath them, confident that a test was indeed being conducted, his entire young manhood one" (*DGS*, 24). Although *ritual* and *test* suggest traditional mythic concerns, Dick's ideal focuses on an image of families united by radio: "Alias Dick Gibson, alias Marshall Maine, alias Tex Ellery, alias a dozen others knew, knew *then* . . . that all this was the truth, that those pictures had it right: Americans *were* in their living rooms, before their floorlamps, on their sofas, along their rugs, together in time, united, serene. And so he felt twinges, pins and needles of actual conscience: he needed to join his voice to that important chorus, that lovely a capella" (*DGS*, 37–38).

Like Flesh and Feldman, Dick chose his vocation through serendipity. He, like many other youths of the depression years, found in listening to distant radio stations a sense of magic and a solace from the constant economic problems of the times, a motif similar to Ernest Hemingway's "The Gambler, the Nun, and the Radio." His father's influence originally pointed him toward broadcasting. In a demonstration tape, he recalls listening with his father to returns from the 1920 Harding-Cox election, and his father told him to " 'remember all your life that you heard the birth of modern radio.' And I have. I was so impressed that . . . I am marked, historically attached to radio" (*DGS*, 21–22).

When Dick chooses this emerging technology, his commitment is absolute, to a self-definition rather than to an occupation that may foster economic and individual growth but is itself subject to obsolescence. This distinction is made during World War II when he and Lieutenant Collins have a battlefield conversation about their civilian futures. Collins plans to enter the emerging broadcast industry, television, whereas Gibson intends to stay in radio, despite Collins's claim that "radio's had it" (*DGS*, 142). Gibson's commitment is not to a profession but to an abstraction about radio as a means of communicating, and thereby connecting, with amorphous America. This concept is developed by Elkin's central metaphor, Dick's apprenticeship.

Literally, an apprentice is someone learning the skills necessary to practice a trade, but for Gibson the notion connotes a mythic intention. He views his career as a series of stages and periodically takes satisfaction in thinking his apprenticeship is complete, only to discover with each new plateau that he must resume it. Often he resents this status: "How weary he was of that apprenticeship" (*DGS*, 102); he left Pittsburgh "to take up the burden of his apprenticeship a second time" (*DGS*, 105); "Behind him lay the long drought of his inland life . . . and apprenticeship, which of late he had begun to grudge" (*DGS*, 318); "What had his own life been, his interminable apprenticeship which he saw now that he could never end?" (*DGS*, 395).

Although apprenticeship denotes preparation for full status in a profession, here it connotes evolution as a personality. Dick's quest, through trial and error, for a format suited to his professional life corresponds with his fumbling toward an identity in relation to the demands of his profession and the culture with which he wants to connect. Thus the apprenticeship is a process by which Dick experiments with various radio roles, working as a disk jockey and news reporter on small-town stations, serving as the warm-up man for network stars, broadcasting for Armed Forces Radio, initiating telephone swap programs at small stations, hosting panel discussions, and finding his format in telephone call-in programs. As he succeeds in each, he hopes the apprenticeship has ended, but Ben Flesh's hearing Dick Gibson's broadcast in *The Franchiser* suggests that the apprenticeship is incomplete when the novel ends.

Figuratively the apprenticeship implies his efforts to discover who he is in relation to America's culture by finding ways to communicate and connect with his anonymous audience. This structure organizes the stages of Dick's professional and personal evolution; paradoxically his progress toward material success and public recognition corresponds directly with his failure to grow as a person. As he recollects meeting each professional challenge, he does not recognize his failure to develop as an individual. This is the principal ironic pattern of *The Dick Gibson Show.*

Dick's first failure to understand how vastly his version of the American myth differs from reality takes the form of an effort to influence the power brokers in a rural Nebraska community. Beginning his apprenticeship at the aptly named KROP in the farm belt, he begins to suspect a political and economic substructure underlying, perhaps challenging, his notion of American family solidarity. The region served by KROP answers to one family, the Credenzas. The eight brothers own most of the farmland in Louis Credenza, Senior, and Sylvia Credenza counties, so local businesses depend on their favor. Each election year, two Credenza brothers compete against two others to represent the counties in the state legislature, so the family also controls the region's political life. Because they own KROP, the programing is designed to cater to their tastes.

Elkin's technique underscores his ironic intention, for Gibson tells the story in a demonstration tape, a recording made to cultivate the interest of hiring stations. He recounts the story with comparative innocence of its implications for his individual growth. This is one measure of Elkin's irony: through the multiple voices of his hero, he communicates implications of which the character is himself unaware. Dick can narrate what happened, but even with several years' hindsight between the events and his making the tapes, he has not comprehended the significance of his KROP adventure. Elkin intersperses omniscient narration among fragments of the demonstration tape to create perspective on the events Gibson describes.

Because KROP is a Credenza operation, Marshall Maine (the name Dick used there) adopts a flunky's attitude that competes with his myth of radio as America's cultural bond. Recognizing that the family—he refers to all the brothers and their families by the collective *Credenza*—listens to the station and makes its history and its members' trivial activities matters of community importance, Marshall eagerly adapts his role as newsman to contribute to the Credenza myth: "I embraced myth then—all myth, everybody's, anybody's. To this day I'm a sucker for all primal episode" (*DGS*, 34). After receiving a complaint from Louis III because he ran a commercial at the wrong time and developing a "notion of command performance" (*DGS*, 32), Maine tailors the news to conform with what he believes the family wants to hear. He reports as hard news auto repairs and telephone calls relating to Credenza; he scours the wire services for the human interest stories they like and occasionally invents these when he cannot find them.

Accepting the flunky's role, Marshall hopes to define his identity by assimilating himself in the Credenza myth. He can acquire importance by being subservient to the sources of wealth and power. His first error is to believe he can combine his professional role as a newsman with the flunky's role he has assumed to cultivate Credenza. He suggests to the most approachable brother that KROP should be like other stations by cultivating his image of the newsman as the voice of reassurance and calm to the public. To his surprise, a delegation visits the station to tell him that his myth of the newsman has no place at KROP.

This scene illustrates the degree to which Marshall is willing to sacrifice professional standards and personal loyalty to gain these powerful patrons' acceptance. Before they voice any objections, "He was prepared to yield at once, to concede to the pressures of what seemed to him their vigilante loomings" (*DGS*, 38). His engineer, fearing a physical attack, draws a knife to defend Marshall, but Poke Credenza knocks the man unconscious: "for all Maine knew, [he] died," and Maine "found himself mourning, grieving for a pal" (*DGS*, 39; compare his battlefield camaraderie with Collins on Mauritius). Yet seeing how little the injury means to Credenza, Marshall chooses absolute loyalty to them over affiliation with his colleague: "Maine was never again to feel comfortable with any of the other employees, seeing them as the Credenzas saw them—not family, outsiders like himself. . . . If he could divorce himself from his colleagues, he felt, he would be that much closer to the Credenzas" (*DGS*, 39).[4]

Maine intensifies his campaign to ingratiate himself with the family, but his effort to win their approval conflicts with his professional conscience. He develops mike fright, "some pinched, asbestos quality in himself of unkindling, some odd, aged and deadened dignity" (*DGS*, 42). Not realizing this is his professional self resisting the accommodations he makes to Credenza's demands, Maine compensates by playing records that need no introduction and goes out of his way to find old-fashioned, obscure records. Because the brothers ordered him to be more cheerful while reporting news of disasters, he becomes almost hysterical, laughing openly while reporting catastrophes. Within weeks, he is making up libel about family members and deliberately opening the microphone so his gossip will be heard.

Maine is unconsciously rebelling against the compromises he has made with his professional standards; he is also making his confrontation with Credenza authority mythic. If he cannot win the brothers' attention by pleasing them, he will gain it by defying them. He seeks "a confrontation, convinced that only through a showdown could he ever hope to negotiate his brotherhood with the Credenzas" (*DGS*, 43). His need to make them take notice, or acknowledge his presence even by hostility, introduces another important motif: paranoia.

Throughout the novel, Gibson's paranoia complements his uncertainty about his identity. This is not to say that Elkin uses the notion of paranoia exactly as Thomas Pynchon does. For Lieutenant Slothrop of Pynchon's *Gravity's Rainbow* or Oedipa Maas of his *The Crying of Lot 49*, paranoia is inverse rationality, an irrational insistence that the universe makes sense. If someone ("they") is out to get one, being victimized has some purpose. Gibson's paranoia is an attempt to reinforce self-esteem and give his random experiences mythic proportion. In this episode, Maine generalizes his futile attempts to win the brothers' approval to a confrontation with "dark, gigantic generals" (*DGS*, 42) or "dark-booted Credenzas" (*DGS*, 43), then to a "single merged *nemesis*" (*DGS*, 51; my italics). This enemy has power to punish, but punishment implies that he has been noticed, and Marshall anticipates visits and telephone calls in which he may be chastised but may also press his fraternal claims. When these do not come, he absurdly expects to be murdered by Credenza and once wonders if their delay intensifies sadistically the torture of a planned electrocution.[5]

This nemesis also has power to reward. Maine hopes that they will, upon punishing him, notice that he is special and take him into their group. Because they embody Nebraska wealth and power, their acceptance would give him a sense of worth he lacks. But the nemesis never responds, and Maine's vanity receives a crushing blow when he discovers the reason for their indifference: "Because one by one we had all stopped listening [to KROP]" (*DGS*, 56).

Even in retrospect, Gibson manifests paranoia when interpreting Credenza indifference to his subservience. Rather than attribute the decision to close down KROP to natural shifts in habit and taste, Gibson takes credit, as did Maine at the time, for ending the station's life singlehandedly: "I ran

KROP into the ground. All by myself. I did it" (*DGS,* 57). Between the announcement and the actual closing, Maine uses the treasured name *Gibson* and, freed from any need to appease his nemesis, inadvertently enacts another cherished professional myth: during bad weather, he thinks of his voice as a consoling influence on some salesman traveling over icy roads. During World War II he discovers that the public with whom he connected was not a salesman but an army officer, and his good deed saves him from facing a court-martial.

Despite his pride that he was solely responsible for KROP's failure, Maine plunges into deep depression over his combined professional and personal failure to attract the Credenzas' approval. The subsequent episode drama-tizes a pattern of psychological regression to the womb.[6] In a Morristown, New Jersey, convalescent home, Maine enjoys a voluntary withdrawal from the world of power (Credenza) and professional commitment.

Going home to Pittsburgh "in disgrace" and actually looking forward to confronting his family with failure ("I had the power of the has-been like a se-cret weapon" [*DGS,* 65]), Maine meets Miriam, a nurse, on the bus and, after a frantic, funny sexual encounter, accompanies her to her new job in "the languishment capital of America" (*DGS,* 71). He originally planned to go home, psychologically to recover an environment that once shielded him from responsibility and failure; but life at home is stressful because the entire family is devoted to role playing, and Miriam, combining sexual gratification and maternal caretaking—because her job pays the expenses and provides living accommodations, Marshall assumes the roles of husband and invalid—offers an ideal alternative for someone who wants to return to the womb. Although their affair begins as torridly sexual, Maine fondly recalls bathing rituals in which Miriam washed him much as a mother might her in-fant, all the while soothing him with stories about her family and her experi-ences as a nurse.

Abdicating responsibility for earning his living, even for personal hygiene, to a mother figure means so much to Marshall that he accepts the cuckold's role when Miriam tires of his passivity and wants him to leave. He refuses to go until "I unlock the secret of your voice" (*DGS,* 82), and she, desperate to be rid of him, begins, or claims to begin, an affair with a patient. Maine ac-cepts the other patients' ridicule, in part because her voice fascinates him, but primarily because he is not prepared to resume his apprenticeship and the re-sponsibilities it entails. After a picnic at which Maine recovers vitality by tak-ing advantage of his health to defeat the invalids he competes against, he discovers the secret of her voice in a "dead room," a chamber built to simulate the silence deaf people endure. There he learns that the secret of her voice was, "You were naked. I'm a sucker for the first-person singular" (*DGS*, 92), and he can resume his apprenticeship by cultivating his voice and accepting the challenge of professional development.

The Morristown episode, then, dramatizes Gibson's response to his defeat in Nebraska by tempting him toward womblike dependency. Moreover, it introduces a supporting motif: Dick's inability to love individuals. He is fond of American culture in the abstract but cannot love any one person. He acknowledges that he "wasn't in love with Miriam. . . . She made me comfortable, more comfortable than I'd ever been in my life" (*DGS*, 81). Years later, when Miriam calls his Miami phone-in show, he neither recognizes her voice immediately nor remembers what she looked like, though he has a nostalgic episode of lust and he undresses in the booth during her call. Both of his other sexual relationships develop this inability to love individuals.

After the climactic Hartford episode, Gibson becomes involved with Carmella Streep, the sister of a guest from his program. Carmella is very like Miriam, and Dick, in her commitment to the ordinary; paradoxically her "very need of the normal was the most fascinating thing about her. It was pathological" (*DGS*, 291). She too is a refuge. Gibson's confrontation with Dr. Behr-Bleibtreau, a psychologist, has shaken his confidence and has challenged his belief in the ordinary. As Miriam offered him sanctuary after his failure with Credenza, so Carmella's passion for the normal reassures him that his dedication to the ordinary is philosophically sound.

He does not love Carmella any more than he loved Miriam, and his fate is to be cuckolded again. She wants to marry a thoroughly ordinary man. Attending his mother's funeral in Pittsburgh, Dick realizes Carmella is falling in love with his brother. He prepares to resume his apprenticeship by taking on the romantic role of the spurned lover who renounces his claims in the interest of his beloved, only to learn they are already intimate, and "now his heart *was* broken. It was a Dick Gibson first" (*DGS*, 298).

In Miami Dick has a brief affair with Sheila, a dance instructor, but he originally sought the company of an entertainer who occasionally "used his shoulder to cry on, though he would have preferred her to call up and tell him about it on the air" (*DGS*, 320). Like Miriam and Carmella, Sheila is a refuge—not from any specific failure but from general disappointment in his life's expectations. She is a one-night stand, but to her he confesses his overall disappointment that his life, although he has found success and his ideal format, has not met his mythic expectations. In confessing, he concedes the paranoia central to his professional life: "What I thought back then was that it [his life] would be touched by cliché. . . . That it would be as it is in myth. That maybe I might even have to suffer more than ordinary men. . . . That I

would even have enemies. . . . Is there a nemesis in the house? . . . That I'd
have this goal, you see, but that I'd be thwarted at every turn. . . . I thought it
would be trite and magnificent" (*DGS*, 323–24). Dick's belief that he is destined to live a life both "trite and magnificent" makes it impossible for him to
love others, and Elkin's technique, especially in the story about his affair with
Miriam, reinforces his alienation.

As a warm-up man, Gibson begins the story while preparing the audience
for Bob Hope's performance, but the scene on the bus is more erotically explicit than would be normal in warm-ups for Hope's kind of comedy. His describing Morristown as a "secular Lourdes" (*DGS*, 72) introduces a subject
that would dampen the atmosphere for snappy one-liners. Finally the autobiographical revelation of Marshall's dependency on Miriam seems highly
confessional for this situation. After most of the story has been told, Elkin indicates that much of what we have just read was not part of the warm-up—
that Hope interrupted Gibson when he mentioned the invalids at
Morristown but after the description of his meeting Miriam. The rest of the
story was told at a roadhouse when members of the cast met after the show.

This assortment of narrative strategies in the Morristown episode casts
doubt on the facticity of the story being told, to say nothing of the meanings
the teller, Gibson, derives from it. A more complex variation on this technique operates in the section describing his participation in World War II.
The bulk of the episode is narrated as "FROM THE ARCHIVES: TRANSCRIPTS OF DICK
GIBSON'S BROADCAST OF / Fabulous Battles of World War II: Mauritius"
(*DGS*, 135), in which Dick broadcasts stories about a military buildup, the
discovery of a survivor of an extinct species, a competition based on an ancient Japanese legend to capture a dodo, and the slaughter of a Japanese force
on Mauritius. It is not clear whose archives these tapes are from, the army's or
Gibson's extensive collection, many of which are later destroyed in a fire, rob-
bing him of some of his past and therefore part of his identity.

One of the most intriguing episodes in the novel, the Mauritius story has
provoked a wide variety of interpretations. Olderman sees Dick's induction
into the army as "the Crisis of the Brute" and the Mauritius episode as a crisis
in which Gibson is a "literal mediator between the magic of Shobuta's myth
and the crass sentiment of Dick Nixon's clichéd version of the Emperor who
saves his people." Bailey argues that parallels between the Shobuta legend
and Dick's experience with the dodo indicate that Gibson misses his opportunity to participate in a truly mythic event and that he trivializes magical
moments suggestive of a "mythic reenactment of sacred events." Bargen,
however, believes Gibson deliberately invents the Japanese ornithologist's

story of the dodo as "a hoax," so the central character in the broadcast is Dick Gibson.[7]

That Dick invents the dodo story and the Shobuta legend makes sense because of both external and internal evidence. In arguing this point, I hope to show that the Mauritius adventure has more in common with the Credenza episodes than has previously been noted.[8] It reenacts the Nebraska misadventure in that what is at stake is a conflict between Gibson's instinct to please those in authority and his obligations as a professional broadcaster. To understand this fully, we must investigate the circumstances that bring Gibson to Mauritius.

Being drafted exposes Dick to a concept of humanity that undermines his myth of the happy American family. A degrading notion of humanity represented by Privates Rohnspeece, Null, Blitz, Laspooney, and Tuleremia equals, in Gibson's mind, "the total collapse of civilization" (*DGS*, 111). Forced into contact with men who habitually degrade one another, destroy one another's property viciously, and gang-rape teenage girls, Gibson discovers that his ideas about humanity were fundamentally inadequate:

Radio had badly prepared him for his new life. He had never suspected the enormous chasm between the world of radio with the sane, middle-class ways of its supposed audience and the genuine article. Only the officers—to the shame of his democratic instincts—were at all recognizable to him. . . . Was he the last innocent man? He was sure that he was not innocent, just less brutal, perhaps, less reckless, more hygienic than the next man. Who broadcasts to the brutes? . . . Who has the ear of the swine? (*DGS*, 116)

Not only do officers comprise the only military alternative to the "brutes," they alone decide who is and is not a brute. They are a military equivalent of the Credenzas, and Gibson cultivates their favor to avoid acknowledging his affiliation with the brutes. If he cannot be an officer—as he could not be a Credenza—he can petition officers to allow him to retreat into his myth of the happy family by resuming his radio apprenticeship. He auditions, carefully adjusting his impromptu broadcast as a captain's interest waxes and wanes, and secures an assignment in Armed Forces Radio, with Lieutenant Collins as his engineer.

Thus Dick resumes his tactic of assuming the flunky's role to escape associating with the brutes and to protect his myth of the ordinary American. Yet broadcasting for Armed Forces Radio, he finds the "rigidity of the format and the endorsed quality of the sentiment burdensome" (*DGS*, 119), then wonders how a brute audience is responding to his neatly packaged patriotism. In the episode that threatens his armed forces broadcasting career, he simultaneously discovers that he has some of the brute within him and that to survive he must cultivate the officers.

During an air raid, he becomes hysterical because Collins insists that they finish the taping before seeking cover in a shelter. He considers shooting Collins and realizes this is how brutes think. His broadcast sympathizes with the brutes as cannon fodder, and he sings parodies of patriotic songs he is supposed to play. Collins arranges to have him court-martialed, but the trial's outcome reinforces Gibson's desire to appease the officer class. A general who remembers the comfort he found in Gibson's broadcast during a storm offers him the choice of facing trial or becoming the man the officers need to "do the color on World War II" (*DGS*, 132). By accepting this assignment, Dick realizes how much he owes the officer class and uses the treasured name *Dick Gibson* when he broadcasts from Mauritius.[9]

That the events he reports from the island are designed to please the officers gains support from his repeated inquiries whether what he is saying conforms with his listeners' expectations. This is the principal technical feature of the broadcasts, represented by this sample: "Is this the sort of thing you want?" (*DGS*, 137); "This broadcast of mine is a little like prayer. . . . That's what you want to hear, right? Am I getting warm?" (*DGS*, 140); his paranoia surfaces when he asks, "It was a test of the equipment. Am I getting warm? . . . It was all *meant* to be meaningless" (*DGS*, 163).

Another way to support the hypothesis that the broadcasts are invented to please Gibson's superiors is to check the historical probability of his story. Although Elkin often revises history to serve his fictional needs, especially in *George Mills,* usually some germ of historical record is behind his anecdote. No such background exists here. Not only is there no account of a live dodo being found in this century on Mauritius or anywhere else, no World War II hostilities occurred on that island. It is more than a thousand miles from the South Pacific war zones; the war's primary impact was that restrictions on trade in sugar, the island's chief export, led to changes in the agricultural economy. There is no record of any thirteenth-century Japanese emperor named Shobuta, and by then the imperial family was, as now, largely a figurehead. Although one emperor challenged a shogun's power in 1221, "as far as political realities were concerned, the emperor and his court had become anachronistic survivals of an earlier age, with no administrative role in the new political order."[10] If warriors like Zamue or, later, Korogachi had political ambition, they would have tried to assassinate the shogun rather than the emperor, and it is inconceivable that the army would have followed an emperor, even one transformed from "the Tender" to "the Jealous," into war without a shogun's direction. Although one Japanese island is called Shikoku—which the ornithologist says is the origin of the Indian word *Chicago* (*DGS*, 145)—it is unlikely that an emperor would have lived there, for the capital was Kyoto, on the island Honshu.

The question is, therefore, Is Elkin exaggerating his habit of playing loosely with history for narrative purposes, or is Gibson making up a fanciful account to win respect, or at least notice, from his superiors? Because the narrative is punctuated by requests for his listeners' approval, the latter explanation seems plausible. That Gibson may be making this up, however, does not diminish its importance to the structure of the novel.

Shobuta's story enacts a culture's yearning for mystery and myth in the face of the ordinary, which is what Gibson is developing as his professional and personal credo. This tale about the miraculous discovery of a survivor of an extinct species and the reverence the Japanese have for it suggests the degree to which Gibson is unconsciously aware of the need for the extraordinary in folklore and myth, among both the Japanese and his Occidental auditors. Elkin has great fun with bogus etymology by having Dick recount the ornithologist's explanation of the word *zoo* as a corruption of the ancient Shikokuan "200," designating a place where animals are exhibited, or asking whether English has expressions like "to gild the lily" (*DGS*, 148), "battle of nerves" (*DGS*, 150), or "locked assholes" (*DGS*, 154). The thrust of Dick's narrative, however, is to trivialize the mystery his story implies by endorsing trickery over mystery and magic.

At the heart of that story is the dodo's transforming Shobuta from "tender" to "jealous," or one of the brutes, and saving Japan in the process. When the dodo saves Shobuta by causing the assassin Zamue to collapse in a peal of laughter, the emperor changes from a mild to a warlike man. When it dies of the din of battle in the final war, Shobuta again becomes "the Tender," who, carrying the bird across the battlefield, brings hostilities to a close, while a deaf warrior slays the rebel Korogachi. With each of its flights— dodos could not fly—the bird saves Japan, and the first flight, disabling the assassin, results in a transference of its invincibility, or *rosichicho* (*DGS*, 153), to the emperor.

In Gibson's narrative, he too has a chance to participate in myth. He temporarily purges himself of the brute within him when he and Collins capture the ornithologist. Gibson threatens Sansoni, muttering clichés from gangster movies, but equates by metaphor the brute with the chevrons on his arm: "My stripes lashed me, driving me to feats of clown and squire" (*DGS*, 145). After hearing the sentimental story about Shobuta and the dodo, Gibson feels that "his story had unsergeanted me, dissolved the chevrons from my arms" (*DGS*, 156). After this apparent purgation, he stumbles on the dodo the Japanese seek in the hope that it can also save Japan, holds it hostage, and develops a fearful awareness of its relevance to him: "I thought of dinosaurs and mammoths and the saber-toothed tiger, and here was I, Dick Gibson, with that other loser, the dodo. *Back,* I thought, cursing it, *back to history, you*" (*DGS*, 160).

The brute is fully reawakened when the dodo bites and excretes on Gibson, and with morning, unable to hide it any longer, he follows Collins's order and kills it, demoralizing the Japanese. When it flies, repeating the miracle that saved Shobuta, Dick too becomes *rosichicho*. Escaping from the Japanese before a British force slaughters them, Gibson trivializes the miracle: "I tossed the bird. . . . It's all in the wrists" (*DGS*, 163).

If Gibson invents or embellishes the story of the dodo and the legend of Shobuta to impress his superiors in London, three conclusions follow: (1) the episode is consistent with the KROP adventure in that Gibson redefines his role as a radio man to seek favor from centers of power; (2) his imagination is truly mythic, for the story he tells concerns human interaction with the rare and mysterious in nature and its capacity to transform a man (Shobuta) and to affect a nation's destiny, but he trivializes the applicability of myth to his own situation by attributing his becoming *rosichicho* to sleight-of-hand, not magic; and (3) his tale dramatizes his worst fear, loss of voice, which will become the key concept in the Behr-Bleibtreau episode, by associating such loss with choice.

Recounting Sansoni's story to the officers, Gibson interprets the dodo's going mad in the racket of battle as a combination of physiology and choice: "Perhaps we have all along paid too much attention to its winglessness and not enough to its voicelessness. Perhaps voicelessness is a choice—the choice of silence. . . . Perhaps even extinction is a choice" (*DGS*, 155). This equation of choice, voicelessness, and extinction, especially if made by Gibson rather than by an ornithologist whose name, "without sound," suggests voicelessness, helps us understand the terror Gibson feels when he meets his projected nemesis—his Zamue—Behr-Bleibtreau.

The broadcast of the "controversy-show" from Hartford is by far the most technically complex, and confusing, set-piece Elkin ever wrote. It is, like the "Circe" section of Joyce's *Ulysses,* in part a play within a novel, and like the Joyce episode it mixes realism and surrealistic, psychological imagery—with the emphasis so heavily on surrealism that Elkin, usually so precise in commenting on the meaning of his works, indicates that the section is intended as a novelistic equivalent of a radio play and concedes, "I don't know whether it's a conspiracy or whether they're [the panelists] playing a joke on Dick

Gibson or not. I don't know if the program is actually being heard. I don't know what the hell is happening. I'm as confused as I hope the listener is. But I know that it ain't real magic."[11]

If the author hopes his readers are confused, he will not get much argument from many who confront the Hartford episode. It represents the main crisis of Dick's career and a logical extension of his dependence on professional identity while offering a focus for his lifelong paranoia. Although the radio play emphasizes progressively intimate confessions by four regulars on Dick's controversy program, the drama centers on an internal conflict within Dick, one he attempts to resolve by attributing his panelists' unruly confessions to the presence of Dr. Edmond Behr-Bleibtreau, a psychologist he can identify as his nemesis. In this section Elkin treats paranoia in a manner quite similar to that of Pynchon, in which defining an adversary and investing that adversary with power to menace one marks an attempt to give rational focus to what is otherwise incoherent and random.

The Hartford broadcast welcomes comparison with the "Circe" chapter in *Ulysses*. Joyce merges realism with psychological hallucination without explicitly distinguishing between these layers of experience. Readers can reconstruct the layers. Literally a drunken Stephen Dedalus accompanies his companions to a brothel, becomes unruly, and is rescued by Leopold Bloom. At the hallucinatory level, the characters perceive images of their unresolved psychological conflicts superimposed on events they witness. Thus Bloom confronts his own cuckolding when Madam Bella becomes Master Bello and his guilt and heritage when he sees the elfin figure of his grandfather; Stephen reenacts his refusal to pray with his dying mother. The hallucinations seem to be simultaneously individual and collective. Something very like this happens in the climactic chapter of *The Dick Gibson Show*.

Literally Gibson moderates an all-night panel discussion show in 1959, fifteen years after the Mauritius adventure. At this stage in his apprenticeship, he has found a forum that allows for limited two-way communication with his audience, who can send in telegrams to propose questions for his panelists. This show's panelists, representing a variety of interests and obsessions, are familiar: Dr. Jack Patterson, a community college associate professor known for flirtations with his female students; Bernie Perk, a pharmacist and crusader for fluoridation; Pepper Streep, the operator of a local charm school; and Mel Son, a radio personality who failed in his try for public office. Each panelist brings guests: Patterson's current girlfriend, Perk's son and daughter-in-law, and so on. The special guest is Behr-Bleibtreau, a psychologist whose books Gibson has never read but whose "major emphasis is the old business of mind over matter" and who is reputed to use "his knowledge of psychology in unusual, if unspecified, ways" (*DGS*, 168). Behr-Bleibtreau brings two guests, neither of whom is introduced to Gibson, and intensifies the mystery surrounding him by saying, "I expect someone. . . . He may come and he may not" (*DGS*, 169).

The drama becomes progressively less realistic when the guests start talking. Instead of a spirited discussion, they conduct monologues in which each reveals a covert personality flaw. Their confessions gather momentum, and Gibson cannot control his panelists' disclosures, which betray progressively secret obsessions. Patterson reveals his fascination with a ten-year-old singer's beauty, indicating that his flirtations with his students express a deep-seated pedophilia. Streep recalls teaching grace to a memory expert, then falling in love with him, only to lose him to his vanity (which her instruction strengthened), but along the way confesses her unresolved emotional and sexual problems. Perk, after attempting to mitigate his fellow panelists' confessions, launches into a long narrative about his fascination with his patients' secret physical defects, an obsession that culminates in his raping one who has overdeveloped sexual organs; in telling his story, Bernie not only reveals his unhealthy obsession with human imperfection but alienates his family as well. Mel Son has chosen this program on which to commit suicide because Gibson's show reaches a wider audience than his own (*DGS*, 262) and, in explaining his desire to kill himself, synthesizes all the panelists' deviant pathologies, a self-love that renders him incapable of meaningful interaction with others.

Unable to account for his usually predictable guests' telling progressively shameful secrets, Gibson wonders if they are under the control of an outside force like the enigmatic Behr-Bleibtreau. This speculation is fueled by each panelist's lapsing into silence after his or her monologue, so Gibson suspects that Behr-Bleibtreau has taken control of their voices.

As readers, we have several options: their confessions generate a momentum the individuals cannot control, so they in effect compete to tell the most shameful secret; they are being forced by Behr-Bleibtreau to confess things they would ordinarily repress; or some portion of what happens in the episode is actually Gibson's projection on the panelists' monologues. Although Gibson prefers the second option, it is the least likely. The first, that the characters compete to tell the most shameful secret, gains support from Elkin's remark that this section is modeled on Chaucer's *Canterbury Tales* and that "the journey to dawn is the journey to Canterbury"; he called the Perk section "The Druggist's Tale" when submitting it to a magazine.[12] This comment, however, raises intriguing possibilities. Chaucer's pilgrims told stories, usually fictional rather than autobiographical, in competition with one another.

Does this imply that Elkin's characters are falsifying their pasts, in effect fictionalizing themselves? This seems likely; if it is, we have yet another connection with Gibson's broadcasts from Mauritius. The final option, projection, is consistent with Dick's paranoia, and he will become obsessed with Behr-Bleibtreau later in his career, to the extent that he waits for the psychologist to call in to his "Night Letters" show in Miami, then expects his nemesis to try to assassinate him at a picnic for the show's audience. Elkin comments, moreover, that Dick's obsession with Behr-Bleibtreau is "baloney paranoia," that the real enemy is "the amorphous public that [Dick] is trying to appeal to."[13]

It is impossible to define exactly when, or to what degree, the account of the Hartford broadcast merges with Gibson's paranoid projection, but we may attempt this reconstruction: the broadcast gets out of hand as the panelists compete to confess the most shameful secret; Behr-Bleibtreau fuels the fire by mentioning, several times, that someone in the studio has a gun (either Mel Son does or Gibson comes to believe he does); and the panelists, exhausted and shamed by their revelations, lapse into semicatatonic stupors. Gibson, trying to make sense of the chaos that has emerged on his show, invests in Behr-Bleibtreau the power to force this descent into psychological and social chaos and elevates him to the position of nemesis, a vacuum he has been seeking to fill since the Credenza episodes.

Behr-Bleibtreau contributes to Gibson's projecting him as adversary. He encourages the panelists to confess by using familiar motivational techniques; he establishes rapport with Patterson (*DGS,* 179–80), encourages Streep to continue (*DGS,* 206), and tells Perk he may use vulgar expressions on radio (*DGS,* 231). His encouraging the panelists toward uninhibited confession challenges Gibson's sense of the decorum appropriate to radio. But this casting Behr-Bleibtreau as adversary responds to needs specific to Gibson's inability to define himself as either a man or a professional. In his crisis, he thinks, "*Because my character is my mind. . . . God knows what Behr-Bleibtreau's, is, maybe his mystery, but mine's my mind, what I think and nothing else*" (*DGS,* 250–251).

When Behr-Bleibtreau "frees" Mel Son to tell his story, the justification for Mel's attempted suicide completes the pattern of the panelists' confessing a self-love so complete that it renders the individual emotionally arid. Mel's sexuality is totally passive, and now that his physical charm has deteriorated, he chooses suicide as an alternative to learning to love responsively. This story obviously exaggerates Dick's own emotional life, and in his imagination Behr-Bleibtreau serves as the opponent responsible for the loss of human speech, associated with Dick's worst professional fear, as well as the inability to love and the denial of the myth of the happy American family, associated with his private fears. Seeking a mythic battle with a defined nemesis, Gibson invents or embellishes a confrontation in which Behr-Bleibtreau openly challenges him, summoning the demon Sordino, who is associated with the power to render one silent.

This projected confrontation with a nemesis reveals three themes central to the novel. First, Dick's complex relationship with his audience is invoked when he seeks their support, through telegrams, to defeat Behr-Bleibtreau, but he is no more successful in getting their help than he was with the panelists or the sandwich man. Second, he places himself in a godlike position in that Behr-Bleibtreau demands that Gibson make a sacrifice, by giving up his voice, in return for Mel Son's life. His response, "The show must go on and I must be on it. I'm the show" (*DGS*, 267), reinforces the association between his professional and his personal identity and also indicates how like Son's self-love Gib[S]on's is. He cannot imagine trading his voice for the sparing of someone else's life.

Most importantly, his fantasy of confronting this nemesis enables him to make final his commitment to the ordinary. Behr-Bleibtreau has challenged his senses (by claiming that colors are not what Dick perceives them to be), his voice, and his control of the show. Behr-Bleibtreau absurdly summons the powers of darkness on the basis of his impeccable virtue, proved by his innocence in major as well as trivial matters, from "because I am without flaw, because I am correct, because I am pure, because I am unblemished and upright, because I am without stain and without aberration" through "because I have never hit-and-run, told fibs, raped, played the radio loud while others were sleeping" to "because I have never clipped, high-sticked, fouled the shooter, never talked back to the umpire or jumped the gun . . . I exercise my right to call on demons, spirits, and avenging angels!" (*DGS*, 269). Sordino cannot quite vanquish Gibson, and a temporary victory over the nemesis is ensured when Behr-Bleibtreau physically attacks Dick, only to be defeated and sent packing.

That we have read the Hartford episode as hallucinated renders its conclusion all the more remarkable. Filling the journey to dawn with a monologue after the guests and "adversary" leave, an exhausted Gibson concludes by denying the mystery his own imagination, projecting on an unruly reality, has invented: "There is no astrology, there is no black magic and no white, no ESP, no UFO's. Mars is uninhabited. The dead are dead and buried. . . . Your handwriting doesn't indicate your character and there is no God. All there is . . . are the strange displacements of the ordinary" (*DGS*, 274). As Gibson trivialized his imagination's ability to respond to wonder when he reduced *rosichicho* to slight-of-hand on Mauritius, he again fails to acknowledge a mystery his mind has invented. He refuses to allow the adventure with Behr-Bleibtreau to challenge his commitment to the ordinary and generalizes his invented or embellished experience to deny the existence of God and life on other planets. It is small wonder that after this experience, Dick seeks the comfort of the pathologically ordinary Carmella.

Whatever goes out over the airwaves, the episode ends Dick's career in Hartford. He resumes the apprenticeship, once calling the station on which the Hartford episode originated to confess his frustrations and midlife crisis. Years later, in Miami, he discovers his ideal format, two-way talk radio. To introduce the technology that enables Dick to find this format, Elkin includes the chapter "From an Address at the Annual 'Annals of Broadcasting Dinner'" (*DGS*, 277) in which an industry spokesman identifies the 6-second tape delay as one of the industry's great inventions, "a fulfillment of what radio has always promised" (*DGS*, 284) and a way to make "every American his own potential star" (*DGS*, 283). This amusing, exaggerated insider's view of the importance of a technology that can create a new niche for an industry rapidly losing ground to television provides a basis for the final stage of Gibson's apprenticeship: his expansion of the radio man's role as mediator with anonymous America.

This technology makes possible the development of Dick's ideal format, one that allows him to connect fully with his audience. For a while, the "Night Letters" program seems to fulfill his myth of a comprehensive American family united by radio. Listeners are organized into "Listening Posts," and the audience obtains community. Alienated individuals share their concerns in a technological extension of the American living room of Dick's Credenza myth. Harold Flesh, perhaps the mystery man of *Boswell* or the convict of *A Bad Man,* calls from Tennessee, and eccentric mail baggers, or regular callers, telephone to share their lives. Soon, however, a note of despair enters the calls, and Dick's cherished dream is again challenged.

The novel ends with Gibson's refusing to take any calls that promise to be jeremiads, including the final call from President Nixon, who with his chum Bebe Rebozo faces insoluble problems. Elkin's introducing the president as a "Night Letters" caller has prompted critics to ask whether a political element, or a literary nonclosure, completes the novel. Olderman connects Dick's tendency to create scapegoats with the media's creation of Nixon as America's scapegoat: "Most likely of all, given Dick's disposition to save himself with scapegoats—he will have found in Dick Nixon the perfect scapegoat to help him prop up his old tired clichés." Olderman also offers the possibility that Nixon and what he stood for may be the "true enemy" Gibson has been seeking, "and Dick will climb from cliché to myth after all," a position with which

LeClair agrees: "Perhaps this is the call to greatness, perhaps it is the call of the enemy."[14] Sound systems suggest affinity between the names; one was called "Tricky Dick," the other calls himself "poor Dick Gibson"; obvious echoes exist between *Nixon* and *Gibson*. We shall, however, concentrate on the reasons for Gibson's refusing to take the calls he has sought throughout his career.

His format has failed him. Rather than create a community with his "Night Letters," he has created a forum for the unhappy, alienated, and dispossessed who really inhabit his America. Cheerful calls dwindle, replaced by callers who need to talk to someone about their misfortunes. One caller was traumatized by her parents' amateurly piercing her ears and their stupid efforts to treat the resulting infection; another, Mrs. Dormer, is dying; Norman, the last descendant of an African caveman tribe, has survived anthropologists and a circus to settle on a farm in America, but his final call suggests that he is about to be lynched for proposing marriage to a white teenager; the Sohnshilds, a gifted lawyer and pianist, gave up promising careers to help the disadvantaged but are consumed with guilt and an overwhelming need to protect their blind baby.

Dick also learns that his own best intentions can compound his callers' difficulties. Henry Harper, an orphan who protects his privacy and offers material comfort to other mail baggers, is forced by Dick to reveal his real name, with the result that greedy people adopt him. Henry has adapted to being an orphan; in fact, his generosity is the most decent gesture in the novel. By forcing Henry to divulge his real name, Gibson has ended his charity and has forced him into an unwelcome family situation.

Predictably, as the calls become more stridently solipsistic, Dick explains the loss of his image of an extended happy family by suspecting that a definable nemesis is behind the breakdown of his program. He thinks a nutty anthropologist who calls is Behr-Bleibtreau: "He was filled with a marvelous sense of relief. An enemy! He had an enemy. An *enemy* had appeared!" (*DGS*, 349). Later he suspects that Henry Harper is simply a Behr-Bleibtreau hoax and that the mysterious man Miriam Desebour now works for is Guess Who?

One final episode from the program suggests both the degree to which Dick reverts into paranoia as his dreams fall apart and the possibility that his paranoia is not irreversible. One caller complains that her son's comic book contains an ad promising to teach children how to make guns, bombs, and toxic weapons. Although reluctant to get involved, Gibson decides that moral imperatives demand a response to this kind of hate-mongering: "There was too much suffering. Too much went wrong; victims were everywhere.

That was your real population explosion" (*DGS,* 395). He decides that, although no one can end all misery, one man must do something, but his decision betrays his fundamental paranoia: "All one could hope for was a scapegoat" (*DGS,* 395). He decides to track down and kill the man responsible for these ads, hoping he will prove to be Behr-Bleibtreau (*DGS,* 397). When he tracks the vendor down, he discovers that evil is not something he can confront in one of the saving gestures he longs for: "It was too shabby—basement evil, the awry free enterprise of a madman. . . . How could he kill *him?* Nothing would change" (*DGS,* 398).

Despite his paranoia, which finally means his desire for a grand, mythic confrontation with the nemesis who embodies all that is wrong in the world, Dick's greatest ethical crisis occurs here, and he rises to it. He confronts the banality of evil, but this too demands a response. Instead of an ego-serving shoot-out, this requires an orderly process of law. Dick does the right thing by turning the evidence over to Robert Sohnshild, who is on the attorney general's staff. This does not, however, mean that Dick is free of his paranoia. He still hopes to confront Behr-Bleibtreau, he reluctantly believes that he must once more resume his apprenticeship, he cannot tolerate any more calls for solace, and his "Miss Lonelyhearts complex" has all but done him in. Faced with an ethical crisis, however, he has done the proper rather than the easy thing.

It would be difficult to overstate the technical brilliance of *The Dick Gibson Show,* Elkin's most innovative novel. This analysis has not done full justice to the variations in style and voice, the pattern of repetition, and the sheer power of rhetoric in this work. Elkin's tactic of calling into question the judgment, and even the ability to remain true to facts, of his character, however, brings to exquisite life his themes: the struggle to define an identity in relation to an amorphous American culture and the risks this quest can involve.

Chapter Five
The Magic Kingdom: What Can We Do for the Dying Children?

While completing his "story machine," *George Mills,* Elkin took up a potentially more challenging project: writing a novel about the practice of offering terminally ill children a dream holiday instead of radical surgical or chemical treatments. This book would challenge even Elkin's artistic resources, for the necessary balance between pathos and humor would be extremely precarious. By maintaining this equilibrium, Elkin would create his most important book to date, in which he explores thoroughly and without compromise the implications of Ben Flesh's discovery in *The Franchiser:* "Plague builds its nests in us" (*TF,* 331).

The Magic Kingdom was inspired when Elkin saw a BBC report in 1980 featuring seven terminally ill children leaving Heathrow for Disney World: "After crying, I said to my wife, Joan, 'What an incredible idea for a novel, but it would be wrong.' The temptation is to be sentimental and maudlin."[1] Although sentimentality is seldom a tendency in Elkin's fiction, a major challenge comes from the demands of the subject matter itself. The emphasis must be on the children, but Elkin's habit has been to explore the implications of a vocation as the generating idea for his novels. These children, however, have no possible vocation unless it is dying. Solving this problem sent him in two directions, both of which contribute to his creating his masterwork. He subtly adjusts the concept of vocation, characterizes the children and their guardians with understanding yet without sentimentality, and uses humor to maintain perspective on the events and subject matter.

His concept of vocation underwent a subtle shift in *George Mills,* in which the main character is a furniture mover, hardly the kind of role that could define someone's identity; but George's true vocation is being a Mills, inheriting and dealing with a curse that has afflicted sixty generations. Who Mills is depends on how he responds to a legacy of being believed to be second-rate. Here, and more thoroughly in *The Magic Kingdom,* Elkin explores the primary meaning of *vocation,* which emphasizes a calling or summons to a course of action rather than the activities deriving from such a calling. As a person entering a religious order can be said to have a vocation, Eddy Bale, the hero of this book, responds to a calling to try to do something, however futile, about the injustice of children's being ravaged by terminal illness.

Some of the novel's richness can be traced to the full dossier Elkin supplies to explain what motivates Bale to assume the burden of his vocation. We never learn what his occupation is, but he had an office job until his son's medical treatments became his primary concern during the four years the Bales sought radical medical procedures to keep Liam alive. While seeking funds to attempt one experimental treatment after another, Bale came to identify himself as "the kingdom's foremost beggar, a man who has passed the hat among the nation's leading industrialists and press lords and brought his case to the public."[2] This role, as England's "foremost beggar," involves hat-in-hand deference to philanthropists and entrepreneurs in which the petitioner assumes a supplicant's role. Moreover, this vocation involves Bale in shamelessly manipulating the tabloid press, which is eager to print gruesome details of Liam's symptoms and prognosis. The night Liam dies, Eddy holds a press conference.

This vocation as the realm's foremost beggar leads us into psychology, philosophy, and Elkin's typical concern with the relation between vocation and personal identity. Adapting to this role, Bale derived perverse satisfaction from the humility and notoriety this vocation required. Ginny complains in her farewell letter, which Eddy postpones reading for months, that he made Liam's illness his reason for being: "Seizing . . . on his illness. Making his disease your cause. Like an entertainer on the telethon, almost, so frenzied you were" (MK, 308). Deriving an almost masochistic self-definition from this role, Eddy faces its loss when Liam dies. It is pointless to be England's greatest beggar when there is no one for whom to beg.

We may infer, then, that in undertaking his crusade for terminally ill children Eddy seeks to generalize the only vocation that has ever given him a stable sense of self. Because the role failed to save Liam and cost him his marriage, it must be preserved if for no reason other than to justify the costs it has imposed on his emotional life. The idea of a dream holiday for terminally ill children permits him to preserve his vocation as England's foremost beggar, but this continuation meets with little success until a very funny scene in which the queen loans Bale seed money to get his enterprise underway. Such a vocation involves unexpected responsibility: "Thinking of it as 'venture,' too, 'operation,' 'undertaking,' the code words more satisfying to him than the 'dream holiday' label the press had taken up" (MK, 25). The identity associated with the venture is fleshed out when an associate, Colin Bible, calls Bale "chief," thus extending Bale's vocation to "the responsible one in the bunch" (MK, 38).

Bale's evolution from beggar for Liam's expensive medical efforts, through beggar for a venture to provide relief for all terminally ill children, to chief in charge of this operation is a psychological compensation for his inability to deal effectively with childhood mortality. It is, moreover, a logical, though zany, philosophical evolution. By considering this transformation, we shall approach one thematic center of *The Magic Kingdom*: the cruel absurdity of childhood mortality and the helplessness and rage we feel in coping with such an unfair, arbitrary issue. By the logic implicit in the novel, dying children, these seven biological abnormalities, are the vehicle of a synecdoche whose tenor is all dying people or everyone whose life contains the inevitable seed of his or her death.

In his interview with the queen, Eddy explains what he has learned about the worth of radical intervention that at best prolongs the life of terminally ill patients: "Where we went wrong. We never rewarded him for his death. He should have lived like a crown prince, Queen. . . . We should have hijacked the sweet shoppe and turned him loose at the fair. We ought have sent him on picnics with hampers of ice cream. We should have ground his teeth down on scones and flan and ruined his eyes on the telly. We should have sent him to sleep past his bedtime. We should have burned out his life, Dynast" (*MK,* 17).

Bale has learned something obvious but unacceptable. By trying to preserve Liam's life, he and Ginny denied the boy what little life he had coming to him. Rather than giving him an opportunity to experience what his life could have been, they subjected him to extreme, painful medical procedures, many of which left him too debilitated to live what time he had fully. Bale's chief regret is that Liam began to have sexual urges a few months before he died. He began to masturbate, and Eddy now wishes he had given Liam a chance to experience sexual love: "Wouldn't we have been better off to have given him a cram course in debauchery?" (*MK,* 17). In one of the book's most touching moments, Bale tells the oldest of his charges at Disney World "what he hadn't dared to tell Liam," because he felt a need "to apologize to Benny Maxine on behalf of everyone who would be surviving him." When Benny asks, "So it's [sex is] all it's cracked up to be, is it?" Eddy can only confess, "I'm afraid so" (*MK,* 183). Further, Bale recalls that Liam, exhausted after experimental medical procedures and pilgrimages of faith—although not Catholic, they took him to Lourdes—wanted only to die in peace.

We may therefore express the key problem Elkin addresses in *The Magic Kingdom* by referring to the title of this chapter: what *can* we do for the dying children?[3] Liam and the children Bale selects for the venture are terminally ill, beyond hope that any medical treatment can improve their condition. All medicine can promise is to prolong their lives and perhaps alleviate their suffering. The cost is not only painful reaction to the treatments but also psychological in that the children are encouraged to view themselves as dying human beings and are advised to prepare for imminent death. Benny, the most glib of Bale's charges, asks, "How do [Bale and his associates] know where a poor *little mortal loser* like yours truly would like to take his dream holiday?" (*MK*, 48; my italics). Another, Noah Cloth, told the hospice lady who tried to prepare him for death, "Well, if I don't [come to terms with the situation], I won't die, then, will I?" The lady calls this "bargaining," but Noah insists, "it's rage" (*MK*, 46).

The Magic Kingdom challenges us to consider the rationality of denying terminally ill children what life they have in order to attempt desperate measures that can at best prolong their waiting for death. At the same time, the novel asks whether it is any less irrational to attempt a bizarre pilgrimage like the one Bale oversees. Elkin does not offer simple answers to this question, but the novel makes it clear that Bale's venture is preposterous and fated from its inception to fail. This is not to say that the failure occurs because of the participants' limitations; it is rather a flawed conception. One child, Rena Morgan, dies on the expedition. Her death is inevitable, so the journey cannot be its cause, though it could accelerate the event. The only value judgments permissible within the structure of the book have to do with intention, Bale's and his associates', on which Elkin's response is quite ambivalent. The other valid criterion is more subjective—whether the children gain anything by their expedition.

On the former, any judgment we arrive at must consider the attitudes and behavior of Bale's associates as well as his own. Bale's motives involve a complex mixture of psychological compensation for his inability to have any meaningful impact on Liam's death and his retrospective discovery that radical intervention is not an effective response to terminal illness. The people he recruits to assist with the expedition create a tetralogue on Bale's ambivalent reasons for organizing the journey. By moving from the simple to the complex in separating these characters' motives and attitudes, we can define those values the novel endorses and those it calls into question.

Bale recruits a nanny, a physician, a "gray lady," and a male nurse to help him supervise his troublesome charges. He knows Mr. Morehead, the physician, and Colin Bible, the nurse, because of Liam's hospital stays; gray lady Mary Cottle comes "highly recommended . . . , a candidate, in everybody's books, of unchurched sanctity" (*MK*, 34), and the nanny, Prince Andrew's former governess, occurred to Bale as a chaperon when he saw her on a BBC program celebrating the prince's military exploits in the Falklands war. Each is a complex combination of humane and selfish reasons for being involved in one of Elkin's "strange displacements of the ordinary" (*MK*, 259).[4]

Of the four, Nedra Carp, the nanny, has the most apparently humane reasons for participating, but these prove superficial. Deliberately developed in the Mary Poppins mode (having seen the film seventeen times, she regards Poppins as "practically my patron saint" [*MK*, 83]), Nedra expresses all the expected clichés about caring for and loving her charges. Yet the omniscient narrator insists that she is "in the wrong profession and . . . one *muy loco parentis*" (*MK*, 83)—a Joycean pun superimposing on the legalistic Latin "in the place of the parent" the Spanish "very crazy." She develops a protective attitude toward those children explicitly charged to her care but a distaste for the others, especially Janet Order, whose heart condition results in a disagreeably blue complexion. Yet Janet has done nothing to incur Nedra's displeasure; in fact, she feels frustrated because "the woman she'd chosen to love did not love her back" (*MK*, 195). Had she been assigned to Nedra's protection, the nanny would probably have felt quite differently about her. Because of Nedra's partiality to those children she oversees, the narrator judges her as "some patriot of the propinquitous" who is "unable to work up any affection that has not actually been bought and paid for" (*MK*, 125).

The novel provides a psychological basis for Nedra's fierce, narrow loyalties. She was the victim of a ludicrous series of parental deaths: when her mother died, her father remarried, then died; her stepmother remarried, then died, and so on, until Nedra became totally estranged from her nuclear family and found her only source of stability in her nannies. She became a nanny not because she loves children or needs money but because this is the only group that ever offered her continuity.

More importantly, Nedra experiences growth as a result of Rena Morgan's death. Fulfilling the nanny's role by advising Rena, she merely affirms sexual stereotypes, such as, "well-brought-up women don't have the upper-body strength for bravery" (*MK*, 130). For her, "forebearance, resignation, and submission" (*MK*, 131), qualities she feels Janet lacks, are those young ladies like Rena should cultivate. After Rena's funeral, however, Nedra the nanny has her arm around blue Janet's shoulder, offering what comfort she can to the grief-stricken child. If her attitudes have not been good for the success of the voyage, perhaps the journey has been good for her.

Mr. Morehead offers a contrasting variation on concern for the children and commitment to the venture's objectives. He heads the pediatric unit at a prestigious London hospital and attended Liam in his final bouts with illness. He has a genius for diagnosis, yet "his gift was a curse. He knew outcomes

. . . . He handicapped death" (MK, 242). He knows how to diagnose ill-
nesses but not how to cure them.

Despite his ability to astonish colleagues with his diagnostic skill,
Morehead is quite mad. His reason for going to Florida has nothing to do
with caring for these children, whom he cruelly calls "goner spawn" (MK,
33). Obviously miscalculating in Rena's case, Morehead selects candidates
for the holiday on the basis of their probable survival of the trip's rigors, by
implication their not embarrassing the attending physician by dying. His reason for taking this assignment—to "see the Jews . . . who have kept him off
the Queen's Honors List" (MK, 32)—suggests not anti-Semitism but an in-
sane professional obsession. He believes that if he can secure family photographs of Holocaust survivors, he will have the proof he needs to confirm his
theory of pathology.

It is indicative of the complex ironies of The Magic Kingdom that
Morehead, who makes the journey for the worst possible reason—to prove a
theory that would bring him fame and honor—is right at a theoretical level.
His "theory about the latency of all pathologies" (MK, 146), while grounded
in a mad scientist's idea of empirical verification, is poetically true of these
seven children and of the overall metaphoric implications of the novel. It recalls Ben Flesh's discovery, "Plague builds its nests in us," a recognition that
our lives contain the seeds of their own destruction.[5] This commonsense notion of disease is ironically supported by the Wordsworth allusion, "The
child, he knew, was father to the man" (MK, 145). All organisms have a pro-
pensity toward a disease that can destroy them. Janet Order's tetralogy of
Fallot is congenital; Tony Word's body chemistry tends toward leukemia;
Noah Cloth's bone marrow incubates cancerous cells.

An obsessive diagnostician who observes works of art for latent pathology,
Morehead comes to ridiculous conclusions—for example, the model for da
Vinci's Mona Lisa suffered from incipient goiter, and Michelangelo's David
was based on imagination, not drawn from life, because such a perfect speci-
men would have lived forever. Elkin depreciates Morehead's diagnostic approach to art when an artist friend jests that scholars have located plaster casts
of Michelangelo's subject. In Disney World, Morehead pays only token attention to his charges and spends most of his time lurking about, looking for
the wrist tattoo that identifies a survivor of the camps. When he finds his
Jew, she is a disappointment. Conducting his examination, he asks for family
snapshots. Hoping for old photos that would enable him to confirm his theory that the Jews in the camps were already suffering from the diseases he diagnosed from the liberation photographs, he spends the afternoon looking at
snapshots of the grandchildren—some adopted—of a thoroughly Ameri-

canized survivor whose family history exhibits none of the anticipated ill-nesses. As evidence accumulates against his cherished theory, Morehead be-comes confused: he "can't say why he needed photographs, old gemütlich formal sepia poses and black-and-white candids" (*MK,* 248). When the novel ends, he is no longer a proud diagnostician fixated on a zany theory to prove the obvious but a defeated physician who could not keep all his charges alive for a week, and he has relinquished leadership of the expedition, both professional and practical, to Colin Bible.

The third chaperon, gray lady Mary Cottle, offers an even more ironic ver-sion of the paradigm of concern for the children and commitment to the ob-jectives of the voyage. She may prove the most difficult character for some readers to come to terms with because Elkin clearly intends his readers to view her sympathetically, but she is the most explicitly derelict among the supervi-sors. Unlike Morehead, she has no personal agenda behind joining the expe-dition. Indeed at no time does she indicate any feeling toward the children other than love and concern.

Her heart is in the right place, but twice her taking care of her own needs nearly undermines the whole escapade. Although all her recommenders cite a serene disposition they attribute to inner spirituality (one associates her with Mona Lisa) and although Eddy is astonished by "her beautiful, blissful face, which seemed never to have entertained the slightest anxiety" (*MK,* 35), Mary is high strung. Her anxiety comes from a reproductive defect, an inabil-ity to carry a healthy baby. Twice in the past, she has aborted deformed off-spring, and she has renounced coitus for life. She told the man she lived with when her condition was diagnosed, "I'm this Borgia madonna. I poison ba-bies" (*MK,* 34), and then she threw him out. Mary copes with her anxiety through heavy smoking and "frequent and furious bouts of masturbation" (*MK,* 34), both of which create difficulties for the travelers. The smoking presents obvious problems for Rena, who has cystic fibrosis; but many of the children's diseases render them susceptible to the effects of passive smoking, especially because Mary prefers strong tobaccos. On the airplane, her charges must sit in the smoking section to accommodate her habit. Janet, suffering from heart disease, is seated next to the chain-smoking Cottle. The smoke wafts forward into the nonsmoking section, and Rena has a minor version of the attack that later claims her life.

Mary's other method of coping, masturbation, results in one serious dere-liction of her chaperon's duty. At the Haunted Mansion, Charles Mudd-Gaddis, who suffers from progeria, or premature aging (a condition Elkin treated in his screenplay *The Six-Year Old Man*), flies into a rage about his wig and throws a tantrum that makes necessary the ride's being stopped and

the attendants' escorting the screaming Mudd-Gaddis, Colin, Mary, and the
other children out of the building. Turning on the lights divests the mansion
of whatever magic it may have had. Overcome by anxiety, Mary steals away
from the group to indulge in restorative onanism. This dereliction leaves
Colin alone to deal with four ill children, one still raging with his tantrum,
who have just been put on public show as they made their exit from the
mansion.

These details suggest that Mary is a less than admirable character, yet the
novel creates an opposite impression. In 1989 Elkin told me he intends her to
be viewed quite sympathetically: "I find her entirely sympathetic. Of course,
she has a real itch, a sexual itch, and she has to scratch." Can we accept the author's judgment, which corroborates impressions the novel itself suggests,
that she is a sympathetic character while acknowledging that her methods of
reducing anxiety result in derelictions of her duty to these wretched children?

We can, if we consider two threads of evidence, one psychological and the
other specific to the structure of *The Magic Kingdom*. First, she refused, when
her "poisoned womb" (*MK*, 33) was diagnosed, to take the easy way out. Her
physician, painting a grim picture of her maternal prognosis, advised tubal
ligation or hysterectomy, either of which would enable her to engage in sex
without adverse consequences, but either would be permanent. Mary chose
to renounce sex rather than to circumvent her biological flaw. When tension
overwhelmed her, she resorted to onanism and eventually became dependent
on this relief. She thus attempts to take responsibility for dealing with her peculiar pathology rather than to accept easy surgical remedies.

Second, her need for privacy allows Elkin to create a real magic kingdom
within the Magic Kingdom within *The Magic Kingdom*. The novel indicates
that Disney's magic is phony, mere manipulation of images. After the
Mudd-Gaddis episode at the Haunted Mansion, Mary's need for privacy
causes her to rent a separate room, number 822, which becomes the truly
magic kingdom. Real magic, literal and figurative, occurs there. When
Benny Maxine discovers Mary's secret place, he "figured he'd found the *real*
Magic Kingdom" and "his hunch *had* been right" (*MK*, 186). For him, approaching death and sexual maturity simultaneously, it is a magic place because, spying Polonius-style "behind the arras" (*MK*, 187), he observes Mary
restoring serenity and gets an initiation into the beauty of the female form.
Others discover magic in 822 as well, and the final scene of the novel occurs
there.

When the children learn Mary has a separate room, they devise ingenious strategies to get in. It becomes their "hidey hole, a sort of clubhouse"
(*MK*, 270) where they find refuge from the public display of their illness

and the future orientation, its implications not lost on these dying children, of EPCOT Center. Another variation on the theme of how we can care for the dying children appears here: these children really want privacy, but even that is disrupted in their secret room. When it is interrupted, a menacing, then strangely benevolent, magic happens.

Menacing magic occurs when all seven children, taking refuge in Mary's room, are assaulted by a false Mickey Mouse and Pluto. While the fake mouse and dog stand outside the room, Benny, telling a ghost story, snaps off the lights, and an image of Mickey and Pluto appears on the ceiling because "the hidey-hole functioned exactly like a sort of camera obscura" (*MK,* 276). Elkin told me privately that this is one of two instances of pure magic in the novel (the other is a snowfall that covers only Disney World), that despite the extended explanation involving reversed protective peepholes, "That's the magic kingdom. . . . I mean, that's not possible. . . . The seven children are in the dark, and a perfect image of Mickey Mouse and the dog appears on the ceiling. The room becomes a kind of camera obscura. Ain't no way that can happen. Physically. But in the magic kingdom, it can happen." This menacing magic yields to terror when the children admit Mickey, actually park entertainer Lamar Kenny, who launches a brutal verbal attack on them. The children feel understandably betrayed when the beloved rodent suddenly spouts reminders of their mortality and Pluto, actually Matthew Gale, another employee who instigates the prank, fails to protect them from the mouse's outbursts. As the children respond hysterically, Rena has an attack of cystic fibrosis, brought on by the confusion and excitement, that ends her life.

Her death introduces figurative magic within this kingdom. The novel's cruelest irony is that love kills Rena. One of the best adjusted among the children, she has learned to manipulate her handkerchiefs (to conceal her nasal discharges) like an artist, and her skill earned the envy of the false mouse, Lamar Kenny, in an earlier encounter. The immediate cause of her fatal attack is a complicated series of misunderstandings in which Kenny becomes confused about the role he is to play. As chaos breaks out among the children, Benny Maxine takes risks to comfort Rena. Her discharge has fouled the bed she lies in; calling the adult supervisors means punishment for Benny, who got the children into the room and who incurred Kenny's wrath in two previous encounters, the first of which involved Benny's insulting Pluto in the hotel; and his fragile body is pained as he holds the dying Rena in his arms. The narrator, moreover, makes it clear that the primary cause of her attack, or of its extreme nature, is her love for Benny: "The great prognostician [Morehead] had simply failed to factor her desire into the equation. He had missed his prognosis because he hadn't taken her sighs into account, the squalls, blasts, and aerodynamics of passion, all the high winds and gale-force bluster of love" (*MK*, 296).

This association of mortality and love brings us to yet another thematic axis of *The Magic Kingdom*. Although associating love and death is hardly new—it is among the most basic and frequent literary themes, and Shakespeare in *Hamlet*, the text to which Elkin alludes most frequently in this novel, never tires of the Elizabethan pun on *die* as both "expire" and "have sexual intercourse"—this novel offers a compellingly stark meditation on this association. Life itself begins as a result of sex, an expression of physical love; but life is by definition movement toward death, accelerated in the case of these children by their genetic inheritance, the flawed chromosomes that brought them into being; yet it is only love that can give their lives fulfillment and meaning; and the experience of love is full of risk, and for Rena, absolute risk. In her case, Elkin has outlined the catch-22 under which all mortal human beings labor. Love is the ultimate cause of human death, and without love life is not worth living. At a less theoretical level, we can say that Rena died of complications associated with the onset of physical love but that her death was inevitable anyway. The only judgment welcomed by the structure created in this novel is that she lived intensely during the moments after she fell in love with Benny and that therefore her death in Disney World, rather than weeks or months later in London, was a fair price to pay for having lived fully, if briefly.

Elkin reiterates this association of our flawed humanity and the dignity of human love in the final scene. Having lost Rena, the chaperons face their mission's failure, and Eddy and Mary Cottle engage in tempestuous lovemaking in 822, her magic kingdom. Except for the final scene of *The Franchiser* and the sermon that ends *George Mills*, this is Elkin's most explicit celebration of human love as the only antidote to universal mortality. Both have refrained from sexual contact because of their imperfect chemistries. Mary has a "poisoned womb," and Eddy, recognizing that Liam's disease originated in his genetic legacy, has avoided sexual companionship since his wife left him.

Their lovemaking is sex for reproduction in spite of the inevitable illnesses the offspring will have: "And accepting infection from him, contagion, the septic climate of their noxious genes. Dreaming of complications down the road, of bad bouts and thick medical histories, of wasting neurological diseases, of blood and pulmonary scourges, of blows to the glands and organs, of pathogens climbing the digestive tract, invading the heart and bone marrow, erupting the skin and clouding the cough" (*MK*, 317). Curiously some reviewers found this scene merely a quantitative exchange.[6] It is much more than replacing Rena with another flawed child. Mary—the omniscient narrator adopts her point of view in this scene—meditates on the essential Elkin theme: the recognition that whomever, or whatever, we bring into this world is fated to suffer imperfection and die. Mary seeks impregnation from Eddy, fully recognizing that this is the human fate. She accepts this destiny and in conceiving with Eddy affirms life in spite of it. As they create their inevitably flawed offspring, Mary meditates on some of nature's other losers, recalling the fate her physician predicted if she did not deny her fertility. At climax, she "calls upon the famous misfits, upon centaurs and satyrs and chimeras, upon dragons and griffins and hydras and wyverns. Upon the basilisk, the salamander, and the infrequent unicorn. *And upon, at last, a lame and tainted Mickey Mouse*" (*MK*, 317). This is extremely funny, but it is also an uninhibited celebration of life, so radically imperfect that every conception is a commitment to disease and death. That Mary and Eddy recognize this and choose to find worth by creating life is magic indeed. It is the thematic mystery of *The Magic Kingdom.*

Although Mary and Eddy create flawed life as the novel ends, homosexual nurse Colin Bible represents the most effective response to childhood mortality. His interest is primarily in the children's needs, and his actions in their behalf are by far the most effective in the novel. We may conclude that his is the response to terminal illness the novel implicitly endorses. Still, Elkin's art remains subtle, and we must first acknowledge motives that seem to cast doubt on the response Colin brings to the Disney World adventure. These doubts create yet another dimension in Elkin's treatment of the obligations of love.

Although Mary and Eddy unite in the final scene, Colin has the only stable loving relationship in *The Magic Kingdom.* It is biologically nonproductive, and the affection may be one-sided. His lover, also named Colin, is a wax artist at Madame Tussaud's museum, and his sending Bible insurance policies on his frequent business trips may hint at compensation for planned infidelities. Bible, however, accepts these possible breaches because of his love for Colin and thereby maintains a stable relationship.

But this love leads Bible into complex ethical predicaments. Because Colin envisions adding exhibits in Madame Tussaud's to memorialize Holocaust and Hiroshima victims, Bible uses his influence as a nurse to persuade terminally ill children to grant permission that they may serve as models for Colin's wax art. This offends even Bale's hardened sensibility about the publicity attending such children, but Liam's dying words indicate that he has accepted Bible's version of his destiny as being a public display. After Bale angrily confronts him on this issue, Bible decides to persuade all the children to be me-

morialized in the wax museum, and executing his plan requires that he take
two "dreadful steps" (*MK*, 125).

The first step is to respond to an invitation from Haunted Mansion employee Matthew Gale to have an affair. This leads Colin into the clichés he
finds revolting: stereotypical, promiscuous, homosexuals lurking in health
spas and then sneaking into Cottle's secret room. Bible's motivation contains
a complicating element of prostitution. He does not actually like Gale,
though he is attracted to him. He is, however, overwhelmed by the technically sophisticated exhibits in the Hall of the Presidents. When he sees these,
he immediately recognizes that Colin, the wax artist, could benefit from
studying the plans. He uses Gale's attraction for him to secure some of these
blueprints, and Elkin's paradox is that he is unfaithful to his lover in order to
express love for him. Although he does this because he loves Colin, the word
for one who exchanges sexual favors for material benefits is *prostitute*. This
transaction has dire consequences. Bible's remorse causes him to break off
with Gale, who, seeking revenge, collects on favors he has previously done for
Lamar Kenny. They assault room 822 as Mickey Mouse and Pluto, and the
result is Rena's death.

Colin's second dreadful step, while not as ethically ambiguous as the relationship with Gale, is far from simple. He acts generously for the children's
benefit, but he always has in mind that he can secure something for Colin by
ministering to them. After his first effective therapy, taking the children to
observe people watching the Disney parade, he gleefully exclaims, "*I've got
their consents in my pocket!*" (*MK*, 229).

Watching the people watch the parade is, however, one of the most therapeutic experiences the children have on their holiday. Thoroughly disgusted
with himself for having used Gale, Bible paraphrases Thoreau—"Like the
poet said, most blokes lead lives of quiet desperation"—and as Flesh discovers that he wants his remission back in *The Franchiser,* Colin finds that he
"wanted his quiet desperation back" (*MK*, 216). To recover self-respect, the
"quiet" in his "desperation," he takes the children to watch spectators while
they observe one of the innumerable parades. He points out the spectators'
imperfections to the children, and soon they are themselves seeing additional
examples of the infirmity that age brings.[7] As they approach a collective,
empathic catharsis, subliterate cockney Noah Cloth passes judgment on the
flawed human race for them all: "Jesus weeps! . . . He weeps for all the potty,
pig-ignorant prats off their chumps, for all the slow-coach clots and dead-
from-the-neck-up dimbos, . . . for all his chuckle-headed, loopy muggins
and passengers past praying for" (*MK*, 227), a description of their own condition so exact that Mudd-Gaddis wonders, "Are they [the people the chil-

dren are watching] on a dream holiday, then?" (*MK*, 228). Now that the children see what they stand to lose by dying young, Bible drives the lesson home: "That's you in a few years, never mind that three-score-and-ten you thought was your birthright. All that soured flesh, all those bitched and bollixed bodies. You see? You see what you thought you were missing?" (*MK*, 228–29). If he later rejoices that he now has their "consents," he has given them a valuable perspective on their deaths. Until now each has resented what he or she would not live to become. Although I doubt that either Bible or Elkin believes life is not worth living because we come to physical decay, this message certainly has more pragmatic value for the children than anything Morehead or Bale can teach them about their condition.

Now restored to self-confidence, Bible assumes moral leadership of the expedition. He takes the children to one more magic kingdom, an artificial island in a man-made lagoon. He hustles the concessionaire to bend the rules and allow them to take out boats, and they dock at Shipwreck Marsh on a perfect Florida afternoon that feels like "time's and temperature's deliverance" (*MK*, 253). They separate into groups, Colin leading the boys and Mary the girls, and the children undress, then sunbathe, with the groups one hundred yards apart. As the children stare across the artificial sand at one another, Elkin reinforces his key themes of privacy and acceptance. The chapter ends with one of the most beautiful paragraphs Elkin, and perhaps anyone else in the 1980s, has written:

And it was wondrous in the negligible humidity how they gawked across the perfect air, how, stunned by the helices and all the parabolas of grace, they gasped, they sighed, these short-timers who even at *their* young age could not buy insurance at any price, not even if the premiums were paid in the rare rich elements, in pearls clustered as grapes, in buckets of bullion, in trellises of diamonds, how, glad to be alive, they stared at each other and caught their breath (*MK*, 257).

This baroque paragraph reads as if Elkin had taught Dylan Thomas or Thomas Traherne about actuarial science and the impossibility of avoiding mortality and as if the combined writer were able to retain the joy and reverence for childhood Traherne or Thomas wrote about. This is magic Disney cannot provide. These children have not recently been "glad to be alive," and very soon they will not be alive, but in this splendid moment of Colin Bible's magic, they have real joy contemplating the beauty of one another's fatally ravaged bodies.

On our second criterion—whether the children gain anything as the result of their expedition—the verdict is surprisingly simple. The book offers a

qualified celebration of the dignity and value these terminally ill children
come to find in their lives. What seems to me an artistic triumph of *The
Magic Kingdom* is that Elkin performs quite a balancing act between sentiment and humor.[8] The concept of dying children has unusual potential for
sentimentality, but this novel resists that by affording each child a differing
response to his or her pathology. Benny Maxine, from a nonkosher Jewish
home, affects the cynic's pose: "I've got this yid disease. Gaucher's . . . the
chosen disease of the chosen people" (*MK*, 50). He complains about his fellow travelers' obvious symptoms and contemplates hijacking the airplane to
force it to fly them to a gambling casino where he could enjoy his dream holiday. Despite his posing as a tough street kid and his justifiable anger at being
on the verge of death just when he reaches sexual maturity, Benny grows because of Bale's trip. He falls in love with Rena, squires her around the hotel,
and in the real magic kingdom, Cottle's room, discovers with her the mystery
of love.

Another indication of the art of *The Magic Kingdom* is that the children,
obviously the center of the novel, are characterized individually and with
compassion but without sentimentality. Elkin scrupulously avoids careless
generalizations in treating the ways they have adapted to their death sentences. Some, like Rena, have mastered the art of concealment. She has
learned to manipulate the many handkerchiefs she must use to control her
discharges so well that Lamar Kenny feels that his art of illusion cannot compete with hers. Others, like Lydia Conscience, less successfully conceal their
afflictions. Suffering from uterine cancer (paralleling Cottle's poisoned
womb), Lydia carries her tumor like a pregnancy and affects a wedding ring
to complete her illusion. Progeriac Mudd-Gaddis, although senile most of
the time, has moments of insight into the children's collective condition, such
as "We're compatible. We're children who die" (*MK*, 113). Noah Cloth,
suffering from bone cancer, bitterly resents that he will never be able to earn
and spend money, but he enjoys one cathartic spending binge when he learns
that the hotel shops will let him charge purchases to his room.

Elkin also avoids the temptation toward facile generalization in the more
subtle area of how effectively each child deals with his or her death sentence.
Benny affects poses to compensate for his anger. Noah feels victimized.
Mudd-Gaddis dreams about Lydia and Tony Word's visiting him at a convalescent home to flatter him and gain his inheritance. Rena seems remarkably well adjusted, and Janet vacillates between generosity and bitchiness.
She frets about how her blue complexion affects others and sees mistreatment
by other children as "opportunities to correct the kids, to make, as she saw it,
the world a better place in which to live" (*MK*, 43). But when the false mouse

assaults the children and Mudd-Gaddis bellows while Rena has the fatal attack, Janet responds with anything but generosity. She denies responsibility for Mudd-Gaddis and tells her "buddy," Tony, "We're each *other's* buddies and have got to make sure nothing happens to either of us. Clearly this isn't a one-for-all, all-for-one situation we have here" (*MK,* 294). Perhaps in this character we have the most effective index to the dignity and compassion Elkin lavishes on his terminally ill children. They are heroic in contending with the unfair hand fate has dealt them, but they are not Dickensian, sentimentalized, suffering children. They can be understandably difficult at times.

Technically *The Magic Kingdom* represents Elkin's narrative art at its highest level of mastery. It is less experimental than *George Mills* or *The Dick Gibson Show,* but the firm command of multiple points of view and complex chronological shifts manifests an artist in complete control over his materials and his themes. Two unique technical features, Elkin's use of collective dreams and his treatment of the logic of cause and effect, add dimension to the themes we have considered.

Collective dreaming is a rare fictional subject, but twice in this book children share a dream. On the airplane, Lydia, the only child who actually wanted to visit Disney World, dreams about being alone on the river trip and enjoying a private look at African scenery while being protected from the gaze of others who see only her swollen body ravaged by disease. Her dream is interrupted when Janet enters the dream in her own fantasy of being in an aquiline blue environment, where her discolored skin blends with her surroundings. They share the dream, but neither acknowledges the other's presence: "Lydia was nowhere about, nor did Janet know that Lydia—she was that neat—had ever occupied it" (*MK,* 69). Later Mudd-Gaddis, Tony Word, and Lydia share a dream in which Lydia and Tony visit Charles at a convalescent home, and he suspects that they are there to be sure he writes them into his will.

Collective dreaming reiterates Elkin's thematic emphasis on the children's desire for privacy and is explained in part by their compatibility because they share imminent mortality. The novel explains Lydia's and Janet's dream by suggesting that each reacts to the odors of Cottle's cigarette, which she lit when her charges fell asleep. This explanation raises the more complicated question of cause and effect in *The Magic Kingdom.*

The novel contains many variations on the clause, "Because everything has a perfectly reasonable explanation" (*MK,* 71), once abbreviated to "*Everything*" (*MK,* 276). It implies a cause-effect sequence in which any effect can be explained logically. The clause offers a multifaceted irony in that a rational cause for childhood mortality cannot be logically deduced; it makes no sense that people are deprived of the opportunity to grow up, even if we know empirically that this does happen. Even granting empirical observation, we are hard pressed to say logically why individual children must die. On the other hand, each child's imperfect chemistry renders his or her fatal illness a "perfectly reasonable" consequence of his or her genetic inheritance, but this still begs the question of why nature creates individuals with genetic configurations that cause their deaths.

The novel employs the clause to explain phenomena that tax our credulity. It is introduced to explain the first collective dream by attributing it to passive smoke from Mary's cigarette. It also explains how the peephole in room 822 functions as a camera obscura, allowing the images of Mickey Mouse and Pluto to appear on the ceiling. It justifies the chaperons' failure to look for the children in the hidey-hole because healthy adults would not understand sick children's need for privacy. In his most expansive treatment of the phrase, however, Elkin gives it global implications: "Everything. Wars, earthquakes, and the self-contained individual disasters of men. Courage as well as cowardice. Generous acts out of left field and the conviction that one is put upon. Everything. Man's fallen condition and birth defect too, those San Andreas and Anatolian, Altyn Tagh, and Great Glen faults of the heart, of the ova, of the genes. They're working on it, working on all of it" (MK, 150). By this logic, there are reasonable explanations for birth anomalies like those affecting the children, for the fates of nations, and for more private acts of courage and generosity. Does Elkin intend, by repeating this clause more than a dozen times, to imply a deterministic theory of matter and behavior?

If so, his refrain contrasts with the tone of this and his other novels in which recognizing our human limitations does not necessitate capitulation before them. One solution to this problem is to look at cause and effect as they occur in fiction, as opposed to the ways these abstractions affect our lives. This is the main theme of Elkin's 1989 response to my question about the clause: "The answer is no, there is not a reason for everything. But in that book, everything does have a reasonable explanation. That's what books are about: to make reasons. Books are little houses of logic." Here Elkin describes his vocation as an artist—to create structures that offer logical consistency to a world that defies our collective wish to see cause and effect work coherently.

"Because everything has a reasonable explanation" functions ironically in *The Magic Kingdom*. Every event in a carefully designed piece of fiction can be explained logically if readers grant the premise upon which the artist works. Even the central subject, disease ravaging the bodies of children, can be explained logically by clinical pathologists, if not by ethical philosophers.

At a broader level, however, the clause suggests something fundamental about the nature of art. It creates logic to satisfy our need for coherence in our human experiences, but by creating that logic it sends us back to our ordinary experience with new doubts and questions.

The Magic Kingdom is Elkin's masterwork, that of a mature artist in firm control of his subject matter and themes. It is the profound theme that distinguishes this from Elkin's other splendid novels. It is at once a searching examination into the justice of the human condition and a hilarious celebration of our flawed nature. We can ask nothing more of art.

Chapter Six
The Rabbi of Lud: Rare Kaddish

The conflict central to *The Rabbi of Lud* is succinctly articulated when the protagonist's daughter screams, "Daddy, our back yard is a *cemetery*! . . . It's *perpetual care*!"[1] The fundamental Elkin theme, mortality and our response to recognizing it, receives a new twist when Rabbi Goldkorn and his daughter engage in a book-length struggle about the propriety of a family's living in a "funerary, sepulchral, thanatopsical town" (*RL*, 18) that exists only to bury the dead. This conflict in turn suggests broad social issues like the existence of a community that depends on death for its life, as well as more individual matters of parental responsibility and the tenacity with which individuals like Goldkorn hold on to their decisions to retreat from the demands of a vital life, even if that retreat places unacceptable costs on those they love.

Coming after the dazzling displays of multiple points of view and complex narrative lines in *George Mills* and *The Magic Kingdom,* this novel is surprising in its narrative simplicity. All but the seventh chapter, Connie's deposition about visits from the Holy Mother, is told exclusively from the first-person central point of view, a method Elkin had not explored in any long work since *Boswell.* There he differentiated between Boswell's first-person narration and the "journal entries" that comprise a substantial portion of that book. In *The Rabbi of Lud,* the primary point of view available to us is Goldkorn's direct account of his youth, work, domestic alignments, and tenure as an Alaskan corporate rabbi. Elkin told me he remained in first-person singular because, having begun the book as Goldkorn's narrative, he discovered that "I liked his voice."

Quite possibly his fondness for this character's voice occurs because it affords the author a grand opportunity for irony, one surpassing even the ironic use of first-person narration in *Boswell.* Although most readers instinctively empathize with first-person narrators, in this novel that instinct is consistently undercut by details laden with ironic implications. This hero is every bit as self-centered as the zealous protagonists of *The Dick Gibson Show* and *A Bad Man,* but he is less candid about his self-interest and more deviously ruthless in making others suffer the consequences of his obsession. He is also more adept than Feldman or Gibson at justifying his selfishness as ethical behavior, and he lacks the zest and intensity of those characters.

Our initial contact with the novel might suggest that Goldkorn is a sympathetic narrator, a wisecracking rabbi whose intellectual limitations restrict his professional options to officiating at funerals for people he does not know, but whose obsessive love for his wife and whose role as the beleaguered parent of a teenage daughter endear him to us. Certain autobiographical details appear to support this impression. The novel was inspired when Elkin's mother was buried in Lodi, New Jersey, and the author, despite his grief, began to ponder the vocation of a rabbi whose job is consoling bereaved members of a family with whom he has no prior contact.[2] As is usual in Elkin's work, this meditation on a vocation and its implications for personality development led to a slightly exaggerated situation. Goldkorn has no living congregation at all; his sole, if lucrative, vocation is burying people he has never met, a situation that produces high comedy when he recalls burying a hat salesman named Feldman early in his career at Lud. Because no one from Feldman's immediate family showed up and because the funeral was scheduled for Saturday until Goldkorn reminded the directors that Jews do not bury their dead on Shabbes, he leaps to the conclusion that the closed casket contains the Nazi Mengele. To get revenge on Nazis and momsers everywhere, he launches into a passionate eulogy and suggests that the man being buried is the Messiah. He soon learns from the funeral directors that the reason no family members came to Feldman's funeral was that he was a petty embezzler.

Another autobiographical detail that contributes to the novel's humor is Jerry's religious training. Because he was the worst student in his Hebrew class, his rabbi located the "Shabbes of the year's shortest haphtarah passage" (*RL*, 12) so he could read the Hebrew text for his bar mitzvah (even then only with the help of a crib), a story Elkin told me is essentially autobiographical. He was bar mitzvahed in July, in Brooklyn rather than in Chicago on his birthday (11 May), because he could not read the haphtarah passage for the nearest Shabbes. Despite his incompetence in Hebrew, Jerry feels a calling to be a rabbi, but no rabbinical academy will accept him, so he pursues his rabbinical studies offshore, in the Maldive Islands: "God's little own welfare cheat. I had no aptitude for what was finally just another inscrutably foreign language to me and not the ordinary, conversational vulgate of God himself. The superheroes in those comic books had more reality for me than all the biblical luminaries and shoguns in the Pentateuch. And this is who He chooses to ride shotgun for Him in New Jersey?" (*RL*, 11). If Elkin chooses as his hero and narrator a rabbi who has no living congregation, who is incompetent in Hebrew, and who practices what we shall call confrontation theology, he subtly undermines our sympathy for this character by means of ironic juxtapositions of Goldkorn's motives, past experiences, and long battle with his daughter to preserve his post as the only rabbi in a town where Jews are buried. This novel traps us in the mind of a character we have difficulty liking and uses irony to explore the implications of such a character's personality.

It is difficult for readers to understand Jerry's attraction to Lud, which he often describes as a wasteland: "We're this company town. (There's no company.) We're this ghost town. (No ghosts either, but plenty of potential). . . . What's responsible for our Luds, those perfectly logical closed systems outside connection?" (*RL*, 9). Jerry is fully aware of the absurdity of anyone's living in, or forcing a daughter to grow up as the only child in, such a place. Throughout the novel, however, he holds tenaciously to Lud and convinces himself that the reason he does not want to leave is his intense love for his wife, Shelley. Because he believes she lacks social skills, he thinks she cannot cope with an urbane setting. He is guilty of three errors, as he learns at the end of the book: he has deceived himself by claiming that this action is in Shelley's interest; he has forced his daughter, Connie, to grow up in an unnatural environment and has obliged her to go to ridiculous lengths to coerce him into leaving Lud; and he has underestimated as well as used Shelley, whom he claims to love, as an excuse for holding tenaciously to his secure position in Lud.

At the heart of the complex ironies of *The Rabbi* is that Goldkorn is afraid to be anywhere other than Lud because there he faces no real challenge. Despite his awareness of the harm this fear brings his daughter, he sacrifices her welfare to remain in a position that promises a good income with many perks, little responsibility, and no commitment to the ministerial or theological concerns appropriate to a rabbi. Evidence supporting this thesis includes the impact his vocation has on Connie, the reasons he decided to retreat into Lud, and the partial recovery of human responsibility he gains while giving the eulogy for his wife's close friend and his former mistress, Joan Cohen. Examining this evidence, we shall recall frequently the supporting motif: Jerry's brand of confrontation theology.

The obvious effect Goldkorn's vocation has on his daughter is to isolate her from her peers, but that isolation produces two unexpected and insidious consequences. The teenager is self-conscious about her home, where she has for daily companionship only the blind son of one of the funeral moguls, an anti-Semitic tombstone carver, and his assistant who suffers from Alzheimer's disease. Her mother, whose empathy with Connie's isolation Jerry underestimates, arranges complex car pools to compensate for Connie's alienation, but the child's unhappiness with living in the town of the dead produces poor school performance, nail biting, and finally rebellion. Goldkorn's response to these undermines his credibility with the reader.

One form his response takes, involving his version of confrontation theology, is cynical and psychologically cruel. Learning that his friend from Rabbi Wolfblock's minyan in Chicago suffers from leukemia, Jerry devotes daily prayers to interceding on Stan Bloom's behalf, an admirable rabbinical goal, but he knows in advance that this intercession will be futile. This has cynical overtones because he involves Connie in the prayers despite his knowing they will not succeed. This cynicism is compounded when he announces to God that "this happens to be a challenge grant. The kid's faith is riding on it" (*RL,* 67), and confides that "what I really meant was her faith in me" (*RL,* 68). At one level, this is consistent with Jerry's confrontation theology, upping the ante with "Teller God of Collections and Disbursements," "Old Sparrow Counter" (*RL,* 67) to include the fate of a young child as well as a middle-aged sick friend in Goldkorn's prayers. More brutally, he knows the prayers will not work—after Bloom dies, his prepared excuse for Connie is, "Hey, kid, I gave it my best shot. . . . Didn't you hear me? The lengths I went to" (*RL,* 89)—so he is willing to risk Connie's faith in a cause he knows is lost. To complicate this motive, Goldkorn admits that his real motive in involving Connie in his prayers for Bloom is to impress the ladies in Shelley's singing group: "I could hear their attention through the thin walls" (*RL,* 68) separating the rec room, where the women rehearse, and the rabbi's study.

When Connie's efforts to persuade or badger her father into moving to another town fail, she goes public to coerce him. Her effort makes clear the effect Jerry's commitment to Lud has on his daughter. Although her grades at school continue to plummet, she spends a lot of time in the library doing research. Why increased library time does not result in better grades becomes apparent when she releases a deposition to the press alleging visitations from the Blessed Virgin. She has been doing research on Mariology (she also interviews Sal the Barber, a Catholic, on miracles) in order to make a case that she has indeed had divine contact. Her motive is to embarrass her father enough to force him to leave Lud or, failing that, to enrage funeral moguls Shull and Tober enough to fire him. In a deposition sure to offend some Jews and Catholics alike, Connie recounts conversations with the Virgin and helping Mary harrow Lud's graveyards. She even tries some harrowing on her own. Her ingenious, if slightly blasphemous, scheme fails. The undertakers are embarrassed by their resident rabbi's family troubles, and mourners do not want him to bury their dead, so Tober and Shull sell Jerry's contract to a realty firm, and his commitment to Lud overwhelms his rabbinical devotion to the

degree that he is willing to conduct seminars in buying cemetery lots—
death's realtor—rather than to seek a real congregation.

Faced with her father's resentment but getting no results in her campaign
to leave Lud, Connie expresses her frustration by running away to Chicago.
Jerry's response to her tale of a lurid sexual adventure illustrates his self-
centeredness. He brutally leads her through a story of a motel assignation
with a preteenager, supplying the most damning details himself: "You sur-
rendered your cherry" (RL, 244). Actually the veracity of Connie's story is
questionable. Obviously she wants to punish her father for not responding to
her pleas and schemes, and she directs her more lurid confessions to him. The
details of the assignation are positively silly, like those an adolescent who
watches "Dallas" on television might make up, and her father supplies many
of these, so Connie merely confirms them.[3] Moreover, she showed great tal-
ent in her deposition for making up stories to embarrass and discomfort her
father.

Whether her story is true, partly true, or pure fantasy to get revenge on
Jerry, what matters most is the callousness of his response. He once regards
forcing Connie into this confession as a tactical error (RL, 246) but shows no
sign of regret that his daughter either lost her virginity or was so frustrated
that she made up a story about having done so. When she, in utter despair,
threatens to run away again, to New York to live as a prostitute, Jerry responds with revealing sarcasm: "Go ahead, . . . run away and turn tricks on
Forty-Second Street. It's not as if you still had your cherry" (RL, 255). Any
parental feeling, or wish to protect the child's self-esteem, must give way before Jerry's obsession with remaining in Lud, and any harm, physical or psychological, that may come to Connie as a result of her father's selfishness is
acceptable if he does not have to leave Lud.

Although it may not be obvious on a first reading, Elkin's handling of the
first-person central narrative method offers substantial evidence that Jerry is
one of this author's most self-centered characters, one willing to sacrifice his
daughter's welfare and in the process to underestimate his wife's intuitive
awareness of what this costs Connie to protect his interest in staying in Lud.
Inevitably this raises the question of motive. Why would Jerry knowingly in-
flict such harm on his daughter, especially when he realizes that Lud is not
even an attractive place to live? Answers to this question can be found in the
longest chapter, Jerry's account of the year he spent as "Chief Rabbi of the
Alaska Pipeline," introduced by the cause-effect sequence, "Leave Lud?
What were they, crazy? I'm Rabbi of Lud! . . . Anyway, I'd done it . . . already" (RL, 94). Examining this evidence, we shall discover that Jerry's motive is not love for Lud but anxiety about the chances one takes when

confronting any vital, protean environment. In Alaska Jerry found that one becomes vulnerable to the schemes and craziness of the world when one takes risks. He comes close to admitting this truth about himself when he and Joan Cohen try, in a Philadelphia hotel, to diagnose his vice, and Jerry speculates, "Maybe that I lie low" (*RL,* 267), a variation on what he discovered after being in a plane crash, then menaced by bears, while on his way to the Alaskan interior, "There's magic in lying doggo" (*RL,* 121). Lud, the symbol central to the novel, is not only a town of the dead but a refuge for the dead of spirit—those who have been burned once and determine never to be vulnerable again. Elkin probably changed *Lodi* to *Lud* to allude to the Luddites, a group of nineteenth-century workmen who destroyed machinery to resist technological change.

Jerry's adventure as "Chief Rabbi of the Alaska Pipeline" makes up chapter 5, the most technically ingenious and most misunderstood in the book. Elkin told me, with a hint of exasperation in his voice, "Nobody knows what the hell the Alaska section means. . . . Nobody's understood what is going on, even, in the Alaska scenes." That the chapter is basic to an understanding of *The Rabbi* is argued not only by its length but by its style and evocation of the fanciful. It resembles the Mauritius episodes in *The Dick Gibson Show* in narrative zest and preoccupation with ways a paranoid personality attributes mythic implications to phenomena.

Because Elkin was generous enough to share his intentions in this crucial episode, I shall modify my critical procedure. First, we shall consider certain meanings I derived from the episode; then we shall examine clarifications the author offered concerning his intentions. In both cases we shall find that the Alaska episodes establish Jerry's motives for being obsessed with staying in Lud, and we shall discover a focal metaphor for the novel, the potlatch.

Goldkorn discovered in Alaska that the world is too complex and dangerous for him to confront; he is not up to the challenge of an actively engaged life. He was a minor part of a great enterprise, laying the pipeline, but that experience persuaded him that he could easily be deceived if he allowed his enthusiasm to operate unchecked in a culture of subtle entrepreneurs, especially in such a vast and unforgiving environment. As a result, he decides to "lie doggo," to hide out in Lud for the rest of his life, so he can never again be victimized.

Goldkorn's original plan in taking the Alaska job was to escape from Lud. The year as chief rabbi was a test of his adaptability to the Alaskan economy and social structure, and if it worked out, he would exchange jobs with Rabbi Petch, who wanted to leave Anchorage because he was obsessed with the weather and would welcome Goldkorn's job if it were in a less severe climate.

As Jerry tells Petch, this "was just supposed to be a break for me, to see how I worked out in the parishes, to see could I handle the pastoral parts" (*RL*, 107). His pastorate north of the Arctic Circle, although it attracts huge congregations, proves that Jerry cannot "handle the pastoral parts." Most of the congregations his zeal attracts are Gentiles, and some are virulent anti-Semites. The Jews in his charge become disaffected and quit coming to services entirely: "What I minded was . . . the sense of having actually *lost* souls" (*RL*, 174). His services become legendary for the size and offerings of the gentile congregations and for the hilarious foul-ups he has with bogus Torahs, so much so that Petch risks Arctic weather to observe Rosh Hashanah and proves, despite his absurd obsession with the climate, to be a brilliant rabbi. He takes over from Goldkorn and reads the service from a blank Torah.

Goldkorn's pastoral failure convinces him that his best option is to stay in Lud, where his duties consist of burying people he does not know and consoling survivors he will never again see. His Arctic efforts to perform traditional rabbinical duties meet with disappointment. He keeps office hours in the camps, but no one comes; he arranges social events, with the same effect. His illusory success comes when he adapts his pastoral duties to the dominant Alaskan economy, represented in the novel by the metaphor, the potlatch, but that adaptation results in his alienating his Jewish congregation.

A potlatch is an Indian custom of hosting a ceremonial feast in which the host gives lavish gifts and the guests are expected to reciprocate. In this novel, the custom, specific to Indians of the northwest coast, becomes a synecdoche for ostentatious concern with materialism, or getting and spending. The concept is introduced when a mysterious "miracle rabbi" whom Goldkorn and Phil meet after their plane crashes tells them about a legendary potlatch hosted by Father John Lookout in which the giving of gifts became so obsessive that the participants destroyed whatever food and belongings they could not give away, including their hunting and fishing equipment (thus undermining the economic base on which their generosity rested), abused their spouses and children, and regurgitated the feast they had eaten. The absurdity reaches its climax when Lookout destroys his most prized possession, a refrigerator, just to show he can do it.

Most of the Alaska episode is dominated by variations on the potlatch in which people practice obsessive and often destructive generosity to show their indifference to material possessions. Such indifference is a deception, for to show ostentatiously one's contempt for material objects assumes that one has accumulated many possessions to disregard. Goldkorn recognizes a despair behind the potlatch: "It was the same instinct that drove them to six-pack the house, that same sporty waste and recklessness lifted to a kind of code. You started with the realization that you only lived once. Then you modified your behavior to spite the bad news. . . . Maybe that was what was so unamiable and cynical about the idea of the potlatch. Maybe that is what Petch objected to in me" (*RL*, 178). Throughout the inflated Alaskan economy, potlatch occurs. Goldkorn explicitly connects "six-packing the house," or buying six beers or mixed drinks for everyone present, with the Indian custom. That practice evolves to subtly ostentatious and absurd lengths, including anonymously six-packing the house and in one hilarious episode, in which Jerry allows himself to be thought the buyer, someone six-packs a Boeing 747. In Anchorage, he realizes that the outrageous price for reindeer steak, which has been flown in a thousand miles for the tourists, is an ostentation; Elkin had the same intuition when he visited Alaska. Jerry's rabbinical success is also a version of the potlatch. He appeals not to the need for religious ritual among his congregation but to their desire for excessive and ostentatious generosity.

The practice, although not called potlatch, occurs in Lud as well. Both funeral directors practice conspicuous getting and spending. Shull, an aging Lothario, owns the latest model of every gadget, buys season tickets to everything, and constantly seeks new ways to make money to support his lavish spending. His explanation of his extravagance recalls Jerry's discovery of the motives behind the potlatch: "Death makes me a big spender. It puts the glow in my cheeks and the stiff in my cock" (*RL*, 79). Whereas Shull is a conspicuous consumer, Tober is a miser, so obsessed with providing for his blind son on his own death that he sends Edward to play on Goldkorn's sympathies, to persuade him to extend his rabbinical duties by selling cemetery lots. One director is obsessed with hoarding, the other with spending; together they represent a New Jersey version of the potlatch, and they scheme to extract ever more profit from the graveyard. Their rumored clients include Mafiosi and the remains of Jimmy Hoffa. Their "bold new marketing scheme" is to provide discreet burials for AIDS victims (*RL*, 81).

In Alaska Jerry learns that his version of the potlatch is not material, but emotional and enthusiastic, extravagance. His enthusiasm carries him into services that are a travesty of the rabbinical function, and his identifying the "miracle rabbi" as the messiah, or at least a tzadik (religious leader), is a result of uncontrolled enthusiasm. When he sees the man, who appears to have flowers in his beard, he leaps to the conclusion that this is a man of miracle. The chap is the pilot Phil's twin brother, but they are from the Tinneh tribe, who grow apart with time, so even Phil seems not to recognize him. Our first clue that Jerry makes more of this "Jewish Lear" (*RL*, 126) than the facts will support involves his beard, which seems to Jerry to be comprised of flowers.

This is the chief evidence supporting Jerry's presumption that perhaps "this was him [the messiah]" (*RL*, 132). When he actually examines the man's face, he finds "that they weren't really flowers, blooms, nothing vegetable at all in fact, . . . but something deep and indigenous in his whiskers and hung across his chin like a fragrant tattoo" (*RL*, 129–30). Despite this empirical awareness, Jerry continues to attribute floral miracles to the beard, and this refusal to act on his awareness causes him to miss other clear indications that the man is no miracle or religious leader. The man asks for a cigarette and justifies his desire for life-threatening nicotine with a fatalism Jerry finds "beautiful" (*RL*, 149). When Goldkorn argues that Palestinians have some proprietary rights in the Middle East, the "tzadik" responds cruelly, "Fuck them" (*RL*, 147). He tells Jerry God created evil for a good purpose because "it shapes our taste" (*RL*, 147).

The miracle man is an illusion Goldkorn's enthusiasm has created, and he ignores the evidence of his senses to preserve this illusion. As the Alaska episode ends, moreover, Jerry realizes this. After Phil's funeral, he offers the miracle rabbi a ride and learns the man is Phil's twin. The "tzadik's" parting words reinforce Jerry's sense of illusion: "Up close, straight on, the beard seemed lopsided, lifeless. . . . 'Ain't no murracles,' old Posypuss said, 'I dud wish dey would was, but dey ain't'" (*RL*, 182). Knowing he allowed his imagination to convert this man into a miracle rabbi convinces Goldkorn that he is safer to stay in Lud, where his imagination only confuses dead salesmen named Feldman with Nazi war criminals.

Elkin's explanation of the Alaska section offers a synthesis of these motifs, with an additional variation. Jerry discovers that he is a pawn in the great Alaska pipeline scam, and the "miracle rabbi" is a con artist. Flowerface spent months on a glacier meditating before finding Jerry and Phil after their plane crashed. He was meditating on an opportunity for a scam created by government contracts affiliated with the pipeline project: "figuring red tape, the long odds of Corporate Life, how the Feds would probably require affirmative action, Prots and Mackerel-snappers and even Jews demanding rabbis, Torahs, the works, and what all this could mean to him at Alaskan prices" (*RL*, 182). When the plane crashed, Jerry found a duffel bag containing a menorah, an ark, some yads, and three Torahs for which the contractor paid nearly half a million dollars. He is shocked because he knows three Torahs should cost $20,000 to $30,000, a value Elkin confirmed while writing the novel. Phil reminds him, "It's like everything else. The price of Torahs is higher in Alaska" (*RL*, 125). When Jerry conducts services, however, he finds that one Torah is an English crib prepared by his mentor, Rabbi Wolfblock. The second is an abridgement Jerry labels, in a joke referring to

Stanley Elkin's Greatest Hits, the "Old Testament's Greatest Hits" (*RL,* 173). The third is blank.

Each Torah is virtually worthless, both as material object and as spiritual icon, but a corporation paid $435,000 for them. Someone has been had. Elkin explains that Phil's brother switched the valuable Torahs and the worthless ones after the plane crash, and if so, this is one smart Tinneh. Meditating on that glacier about affirmative action, he must have planned to have worthless Torahs to switch with the real ones, and presumably he had plans to sell the valuable ones at Alaska's inflated prices. Because the quotation about Flowerface's meditating on the glacier indicates that Goldkorn is aware of his having been used in this scam, we have more support for our governing hypothesis: that his Alaskan adventure convinces him that he must stay in the safety of Lud, no matter what it costs his daughter or anyone else.

The culminating irony of *The Rabbi* is that Lud is not safe either. Despite Goldkorn's fervent holding to this risk-free environment and the prices he has exacted from Shelley and Connie for his cowardice, he learns in the final sections that Lud, while it may protect him from having to compete for a living congregation, cannot guarantee the emotional invulnerability he sought. Physical danger is present in the person of Bubbles, an ostentatious hit man being shaved by Sal. Although there are rumors that the Mafia use Lud to bury their embarrassing dead, this is a real hit man with a visible gun. That gun is not used, but another, fired by a hunter, kills Joan Cohen, Shelley's friend and Jerry's mistress. Her death forces Goldkorn to come to terms with the price his retreat has imposed on his family and to recognize that one cannot hide entirely from the human community. Charged with giving the eulogy for someone he not only knows but has been intimate with, Goldkorn faces his cowardice and rediscovers the ethical humanity he has so long buried in Lud. In this process, he finally makes a meaningful declaration of his confrontation theology.

The primary benefits of being in Lud are a secure job entailing little risk and emotional isolation. He performs services without any emotional involvement in the human grief that attends a death. Joan's death shows him that his emotional isolation does not work. Her friends insist that Jerry conduct her funeral, despite his reluctance, and in preparing and delivering her eulogy he has an epiphany in which he realizes the cruelty of what he has done to Connie and Shelley, makes meaningful his brand of confrontation theology, and recovers some dignity.[4]

Throughout the book, Goldkorn has challenged God to prove His justice in human events, a motif Elkin explores in *The Living End* and *George Mills.* He offered prayers for Stan Bloom as a "challenge grant" to confirm

Connie's faith, and his epithets for God throughout the book, while funny, are extremely confrontational: "Because where, in Torah, is God's name? *Where is it written?* God, Jehovah, Lord, and Yahweh. All aliases—the noms de plume and a.k.a's of Agency, your basic top-secret, undercover, cloak-and-dagger, off-the-record, ambush-laying Pussyfoot. Peekaboo to you from the burning bush!" (*RL,* 6). His concept of God is strangely adversarial for a rabbi: "God is no humanist, no One Worlder, and is hostile to the very concept of brotherhood," so He "knew what He was doing when He invented the Diaspora. Hansel'd and Gretel'd the Jews and lost ten tribes of Israel" (*RL,* 58).

Until he prepares Joan's eulogy, however, Jerry's confrontation is primarily bluster and posing. Many of these histrionics have self-serving motives. His "challenge grant" is intended to impress the ladies from Shelley's singing group; he thinks his rabbinical gear sexually excites women and tells Debbie Grunwald in Alaska that certain clerics get girls because they have "God's ear, a line on the mysteries" (*RL,* 172). When Shelley refuses to sleep with him while Connie is in Chicago, Jerry attempts to win her affection by strapping on "my phylacteries, . . . girding myself, a Jewish Crusader" (*RL,* 226). When he has an assignation with Joan after an accidental meeting in Rutherford, he believes his attraction for her is as "the surrogate, the middleman, her humble conduit to the Lord" (*RL,* 249). From this evidence we may conclude that some of Jerry's encounter theology is not serious questioning of the ways of God to man but is rather a tactic for enriching Goldkorn's ways with women.

When preparing the eulogy, he struggles to find a balance between his erotic memories of Joan and the decorum her family will need to comfort them. Deciding to "play it straight" (*RL,* 270), he launches into a eulogy that gets out of control, moving his audience from tears of empathy to expressions of shock and disbelief. Under the spell of his rhetoric, he comes to a meaningful definition of his confrontation with God's justice and a self-indictment that leads him toward human value and decency. Like the sermon at the end of *George Mills,* this rhetoric leads to an affirmation of our shared humanity.

First, he discovers that to account for Joan's untimely death, he must accuse God of capriciousness: "The Book of Life she prayed and petitioned a loving and forgiving God to inscribe her in. Who wouldn't do it. Who heard what He heard and *still* wouldn't do it. Who *must* have heard her. Who heard her, all right" (*RL,* 274). As the caprice of Joan's death dawns fully on her ex-lover, he asks, "We spoke of keeping God honest? . . . So *honest?* My God, my friends, He's positively *fussy!*" (*RL,* 275). If he cannot reconcile himself to the discrepancy between God's ways and human notions of justice, he can make a confrontational statement that does not contain any element of posing. In fact, it has an opposite effect on the mourners, who are increasingly uncomfortable with his rhetoric. He also discovers, while saying prayers of forgiveness, that God's apparent indifference makes human beings fully responsible for their ethical choices.

As he asks for general forgiveness, his prayers approximate public confession, or mea culpa. Those sins upon which his prayers center are his: "the sins we have committed against Thee by seeking to lie low and maintain a low profile" (*RL*, 276) explicitly refers to "lying doggo," and he seeks forgiveness for sins of the flesh. Most importantly, he asks forgiveness for his sins against Connie, but it costs him a careful revision to do so:

> "For the sins we have committed against Thee by living in the wrong communities," I said.
> That wasn't it. It wasn't even more like it.
> "In which we raised our children," I amended.
> "Our daughters," I revised.
> "*My* daughter," I atoned. (*RL*, 276)

Confession, they say, is good for the soul if not for the public image. Relieved of the burden of his accumulated guilt by public confession, Jerry moves toward renouncing the spiritual cowardice that led him to hide out in Lud and has at least acknowledged how much this has cost his family. His soul relieved by confession, he offers an affirmation of human community very like that at the end of *George Mills*: "Just before I said the El Moley Rachamim for Joan Cohen, I recited special blessings I'd learned in yeshiva. I offered the broches you say when you see a rainbow, when you eat ripe fruit, when you hear good news, when you laugh out loud, when you buy new clothes, when you kiss a woman, when you repair an appliance, when you touch a giant, when you smell sweet wood" (*RL*, 277).

It is a little short of miraculous how far this rabbi has come: from the most deviously selfish character in the author's canon to someone capable of seeing the divine in the trivial (buying clothes, fixing appliances), the miraculous (touching giants), the joys of community (hearing good news, kissing), and the simple pleasures of the senses (seeing, tasting, smelling). If Jerry's life has not led to spiritual wisdom—he still thinks God is fussy—it has led, through epiphany, to acknowledgment of responsibility and the intuitive wisdom that creation is an eternal source of mystery.

Chapter Seven

Searches and Seizures and *The Living End:* The Novellas

The novel is Elkin's strong suit, but he also excels in briefer forms, especially the novella. His most popular work, *The Living End,* combines three stories he wrote during consecutive summers while composing *George Mills.* Earlier he had completed the novellas constituting *Searches and Seizures* between the publication of *The Dick Gibson Show* and the diagnosis of his multiple sclerosis, making final revisions for this collection the day before he entered the hospital for tests.

This form appeals to Elkin because it combines the concentration of the short story with the freedom for verbal inventiveness of the novel. Although he is a talented short story writer, he has not been entirely comfortable with that form's demand for compactness and simple narrative line. He printed one collection of short stories early in his career but has published only a few stories since. The preface to *Searches and Seizures* indicates that writing "The Making of Ashenden" was a process of discovery: "But I was hooked; I had enjoyed writing the novella, enjoyed . . . writing at that length more than at any other. Hence, when an interviewer asked me about my next book, on the spur of the moment I told him I was working on a collection of novellas. I wasn't, but as soon as I said it I knew it was something I really wanted to do."[1] Asked about the special appeal of the novella for him, Elkin told me, "I like the length. It seems more important than a short story, and more manageable than a novel," and he mentioned that a project he plans to take up after completing *The MacGuffin* will be a novella titled "Her Sense of Timing."

This appeal is grounded in Elkin's fascination with rhetoric and the ways in which circumstances affect character. The short story, encouraging uncomplicated narrative line and relatively one-dimensional characterization, has never been an ideal medium for him. The novel, on the other hand, gives the writer space in which to explore the implications of his rhetoric, but its length works against the intense concentration Elkin's language requires. Novellas, however, allow the author to explore more than one dimension of the character's experience and the full implications of the character's and narrator's rhetoric but are brief enough to be read at a single sitting, so the rich rhetoric of such texts is enhanced by the reader's ability to recall details and verbal echoes over an uninterrupted reading.

Each collection, moreover, works by an incremental aesthetic strategy; that is, neither is a group of discrete stories but a collection possessing its own structure. The author alludes to the medieval concept of the triptych, or set of three related carvings or panels often used in church decor, to describe *The Living End,* which develops common characters and themes among "The Conventional Wisdom," "The Bottom Line," and "The State of the Art" (the titles are clichés from business or technology). One can read any story separately and derive aesthetic pleasure from it. But to read the story in conjunction with the others produces a higher order of pleasure.

Searches and Seizures works by a similar aesthetic principle. These stories do not share characters or locations, but they build an incremental logical structure indicated by their order in the collection. The first novella Elkin wrote, "The Making of Ashenden," is second in the collection. The final story written for this collection, "The Bailbondsman," appears first. The second in order of composition, "The Condominium," concludes the book.

This ordering reflects an intention to suggest resemblances and developments among the stories. All are, as Elkin mentions in his preface, about bachelors concerned in differing ways with mortality (the British edition is entitled *Eligible Men,* a reminder of this bachelor status; Elkin's friend Al Lebowitz, a lawyer, suggested the American title, which alludes to the Fourth Amendment to the Constitution). Incrementally these "searches" and "seizures" treat ways the characters deal with their mortality. The hero of "The Bailbondsman" zealously embraces his professional craft to avoid acknowledging his mortality; Ashenden is an unfamiliar type for Elkin, a refined WASP initiated into a crude, vital relationship with nature; Marshall Preminger in "The Condominium" is also atypical of this author, a man whose brooding on his alienation produces the only suicide among Elkin's protagonists. He indicated in a conversation that the technical challenge of writing about a suicidal person was one motive behind his novella: "I say to my writing students that I don't want anybody killing himself in a story they write for me. It can't be done successfully. So I tried to do it successfully."

The overall effect of *Searches and Seizures* is therefore more than the sum of its parts. The collection moves from enthusiastic immersion in a vocation, through discovery of the need for a vital relationship with the surrounding world, to the despair to which one can succumb when facing existential dilemmas without philosophical or vocational alternatives.

Searches and Seizures

Alexander Main, "The Bailbondsman," is the prototypical Elkin hero in his obsessive devotion to his business, providing liberty to accused criminals. Elkin once asserted that "I, myself, am closer to Main than any other character," and one critic calls Main the "Elkin omnivorous man . . . to whom the world is an affront because it and he are separate."² The sleazy world of prisons and courts gives focus to his immense energy and purpose to his life, but the day in Main's life represented in the novella is his existential crisis.

Elkin was inspired to write the story when, reading *Boss*, Mike Royko's book about Chicago's Mayor Richard Daley, he was struck by the word *bailbondsman* in a description of a saloon patronized by cops and bailbondsmen. Although he knew little about bondsmen, the word excited his imagination, and Elkin began to reflect on the vocation. He told me that one fascinating element of the job is the bondsman's unique power over anyone who jumps bail: "these guys can kill you." Main takes sadistic pleasure in pointing out the contractual clause in which someone needing bond consents "to the application of such force as may be necessary to effect your return" (*SS*, 116) and delights in bailbondsmen's powers of arrest, "stronger even than [the cops'] own" (*SS*, 25).

Years in his vocation have made Main the most overtly cynical of Elkin's heroes, and habitual association with felons and prison guards he can intimidate or bribe has reinforced his latent nihilism. Family life was unrewarding because his wife insisted on activities like picnics that Main found boring— "Nobody could *want* to do that crap"—and he accepted her terminal illness with relief: "her leukemia went my bail" (*SS*, 66). He frequents prostitutes, often black teenagers whose bail he has gone, to placate his "vicious . . . kinky catered lust" (*SS*, 12). He is a racist, adept at parodying the street lingo of urban blacks and too ready with racial slurs. He despises his clients and enjoys manipulating authority figures, like a judge he "chats up" while arranging bail for someone the Mafia hired Main to get out of jail so they can kill him (*SS*, 47–50) or loudly bullying in a barber shop a prestigious divorce lawyer representing a client Main fears may jump bail (*SS*, 72–76). His egocentrism is represented by "Alexander's ragtime bond" (*SS*, 70), his will stipulating that all his cash will be buried with him.

Despite these characteristics, most affiliated with latent cynicism nurtured by the shady associations his vocation requires, Main is among Elkin's most philosophical, or at least speculative, characters. He is preoccupied with time, a concern expressed in reflections on the past and the future. He makes up a history of a bailbonding craft invented by the Phoenicians, from whom he claims descent, and insists that *bail* derives from the Hebrew *Ba'al*, not medieval English law (*SS*, 6; bogus etymology also provides humor in the Mauritius episode of *The Dick Gibson Show*). He habitually visits a museum, this day skipping an important business luncheon to do so, to study one exhibit, fossilized teeth. This scene illustrates Elkin's concept of research for a novel. He often visited London's Victoria and Albert Museum of Natural History to study a similar exhibit: "I didn't make up a single thing in the descriptions of teeth. . . . I went with a pad and pencil and copied down the shapes of those teeth."[3] Main's preoccupation with fossils is a reminder of mortality that produces his only display of authentic emotion:

It is teeth that he comes back again and again to see, as if these were the distillate of the animal's soul, the cutting, biting edge of its passion and life.

He is thinking in geological time now, in thousands of millions of years. . . . He is weeping. (*SS*, 60).

His emotion is not motivated by sympathy for extinct animals. That merely raises the ironic issue that he feels compassion for dead animals but not for live people. The principal reason for Main's emotion introduces another theme, explored fully in *George Mills*: that one can never achieve complete understanding of one's world. Main regrets his dependence on cards in the museum to tell him which animal's tooth he is examining and feels "furious with himself" (*SS*, 85).

If Main feels insulted by his fragmentary knowledge of the past, he feels like a blockhead when he contemplates the future. He has a vision that depresses him, not because he anticipates a future worse than the present but because people then will know so much more than we do now: "How he envied them. . . . Their 90 IQ's would encompass wisdoms that the greatest minds of today could not even begin to comprehend" (*SS*, 108–9).

Main's irritation over his limited knowledge of the past and total stupidity about the future suggests his central motive and the story's primary theme, expressed in the marvelous sentence, "What do I do with my wonder, I wonder?" (*SS*, 124). Main differs from his environment because he has a profound sense of mystery, and this is probably the quality with which Elkin identifies in saying he feels closer to Main than other characters he has created. During the luncheon Alexander skips, other bondsmen suspect that "that goddamn Phoenician," who is probably "off beating our time" (*SS*, 57), will not cooperate in the strategy they have devised to cooperate and thereby minimize losses liberal court rulings impose on the business.

This professional separateness is a synecdoche for Main's philosophical

isolation from his environment, an alienation caused by his capacity for wonder and mystery. This in turn motivates his choice of profession: "Mystery.
The reason he was a bondsman. The meaning of his life. The way he came to
terms with what engined it. Mystery. Why he lived with the cops and the
robbers. . . . Crime was the single mystery he could get close to" (SS, 106).
Being a bondsman addresses Main's need for wonder, which "engines" or
drives his life, by enabling him to probe deeply into his clients' lives, to exercise control over them, and to influence those in authority by bribes or bullying. Lamenting his ignorance of mathematics, physics, chemistry, and
languages, he throws himself compulsively into a business that involves him
with the seamier side of American life but challenges him to control his
environment.

This control is manifested in the management of his office, as well as in his
dominating judges, prison guards, and accused criminals. He forces his secretary to comport himself like a functionary in a Dickens law office by using
quill pens and sitting at a scrivener's desk; Main admonishes him for not
wearing a nightgown and sleeping cap he provided, thus extending his influence into the secretary's private life and illustrating his compulsive need for
control.

His obsessive response culminates with Oyp and Glyp, two fugitives
who got away.[4] Throughout the day, he recalls having dreamed about them
(SS, 28, 29, 63), and today's dream, in a hotel room, marks an existential
crisis in his professional life. Because they are the only clients ever to escape
Main, he has elevated them to mythic stature. In his dream, they become
robbers of a pharaoh's grave, expert vandals, defilers of religious icons, and
ghouls who rip the mummy's heart out. Captured red-handed, they present an ultimate challenge to the bondsman, who tries to persuade Egyptian
authorities that their crime, however heinous, is technically bondable because no statute explicitly forbids bond in such cases. Main offers to under-
write a $20 billion bond, despite his inability to raise such a sum and Oyp's
and Glyp's inability to pay the retainer, because this would be "a feather in
my cap!" (SS, 104). The judge denies bail but preposterously frees them
because their crimes "must be of such magnitude that no punishment can
redress them" (SS, 104).

This bizarre, erotic dream shakes Main to the core of his being. He first explains his dream by giving Oyp and Glyp mythic stature greater than that he
has already invested in them: as "fugitives from fugitiveness itself" they create
"limits to his power and his own precious freedom" (SS, 105). As he reflects
on the dream, however, he redefines their importance. He realizes that because they got away, he was elevated these "ordinary car thieves" to the status

of "masterminds" or "arch criminals" (*SS,* 106). He recognizes that they are not master criminals but ordinary punks who escaped his enforcement of the bondsman's unique authority. He announces their death and searches to assert himself in the only way he knows—by pursuing a fugitive.

To fill the void this reassessment of Oyp and Glyp creates, Main declares open season on Crainpool, whom he brought back eleven years before and rehabilitated as his clerk. With no master criminal to hunt, Main's identity is in jeopardy. He shoots Crainpool in the hand to overcome the stunned clerk's apathy, and the chase is on; now Main has a fugitive to hunt, a role as a bondsman. He is surely creating another Oyp and Glyp by imposing on the mild-mannered Crainpool the role of archcriminal, but the chase will give his life purpose until he either kills Crainpool or has another epiphanic dream.[5]

The alternative to pursuing Crainpool is dealing with entropy.[6] Discussing Einstein's theory of the expanding universe with Crainpool, Main reflects on a mystery his mind cannot encompass or deal with: "I'm an honest man. Upright and respectable in this universe I inhabit. I'm honest, but the fucking laws are leaking, the physical constants bleeding into each other like madras. God himself is nothing but a slow leak, some holy puncture, Nature's and reality's sacred flat. Matter and anti-matter" (*SS,* 122–23). He can neither comprehend relativity's implications nor tolerate the confusion they produce. He can, however, grasp the bailbondsman's freedom from legal restraint, and he clutches compulsively to this vocation, elevating the docile Crainpool to mythic status to give his life purpose and his environment radiance and wonder.

If Main is Elkin's typical protagonist, combining Boswell's obsessiveness, Feldman's cruelty, Gibson's mythic imagination, and Goldkorn's self-centeredness, the hero of the second novella (the first written) is quite uncharacteristic of this author. Brewster Ashenden is rich, cultivated, courteous, eminently honorable, and devoted to American blueblood norms of conduct. His personality recalls a type E. E. Cummings satirizes:

> —yon clean upstanding well dressed boy
> that with his peers full oft hath quaffed
> the wine of life and found it sweet—
>
> a tear within his stern blue eye,
> upon his firm white lips a smile,
> one thought alone: to do or die
> for God for country and for Yale.[7]

In brief, he is a vacant skull containing a decadent elitist culture's clichés. Elkin's story, however, is about "The Making" of Ashenden, and "making" implies the familiar euphemism for sexual activity but has a more serious meaning too. By being forced to have sex with a bear, Ashenden is remade: from an embodiment of elitist clichés to someone who acknowledges the primitive and earthy element in humanity.

Until he meets the bear, Ashenden is a dilettante modeled on the rich, cultivated, often naive Americans in Henry James's novels. Ashenden alludes to this by describing the inevitable response to any mention of Jane Lowes Lupton, the enigmatic object of his search, as "round Henry James 'Ah's'" (SS, 150). The language of their interview, after he finds her, recalls the circumspect rhetoric of James's courtship scenes. With her life of service to others and her insistence on absolute purity as a condition for marriage, Jane is a modern Milly Theale wasted by lupus.

She is also the perfect companion for this heir to fortunes in the four elements (real estate, oxygen tanks, bottled mineral water, and matchbooks) who, despite serving in armies, relieving earthquake victims, counseling women victimized by cads, and dueling other cads, has accomplished less than his father, whose life's work was inventing the matchbook slogans "Close Cover before Striking" and "For Our Matchless Friends." She is his ideal companion because of her taste, charity, and purity but primarily because of her disease. This illness and Brewster's willingness to share it, though he knows it is not contagious, become Elkin's symbols for the romantic posturing this character must overcome.

The silliness of Ashenden's romantic pose is exemplified by his passion for Jane and his acceptance of the task she sets before him. Although he was wife hunting when he heard about her (after his parents' deaths, he felt that "honor did subsist in doing right by the generations" [SS, 144]), he falls in love with a reputation but has never seen Jane when he decides to spend the rest of his life with her. His purpose in wife hunting was to perpetuate his dynasty, to do "right by the generations." In the advanced stage of a fatal disease, Jane cannot perpetuate any line, so the end of Brewster's quest contradicts the beginning. He decides that if she cannot live with him, honor dictates that he die with her.

The antilogic and silliness of Ashenden's Byronic pose as the "heroic man" (SS, 132) culminate in Jane's task and Ashenden's response. They are clearly soul mates, although their ability to read one another's thoughts suggests that they are in love with images of themselves,[8] but Jane demands that Ashenden recover his virginity before marrying. Accepting this challenge is silly because virginity is irrecoverable, but Ashenden practices self-deception worthy of Dick Gibson by meditating on his past moral failures and recalling scenes of innocence and then superimposing these to achieve "shame like a thermal inversion, the self-loathing that *is* purity" (*SS*, 167). In this state of self-deception, he meets his fate in the form of a young bear in her first estrus cycle.

His belief that he has purified himself is reinforced during his stroll through his friend's animal preserve. Observing scenes that suggest backgrounds for famous paintings, he concludes, "I am in art" (*SS*, 172), a civilized assessment of his new purity. As he realizes what the bear requires of him, he undergoes a gradual loss of his illusions.[9] He first suspects that the bear's demand transports him into myth: "Is *this* the test? Oh, Lord, first I was in art and now I am in allegory!" (*SS*, 179). He thinks that satisfying the bear is a test that restores his virginity and wins Jane's love. His deceptions begin to unravel when he discovers that, telling the bear his erection belongs to Jane, he is deceiving himself. Jane is no longer on his mind, and he finds that "my life has been too crammed with civilization. . . . I have been too proud of my humanism, perhaps, and all along not paid enough attention to the base" (*SS*, 179–80, an ironic echo of *King Lear* 3.4.32–33). His encounter with the bear produces blood, from the virgin bear and a small wound on his penis. The blood suggests that, figuratively, he has won virginity by moving away from the artificial world of Luptons and Ashendens into a less antiseptic definition of nature. He abandons his quest for Jane and what she represents and compounds his "Ashenden-elements" this way: "Air. Water, he thought. Fire, Earth, he thought. . . . And *honey*" (*SS*, 188), which one critic takes to mean he learns that the "genuine bears inside the cherished landscapes of Western culture . . . make simple and savage demands on the basic functions of the real body," whereas another concludes that the real "making" of Ashenden is "his freedom" from elitist conventions.[10]

Because Elkin wrote a dissertation on Faulkner and echoes Faulkner's style and method in *George Mills*, it may be tempting to hear echoes of "The Bear" in "The Making of Ashenden." Fortunately most critics have resisted this temptation. The bears in Faulkner and Elkin are of a differing kind and degree. Faulkner's bear represents the possibility of reverence for nature in an increasingly technological society, whereas Elkin's suggests a vital force that draws a limited man away from artifice into the ambiguity of freedom. Elkin denies any intended reference to "The Bear" when explaining how the story was conceived. While writing an autobiographical story about a man recovering from a heart attack and playing softball, he heard from his editor an anecdote about a man who, like Plympton in the novella, owned an animal preserve and was attacked by a bear. Hearing him scream, family members

rescued him by prodding the bear with poles, but as Elkin listened, "It occurred to me it would make a terrific story but that Joe [Fox, the editor] was
telling it all wrong. He's . . . got to be saved by poking at the bear with his
own long pole, by screwing the bear. . . . It had nothing at all to do with
Faulkner's bear."[11]

Ashenden's quest is successful by Elkin's definition. He learns that what
he was seeking before the bear "seized" him was an illusion, and he is ready at
story's end to search for a comprehensive definition of his humanity. The
hero of the final (second in order of composition) novella, Preminger, fails to
come to terms with his experience. An intellectual who cannot cope with the
demands of an urban environment, he is the only suicide among Elkin's protagonists. If Main adapted to losing Oyp and Glyp by creating a new fugitive
to hunt and if Ashenden adapted to losing his romantic illusions by accepting
a more comprehensive range of experience, Preminger's "seizure" suggests a
thematic contrast with the "searches," a failure to adapt.

A metaphor, the expanding universe, clarifies each novella's meaning. The
concept is introduced literally in "The Bailbondsman" when Main is intimi-
dated by Einstein's theory and takes refuge in his vocation so he can impose
limits on his universe. Ashenden is forced by confronting the bear metaphorically to expand his universe, to add "honey" to his list of elements, and thus to
add the wild and the gross to his world's antiseptic qualities. For Preminger
the universe does not expand; it contracts. Returning to Chicago from the
open spaces of Montana, he finds his territory limited to a condominium his
father willed him. Formerly an itinerant lecturer, he now accepts the stultify-
ing job of lifeguard at the pool. Sitting shivah for his father, coyly wooed by
his father's mistress, and besieged by the mendacity of the condo's board of
governors, he finds his universe contracting around him, so he despairs, goes
mad, and ends his life in a theatrical leap from the balcony of his new home.

"The Condominium" is not just a story about the way circumstances affect
character. Marshall brings to the condominium he inherits, with its legacy of
encumbered value and unmistakable evidence that his father had become a
fatuous conformist with a trendy youth culture (his hair styles, polyester
clothing, sleek expensive furniture, and affair with Mrs. Riker challenge
Preminger's sense of paternal decorum), a belief in the primacy of place that
makes him vulnerable to the influence of the condo and the mindless conformity it represents. He writes in a lecture he is preparing, "A place to live, to
be. Out of what vortical history came spinning this notion of a second skin?"
(SS, 192). Marshall brings to Chicago an existentially dangerous equation
between the place one chooses and the quality of life one has. When that
"place to be" proves hopelessly artificial and trivial, he has no definition of

self through vocation or innate character to fall back upon and risks madness and despair. Thus, while "The Condominium" welcomes reading as a commentary on the banality of a life-style that has developed in recent decades— "You rejected nationhood for neighborhood!" (*SS*, 198)—the life Preminger chooses can destroy him only if he, aware of the banality it represents, elects because of a character flaw to accept this life, to become "a pioneer in reverse" (*SS*, 234) who cannot adapt from a relatively free style of life to a constricting one.

The Living End

Although Elkin once said the stories in *The Living End* were written primarily to provide material for the reading circuit and although they were created as a diversion while he was writing the complex *George Mills,* this collection is his most popular work. Its sales far exceed those of other Elkin books. It was reviewed enthusiastically and earned the Rosenthal Foundation Award.

This popularity is a mixed blessing. It enriches Elkin's coffers and provides him freedom to pursue his innovations without too much concern for sales. *The Living End* is a funny, outrageous, and thematically daring book, but its popularity creates certain expectations in the minds of readers, and it is not in my judgment an ideal introduction to the author's work for these reasons. First, except for portions of "The Bottom Line," it is technically less rich than novels like *The Dick Gibson Show* or *The Magic Kingdom.* Second, it can be seen by some readers as merely comic, and by humanizing God and the Holy Family it can offend some readers as blasphemous. And third, with its funny apocalyptic mode, it lends itself to reading as satire or black humor, literary conventions Elkin rejects. Any of these possibilities, unchallenged by familiarity with Elkin's other books, can lead the reader to expect such features in Elkin books he or she may subsequently encounter. With such expectations, the reader may force these elements on works in which they are minor. It is therefore best to approach *The Living End* with a knowledge of more typical Elkin works like *A Bad Man, The Magic Kingdom,* or *The Franchiser.* In this way, the reader should see that *The Living End,* while not typical of the author's canon, is his most daring approach to the task Milton set before himself, justifying "the ways of God to men."

Elkin alludes to *Paradise Lost* when God calls the "rebels and organizers" in hell "Beelzebubs, . . . iambic angels in free fall" (rebels and Beelzebub are central to the epic, written in iambic pentameter), but the allusion is certainly ironic.[12] Milton saw in "Man's First Disobedience" a justification of God's ways to people: His decree that we must suffer, live in an antagonistic relationship with earth, then die. Milton holds that God's ways toward human beings are ultimately benevolent, that He offers redemption through sacrifice to save people from the damnation they deserve through Original Sin.

Elkin's novella raises disturbing questions about the Creator's justice and benevolence, and for that reason, especially with its apocalyptic mode (God decides to end creation: "All right, that's it! *Karios!* Doomsday!" [*LE*, 144]), *The Living End* invites discussion as satire. Melvin Raff argues that despite Elkin's objections to the label, the novella is Menippean satire that "confronts us with our beliefs made concrete."[13] There is great merit in Raff's interpretation of many details, but the label *satire* is not entirely convincing. Grounding his discussion in Northrop Frye's category, satire as the mythos of winter, Raff does not demonstrate how Frye's principal definition of satire, "militant irony: its moral norms are relatively clear, and it assumes standards against which the grotesque and the absurd are measured," applies to Elkin's text. Raff's contending that the point of the novella is that "there is no message," only the "energy of creation," finally argues against the "relatively clear norms" Frye's definition demands.[14]

At a less theoretical level, here are some questions Elkin raised when asked whether this is an exception to his practice of not writing satire: "But what am I satirizing? Heaven and Hell? I mean, that's crazy. . . . I sure as hell don't see it as satire. . . . That book came to me altogether, all at once. I got up in the middle of the night. I wasn't dreaming, but the question suddenly occurred to me, 'What would happen if everything was true?' You know, the morning line on Heaven and hell, God and the devil, everything. What if it turns out that none of it is made up, but it's all true?" (conversation, 1989). What, indeed, does *The Living End* satirize? Religious belief? That is hardly a relevant concern, for none of the characters is a believer, and it requires some stretching to see Ellerbee, Ladlehaus, Lesefario, and Quiz, four victims of God's arbitrariness, as representing theological options. Heaven and hell? Elkin's account of the origin indicates that he wanted to ponder the truth of all the conventional wisdom (thus the first story's title) about heaven and hell, and when Ellerbee arrives in heaven he discovers that everything he ever heard about it is true: pearly gates, golden streets, glorious harmonies, radiant light, tearful reunions of the blessed (*LE*, 25–30). In hell he discovers that all he heard about it is also true: the "ultimate inner city" (*LE*, 30) is unformed chaos, where the damned are tormented by physical pain, the horror of one another's company, the pain of losing God's presence (*LE*, 33), and the burden of endless time, which Ellerbee fills by exploring, making channels in the brimstone, and ministering to the wounds of his fellow damned; Dante's slogan, "Abandon Hope, All Ye Who Enter Here" (*LE*, 34), adorns the entry. To say *The Living End* satirizes heaven and hell, then, defies both the author's professed intention and the satiric convention of providing moral norms that are relatively clear, in that the point of such satire would be ambivalent.

The most likely candidate for satire is the central character, God, and by extension belief in God. This intention Elkin explicitly denied when I asked about God's capacity for error in the novella: "He makes a tiny mistake every now and then. So what? He's God. He's entitled. That was the whole idea, don't you see? Creating somebody so powerful, so immensely powerful, that he can do anything he wants to. God's not subject to the kinds of laws we're subject to." An intention to satirize God or belief in a supreme being seems to be ruled out by his statement emphasizing the absolute power of God, a character the author believes cannot be judged by human standards.

Unlike heaven and hell, however, Elkin's God is anything but an embodiment of conventional wisdom. Neither He nor the Holy Family conforms with popular mythology. The Blessed Virgin, who also appears in *The Rabbi of Lud*, is bitter that the myth of her chaste sexuality is used as "the Hook" (*LE*, 112) to interest primitive people in Christianity. Joseph is a stereotypical Jew who refuses to accept his stepson's claim to be the Messiah. Jesus is a bitter, whining cripple who has never forgiven God for forcing Him to go through with the Crucifixion because "I loved it there. . . . I loved being alive" (*LE*, 107).

While these are unconventional portraits of the Holy Family, such presentations hardly qualify as satire. The tensions within the Holy Family remind us of those between Ellerbee and his wife in Minneapolis and suggest that even in eternity conflicts are not fully resolved. All these tensions have their origin, as do all conflicts in *The Living End*, in the capriciousness of God. To see what Elkin implies by his characterization of the Creator, we shall examine His relationship with the principal human characters, a structure that defines contrasting responses to the caprice of absolute power.

"The Conventional Wisdom" focuses on Elkin's most decent human character, a liquor store owner. Ellerbee is a modern Job, a good man subjected to multiple misfortunes. Ellerbee alludes to this when he insists that God justify his damnation: "no Job job, . . . an explanation!" (*LE*, 43). His house was destroyed by fire, and his store, in a deteriorating neighborhood, was robbed twice; one clerk was killed and another permanently disabled. Ellerbee suspects that the robberies were staged by a corporation that buys up failing businesses. Despite his wife's objections, Ellerbee paid medical and funeral expenses and still pays each clerk's salary. Reluctantly he sells the business and opens a new store in a suburban mall. There he is murdered in a holdup, and his last thoughts express his decency; his wife and others have had racist reactions to the robberies, but Ellerbee feels "oddly justified" to see that his assailants are white (*LE*, 18).

By any reasonable ethical standard, a man so compassionate and charitable is a candidate for sainthood. Sadistically Ellerbee gets a guided tour of heaven and, his appetite whetted for eternal bliss, hears this stunningly literal cliché from Saint Peter: "Go to Hell" (*LE*, 30). One nucleus of the Ellerbee story's meaning is the series of technicalities God offers for damning this good man. After sixty-two years in hell, Ellerbee challenges the "Boss of Bullies," "Old Terrorist," "God the Godfather" (*LE*, 41) to justify His ways to him. He learns he is damned for violating certain commandments: he occasionally swore (III), failed to keep the Sabbath (IV), did not honor his parents (V), and once coveted his neighbor's wife (X). He is technically guilty. He kept his store open on Sundays to cover relocation costs, but he simultaneously paid the salaries of two former clerks and retained all the employees at his new location. He was a dutiful son, but God reminds him that he was adopted and could not honor his biological parents because he did not know them. When the beautiful wife of the injured clerk he still supports became amorous in showing her gratitude, Ellerbee developed an erection but resisted this and subsequent advances.

God, then, has a legal right to damn Ellerbee, but that right's being based on technicalities renders the verdict capricious. It seems that Ellerbee's many virtues should outweigh technical violations of selected commandments, but when he presses this argument, God discloses one other reason Ellerbee was damned: "*You thought Heaven looked like a theme park!*" (*LE*, 44). Although he thought this (*LE*, 25–26), no covenant guarantees damnation to everyone who thinks heaven is like Disney World. This seems like more of God's egocentric arbitrariness, but Elkin is foreshadowing the reason for Armageddon in "The State of the Art." Like everyone else, Ellerbee fails to appreciate creation. Trying to express his awe at heaven's beauty, he can only compare the zenith of God's creation with something humanly contrived and banal.

Like Robert Frost's "A Masque of Reason," Ellerbee's story is a modern version of Job's trial. Elkin and Frost question God's capriciousness in victimizing good people for His own inscrutable purposes. The biblical story is an account of trial and reconciliation. Job's faith is tested, and when it does not waver despite many misfortunes, God rewards him with honor and material goods. Ellerbee's is a test of works, not faith. He is not a believer but an ethical man. And his progress is not toward reconciliation but toward alienation. He is furious with God for condemning him, yet his fury exhibits supplication. He prays for God to "kill us, to end Hell, to close the camp" (*LE*, 45). When God refuses, Ellerbee attempts another course of passive defiance: forgiving Ladlehaus, his killer's accomplice.

A major irony of *The Living End* is that Ladlehaus, a petty criminal who advised the killer that Ellerbee "knows too much" to stay alive (*LE*, 20, 21), survives for almost a century and is condemned to exactly the same punishment for his life of crime as Ellerbee was for technical infractions of four commandments. Both are victims of divine caprice. When God visits hell and challenges the rebels to ask questions, someone wisecracks, "Is there Life before Death?" (*LE*, 54), and God banishes Ladlehaus: "He means me, He makes mistakes," but the damned could not hear "God's under-the-breath 'Oops' when He realized His mistake" (*LE*, 57).

Although God is omniscient—He squares the circle, divulges the name of President John Kennedy's assassin, and discloses what was on the gap in the Watergate tapes (*LE*, 137–38)—He is not beyond error. Ladlehaus pays for His error by becoming "the only man in the long sad history of time ever to die" (*LE*, 69), moldering in a grave ridiculously located in a St. Paul high school's athletic complex. There he discovers that not-being is worse than hell's pains. In itself, this indicates that Elkin is not mocking the concept of an afterlife, for Ladlehaus actually misses suffering hell's tortures. Those torments are replaced by insidious, vindictive deceptions practiced on the helpless Ladlehaus by Ellerbee's opposite, a paranoid, hypertensive groundskeeper.

Quiz is as vicious as Ellerbee was kind, yet in the final story Quiz is in heaven and Ellerbee in hell, another indication that the universe of *The Living End* is irrational. Plagued by a dead man talking to him, Quiz develops increasingly nasty strategies to punish Ladlehaus. He urinates on his grave and enlists children to simulate a war between Minneapolis and St. Paul, a deception that causes Ladlehaus to despair because "history had gone out of whack" (*LE*, 71). When the children tire of this play and discuss eternity with Ladlehaus, Quiz drives them away by preying on their superstitions, then mounts, in the most technically complex section of the book, a vicious charade to convince Ladlehaus that he is alive but on life support and has wealth and a beautiful wife to lose by dying. The deception involves a court order to turn off the life support system. When Irene Quiz, playing the nurse, pulls the plug, Ladlehaus loses the false hope Quiz's deception caused him to entertain. The only dead man in the universe dies "once again, and kept on dying, in their presence dying, dying beneath them, with each spike and trough of their laughter" (*LE*, 89).

As Quiz's ethics oppose Ellerbee's, his journey inverts the kind man's.

Ladlehaus, knowing God makes mistakes, takes advantage of God's visiting an amateur musical performance to get revenge on Quiz and God. Unable to prevent God's taking the child Flanoy to heaven because He likes his music, Ladlehaus tells Him Quiz is a composer and "God, who . . . owed Ladlehaus a favor, struck Quiz dead" (*LE*, 95). In hell Quiz reverses Ellerbee's strategy of praying for an end to hell, which would end his and everyone else's suffering. Quiz feels that he alone has a raw deal, that everyone else deserves damnation. He complains constantly and eventually gets relief from his burning. The damned confuse cause and effect and suspect that his complaining is the cause of his coolness, a logic endorsed by one critic who says, "Hell nourishes the obsessive, and Quiz flourishes."[15] With his griping and its apparently consequent reward, Quiz becomes a "miracle" who, believing his complaining caused his relief, is transported to heaven.

Quiz and the damned are wrong. His complaining had little to do with his transformation. Ladlehaus was getting even with Quiz for tormenting him, but he was also getting revenge on God for dismissing him for hell. God regrets having "overreacted" by taking Quiz, so He asks Christ to do "what you do for those other poor bastards. Absolve Me, shrive Me, wipe My slate" (*LE*, 106), and Jesus reluctantly intervenes on Quiz's behalf, not because Quiz complains but because God, while omnipotent, makes mistakes and needs forgiveness.

The universe of *The Living End* is irrational because its origin, God, is omnipotent and omniscient but arbitrary and mercurial. Whatever their ethical positions, men and women must operate within this incoherent ethical framework. In a way, however, the good man has the last word. Although he virtually disappears from the novella early in "The Bottom Line," Ellerbee prayed for an end to hell, and God inadvertently answers this prayer by destroying creation. He does not annihilate creation to grant Ellerbee's wish but for reasons that add one final thematic texture to *The Living End*.

By most religious or mythological standards, God is first and foremost the Creator, defining and organizing laws by which the universe operates. When Elkin's God tells the blessed why He chose covenants as his means of communicating with His people, the explanation suggests many analogies between God and the creative artist, a point developed by several critics.[16] While the blessed fumble to explain the trial-and-error process of a God who "could have gotten it all right the first time, saved everyone trouble and left Hell unstocked" (*LE*, 143), they come up with ethical clichés like "free will" and "goodness," to which God responds, "It was Art! It was always Art. I work by the contrasts and metrics, by beats and the silences. . . . *Because it makes a better story is why*" (*LE*, 144). God created the world to embody an aesthetic that includes human conflict and suffering. This aesthetic may involve injustices like Ellerbee's damnation or Quiz's salvation, but the standard is ultimately aesthetic, not ethical.

Explaining his decision to end creation, God again alludes to an artist's alienation: "Because I never found my audience. . . . You gave me, some of you, your ooh's and aah's, your Jew's hooray and Catholic's Latin deference—all theology's pious wow. But I never found my audience" (*LE*, 148). Worship is not what God wants; he has plenty of that. He wants to be appreciated in terms appropriate to the magnitude of His creation, and no created entity can do that. Ellerbee, that well-intentioned soul, reduced the wonder of heaven to the glitz of a theme park. And if creation exists by the fiat of God, then God logically has a right to terminate it whenever He pleases.

The point *The Living End* makes is daring and the episodes are funny, but it is not satiric. If we conceive of God as God, such alienation and power are beyond our comprehension. If we are incompetent audiences because of our limited capacity to appreciate true wonder, we are certainly not competent to judge ways we cannot even appreciate.

This, Elkin's most popular book, gives convincing proof of his mastery of the novella form and his uncanny ability to amuse, shock, and disturb us profoundly through the medium of charged and funny rhetoric.

Chapter Eight

The Short Stories

Most novelists begin as short story writers, and Elkin, a student at the University of Illinois and a reader at *Accent*, wrote several stories in the 1950s and early 1960s. Many novelists, like Faulkner, Bellow, and Updike, continue to collect stories every few years, whereas others, like Joyce and John Dos Passos, concentrate their energies on the more flexible novel form, so it is tempting to view their work in the short story as apprenticeship toward the novel.

Elkin belongs in the latter camp. His only story collection, *Criers and Kibitzers, Kibitzers and Criers*, appeared in 1966. Since then he has published occasional stories, including "The Graduate Seminar" (1972) and "Corporate Life" (1985), in magazines. In 1985 he brought out *Early Elkin*, collecting some early stories.[1] Additionally he served as guest editor and wrote introductions for two collections, *Stories from the Sixties* and *The Best American Short Stories 1980*.

Although he has written relatively few stories, many have received awards, and some are frequently anthologized. Despite this recognition, the short story is not Elkin's ideal form because limitations in space inhibit the author's fully exploring the rhetoric of the story and require comparatively one-dimensional characterization. Elkin's stories are lengthy by the standards of writers like Updike, in itself an indication that the form poses restrictions against which the author chafes. This study contends that Elkin is at his best in more leisurely forms like the novella or the novel. This does not imply that the stories are not worthy of study but merely defines priorities from which any critical study must proceed. Consequently this treatment of the stories is brief, with extended discussion restricted to stories that are frequently anthologized.

The stories differ from Elkin's novels not only in length, scope, and rhetorical inventiveness but in the kinds of characters with which the fictions are concerned. The novels generally treat characters who are exceptional because of their obsessive commitment to a way of being. Feldman's egocentrism in *A Bad Man* traces to his dedication to the art of merchandising, or Gibson's to his desire to communicate with America. Flesh in *The Franchiser* is obsessed with "costuming America," whereas Eddy Bale in *The Magic Kingdom* tries heroically to do something, however zany, about childhood mortality. The heroes of the stories, by contrast, are usually schmucks, ordinary people facing typical human situations. The exception to this rule is "A Poetics for Bullies," Elkin's favorite among his stories. More typical is the hero of "On a Field, Rampant," who believes he is royally born and searches for his kingdom and regal acceptance but refuses at his existential crisis to accept a proletarian role as spokesman to the powerful about the misery of the disadvantaged. Richard Preminger in "Among the Witnesses" stays at a Catskill resort after being discharged from the army in order "to get laid in Jewish . . . to abandon himself" (*CK*, 73), but having witnessed a child's drowning that may involve negligence by the lifeguard and the resort owner, decides to find a job and ask Norma, a very conventional Jewish girl, to marry him. The narrator of "Cousin Poor Lesley and the Lousy People" cannot assimilate his memories of a childhood group, the lousy people, whose charismatic leader became an institutionalized catatonic, whereas Lesley, a schmuck from a "Certified Public Accountant family" (*CK*, 220), joined the marines, and was killed. The anthropologist of "Perlmutter at the East Pole," probably the supporting character from *Boswell*, has collected data from all over the world to "close in on the truth" (*CK*, 257) in New York City, only to become one of the Sunday morning nuts who give speeches about their private obsessions in Union Square.

Except for "A Poetics for Bullies" and "The Guest," the stories are more realistic or mimetic than Elkin's novels. Most were written before 1965, when the Joyce and Hemingway legacy of realism in the short story was in vogue and before the radical innovations of John Barth, Donald Barthelme, and Robert Coover altered the genre. In Elkin's stories, an ordinary man faces an oppressive but identifiable reality and usually succumbs to it.[2] This situation produces characteristic Jewish-American art in the title story, which defines the range of characters in the collection as criers, "earnest, complaining with a peculiar vigor, . . . their despair articulate, . . . their sorrow something they could expect no one to understand" (*CK*, 13–14), and kibitzers, "deaf to grief, . . . their voices high-pitched in kidding or lowered in conspiracy" (*CK*, 14). The hero discovers limitations in each existential view: "The criers, ignorant of hope, the *kibitzers*, ignorant of despair" (*CK*, 35).

Because Jake Greenspahn operates a grocery facing reversals, the title story anticipates the masterful treatments of merchandisers in *A Bad Man*, *The Franchiser*, and the Ellerbee sections of *The Living End*. Greenspahn is not, however, the enthusiastic entrepreneur Feldman or Flesh will be. He is so burdened by the demands of his store that he seriously considers selling the business. He sees merchandise not as an opportunity to sell but as endless accumulation: "That much less to sell, he thought bitterly. It was endless. You could never liquidate" (*CK*, 17). He feels antipathy toward his customers, especially an elderly lady who buys only loss leaders and a physician's wife who tries to cheat him, whom he eventually throws out of the store. He feels alienated from his employees, the most competent of whom he fires over Frank's shaking down a shoplifter. His butcher and cashier are having an affair, and the fact that his business associates know about it embarrasses Jake.

Greenspahn is thus Feldman's opposite. The "bad man" of the novel is a consummate hustler who enjoys manipulating customers and employees and sees merchandise as a challenge to his energy. Greenspahn's only Feldman-like quality is spitefully parking his car in front of a competitor's store to make customers' access difficult. Greenspahn recalls the struggling shopkeeper of Jewish-American fiction, like the saintly grocer in Malamud's *The Assistant* or the seething hero of Edward Lewis Wallant's *The Pawnbroker*. Greenspahn's repressed rage and misery, both symbolized by his constipation, may combine the qualities of these characters. Certainly this story is Elkin's principal contribution to Jewish-American fiction.

This association is reinforced by the overwhelming grief over his son's death that brings Jake's frustration with his business into focus. His deliberately repressing Harold's theft from the cash register is also associated with the dominant symbol, his constipation, but in a dream he must come to terms with his son's cheating. This stealing is a blow to Jake's self-esteem because he built the business for his family and sees this behavior as an insult to everything he has created: "When Harold was alive was it any different? No, . . . he knew plenty then too. But it didn't make as much difference. . . . Now there wasn't any reason to put up with it" (*CK*, 9). With Harold alive and with hope for a future, he could put up with the criers, kibitzers, and podlers (thieves) who make up his world, but without hope for the future he cannot accept a universe of whiners, jokers, and cheaters.

Greenspahn becomes partially reconciled with the radical imperfection of his world in a dream that takes place significantly in shul. Praying for Harold, he comes to terms with the waste of his death: "twenty-three years old, wifeless, jobless, . . . leaving the world with his life not started" (*CK*, 36). More importantly he accepts Harold's guilt and, with it, by implication, that of his customers and employees, all of whom he must forgive in order to forgive his son. Although the reconciliation is not complete, it is a step toward accepting the world as it is.

This is more than the hero of "I Look Out for Ed Wolfe" can do. Ed's problem is alienation, symbolized in the story by his obsession with being an orphan, an insistence that leads some critics to treat orphanhood as a central

Elkin motif.[3] For Wolfe, being an orphan means lacking an inherited identity and defining his worth in the material or vocational terms the culture offers. While working as a loan collector, he has an identity. Fired for doing his job too vigorously—his boss says he approached the collection game like "an artist. You had a real thing for the deadbeat soul. . . . But Ed, you're a gangster" (*CK*, 43)—Wolfe faces the crisis that without deadbeats to bully around, he has no identity. Both a chiropractor and his boss advise him to "look out for Ed Wolfe" (*CK*, 38, 44), but with neither a history of parental care nor a job to do, there is no one to look out for Wolfe except Ed.

How he looks out for Ed Wolfe introduces another thematic link among these stories, again excepting "A Poetics for Bullies." Ed begins to divest himself of his possessions, much as Greenspahn wishes to liquidate his inventory—an extreme contrast to the acquisitiveness of the heroes in the novels, especially Feldman and Flesh. In Wolfe's case, however, the liquidation is not an effort to divorce himself from the burden of material things but an attempt to convert the concept of selfhood into cash equivalency. Feeling that as he sells his possessions he sells himself, he discovers a new role as a "born salesman," a "disposer, a natural dumper" (*CK*, 49), and he associates the possessions he sells or pawns with elements of himself. Cashing in his life insurance becomes selling his future, selling his books means selling his mind, and so forth until he has only "my things" (*CK*, 53) to sell. When he has disposed of his inventory, he places a bitter value on his identity: "That was the going rate for orphans in a wicked world. Something under $2500" (*CK*, 55).

At this point in its development, "I Look Out for Ed Wolfe" is a story of the first order of importance, a skilled and searing inquiry into ways in which a capitalistic culture distorts human worth into material equivalencies. Elkin, however, told me he regards the ending as "contrived. Nobody would throw money away." The ending, while theatrical, works on two symbolic levels. First, Ed, living on his principal, finds his assets, and therefore his self-esteem, diminishing at an alarming rate. He is looking for an opportunity to gamble his remaining worth in the hope of accumulating more when he meets Oliver, a black man who reads the *Wall Street Journal* in hotel lobbies because it "looks good for the race" (*CK*, 59). He asks the desk clerk, the bell captain, and Oliver the same question, "Where's the action?" (*CK*, 56–57). His accompanying Oliver to a black club, aware that he may be walking into trouble (*CK*, 60), suggests a more intimate kind of gambling, in which what is at stake is his life as well as his self-esteem.

That Ed is gambling with his life receives support from the second symbolic level on which the ending works: his antagonistic identification with the blacks in Oliver's club. An orphan who may be Jewish, he sees himself as an outcast but also recognizes that black people are outcasts in a predominantly white society:[4] "An orphan's like a nigger" because he "doesn't have to bother with love" (*CK*, 65). Telling Roberta Mary he is a "salesman" and "pusher" (*CK*, 63), he ignores his former boss LaMeck's advice, "detachment and caution" (*CK*, 44, 64), and outrages the blacks by attempting to sell Roberta Mary in a parody of a slave auction. When no one bids, he throws his money to the crowd to purchase her. The gesture is theatrical, insulting, and suicidal, but as he dismisses Roberta Mary he sees, in her rich brown hand, "his own pale hand, lifeless and serene, still and infinitely free" (*CK*, 66). Is Ed free because he has virtually committed suicide? Is he free because giving away his money frees him from the illusion that he can calculate his worth in monetary terms? Or is he free because the parody of the slave auction was a transference of his equation of material value with human worth onto this woman, and, by extension, black people in general? Each of these possibilities may be true, and therein lies the rich ambiguity of "I Look Out for Ed Wolfe."

A different kind of liquidation energizes "In the Alley," in which Feldman (not the hero of *A Bad Man*; many early stories, including "The Party" and "A Sound of Distant Thunder," feature heroes named Feldman) discovers that his problem is not mortality in the abstract but a diagnosed terminal illness. After his optimal life expectancy has passed, he has to decide what to do with his death, how to confront it and thereby validate his life, but he learns that conventional formulas for facing death are fitted for abstractions, not for real death. He tries several strategies to endure his mortality: heroic suffering, which would be a sacrifice for his family, ignorant of the seriousness of his illness; patient endurance, but he cannot cope with the fact that family members take his imminent not-being more literally than he has; a community of the dying, in which he enters a hospital to share his death with those like him but finds that they are unable to suffer like gentlemen, so he "blackballs" himself from this "fraternity among the sick" (*CK*, 140).

He chooses his death in an ethnic bar in a factory neighborhood, when a young woman confuses, as Feldman has, his desire to tell her about his dying with lust, and she and her friends beat him unconscious, then leave him in an alley to die a victim of ethnic prejudice. Annie made anti-Semitic comments (*CK*, 146), and his tormentors pin a sign to the dying Feldman, "STAY AWAY FROM WHITE [non-Jewish] WOMEN" (*CK*, 151, 152). His death was inevitable, but he moves beyond romantic posturing about dying for others and in a way chooses his mode of death. One critic says he "outwits the terminal disease that was supposed to kill him by actively seeking a different death,"[5] perhaps overstating his intentionally seeking death by beating and underestimating the degree to which his cancer forces him into the bar but perceptively indicating that this scene suggests that even a dying, powerless man has some choice about his life and its end.

Another story about choice is the more experimental "The Guest," in which Bertie, a moocher and failed jazz musician who invokes Charlie Parker as his hero, occupies and then trashes the St. Louis apartment of Richard and Norma Preminger, thoroughly domesticated incarnations of the characters in "Among the Witnesses." Energized by dependency but holding off despair by cherishing a poison he will use to commit suicide, Bertie concludes that the Will is not merely free: "Free? Hell, it's positively *loose!*" (*CK*, 112). He scrupulously rations his drug intake and fantasizes about power as a scientific researcher, a rental agent, the cop who harasses his enemy Klaff, and a soldier in a foxhole. Stoned on his last narcotic, he learns the meaning of life from a Chinaman he sees in a vision, but trying to tell a friend about it on the telephone, he forgets what life means. He is contemplating suicide and the effect this will have on his friends when the apartment is robbed. He decides to claim the robber's identity and thus give his failed life meaning: "How they would marvel! . . . How they hounded you if you took something away from them!" (*CK*, 126). He expects to be caught, perhaps to become a prisoner like his nemesis Klaff, but in the outlaw's role he will force the Premingers to take notice of him, not to treat him with the condescension he has sought up to this point.

Elkin's art as a short story writer is impressive, even if he has not produced a large number of stories. His best, however, gives a clear preface to the genius he lavishes upon his novels. "A Poetics for Bullies" is more technically innovative than the other stories in *Criers and Kibitzers, Kibitzers and Criers*, if not as daring as "The Graduate Seminar," which evolved from a review of an Anthony Burgess book. Elkin attributed his remarks on Burgess to the character "Professor" and created a context around this character.

Like *Boswell* and *The Rabbi of Lud*, "A Poetics for Bullies" is an experiment in voice. Whereas Elkin uses irony in the novels to criticize his narrators' attitudes, in "Poetics" he uses a startling literalism to endorse the values of Push, his hero, and thereby achieves thematic richness. Push is, like Feldman, a "bad adolescent," a bully who sees it as his vocation to be a "chink seeker, a wheeler dealer in the flawed cement of the personality, a collapse maker" (*CK*, 206)—someone whose life's work is to rub his associates' imperfections in their faces.

Despite the fact that the story originated in an unpleasant experience Elkin's son Phil had with a neighborhood bully who promised to return two arrows if Phil let him hold one, then broke the arrow in half,[6] a prank Push executes in the story, and despite the fact that antagonist John Williams is based on the hero of "On a Field, Rampant," Elkin intends the reader to empathize with Push's values. This is not easy to do, for Push is a manipulator and his vocation springs from envy. He "loves[s] nobody loved" (*CK*, 197) and executes his bullying because he envies qualities his schoolmates have. He compensates for his feelings of inadequacy by reminding others of their imperfections: "Nothing could ever be forgiven, and I forgave nothing. I held them to the mark" (*CK*, 206).

Although his bullying is a compensation for low self-esteem, Push operates by a curious set of rules. He will not use physical force to intimidate his victims and has given up training because "strength implicates you"; those who use size or strength are not bullies at all but "*athletes*" practicing a "sport" (*CK*, 197–98). He uses cunning and charisma, "sleight-of-mouth, the bully's poetics" (*CK*, 199), and thus the story's title and one element of Push's appeal can be explained. "Poetics" describes the craft by which an artist works, and Push is figuratively an artist, someone who knows there "*is* no magic. If there were I would learn it" (*CK*, 198), but he operates within a limited medium—the restrictions he voluntarily places on his bullying—to affect his environment. Until he meets Williams, his bullying produces unexpectedly benevolent consequences: "Who else cared about the fatties, about the dummies and slobs and clowns, about the gimps and squares and oafs and fools, the kids with a mouthful of mush, all those shut-ins of the mind and heart, all those losers?" (*CK*, 206–7). Most of his victims are losers, but his bullying gives them a sense of importance.

His "poetics" is challenged by the new kid at school, John Williams, a "paragon" (*CK*, 207), a "glass of fashion, mold of form" (*CK*, 208; cf. *Hamlet* 3.1.156), and perpetual do-gooder who embodies every imaginable cliché about adolescent excellence. He is a world traveler, a bon vivant, an exceptional student, the teachers' pet, a gifted athlete, a heartthrob to every girl in school, and a volunteer who dispenses charity to the old, the desperate, the poor, and the slobs and losers Push torments. Williams is without flaw and therefore impervious to Push's tactics. The exemplar of establishment virtue, he anticipates Behr-Bleibtreau's claim to impeccable virtue in *The Dick Gibson Show*, as well as Warden Fisher's gospel that "life is ordinary" in *A Bad Man*.

Push intuitively realizes, however, that Williams is another bully with a different "poetics." Although it appears that he acts selflessly by tutoring the stupid Mimmer, double-dating with the ugly Clob, or teaching the cripple Slud weight lifting, John, like Warden Fisher, forces his paradigm of perfection on those who can only be frustrated by their continued inability to reach

Williams's level of achievement. Until Williams offers to "help" him, Push remains "alone in my envy, awash in my lust" (*CK*, 211). When John tries to bully Push into conformity with his view by helping him "to be happier" (*CK*, 212), Push defies him and asserts his "poetics" against Williams's.

He initially tries to beat Williams at his own game but fails. By forcing a fight, Push hopes to engage John in a no-win situation: if he wins, he will diminish John's reputation for invincibility; by losing, as he expects to ("my strength is as the strength of ten because my jaw is glass!" [*CK*, 213]), he will expose Williams as a bully and, in Push's aesthetic, a mere "athlete." Williams is too adept in fighting and postcombat etiquette to fall into this trap, so Push discovers "real magic at last" (*CK*, 216) in that reserve of untouchable selfhood that is the core of Elkin's heroes in the novels: "I will not be reconciled, or halve my hate. *It's* what I have, all I can keep. My bully's sour solace. It's enough, I'll make do. . . . *I push through*" (*CK*, 217). Refusing to submit to Williams's poetics of bullying, Push has validated his own and has asserted that intractable selfhood central to Elkin's theme and aesthetic.

It is tempting to speculate that had he continued to write stories, Elkin might have become a master of that form. His stories are often brilliantly conceived and executed, and the best among them, especially "A Poetics for Bullies," "I Look Out for Ed Wolfe," and "Criers and Kibitzers, Kibitzers and Criers," make an important contribution to the short fiction of the 1960s. But his talents lay in the more flexible novel form, and his achievements there compensate more than fully for any loss we might project in the medium of short fiction. We may therefore look upon the stories as aesthetically satisfying preparations for his life's achievement as a novelist—the work of a most precocious apprentice.

Conclusion

Over three decades, Stanley Elkin has been associated with many groups of writers. He has seemed to various readers a satirist, a black humorist, an absurdist, a comic novelist, a Jewish-American writer, a cultural cataloger, and a metafictionist. He prefers to be considered an individual artist, concerned with his unique styles and methods of communicating his vision. While any of these labels describes elements of his art, his work almost successfully resists categorization. Although he has not attracted a wide general readership, he enjoys great respect among his fellow novelists as an innovator and as a distinguished voice. He continues to make his presence felt in contemporary American fiction through his unique rhetoric, worldview, and wit.

When asked about his fiction, Elkin invariably encourages the image of himself as a wordsmith, a craftsman of metaphors, sentences, paragraphs, and catalogs. Almost any page from any novel yields unexpected rhetorical treasures. The quotations I have analyzed were chosen to illustrate themes or developments central to the work under discussion, but except in rare cases—like the final paragraph of *The Franchiser* and that ending the scene at Shipwreck Marsh in *The Magic Kingdom*—alternatives as splendid could have been chosen. Virtually every rhetorical tactic available to writers—from the cliché given new life by its literalism, though outrageous puns, to subtle allusions—energizes the rhetoric of his works.

Elkin's comments on the priority of rhetoric in his work may mask the subtlety and craft with which he manages his language to develop a cohesive and often profound picture of our shared human condition. His comments on the priority of rhetoric in his fiction, especially early in the 1970s, may have discouraged critics from approaching his fiction thematically. In 1989, however, he told me he considers himself a "philosophic" novelist who, while not as preoccupied with abstractions as Saul Bellow, is concerned with ways in which our thinking affects our being. His preoccupation with the ordinary vocations of people who become extraordinary because of their commitment to their occupations contributes to the philosophic richness of his work and exhibits a unique approach to the vocations by which many contemporary Americans earn their livings and to some degree define their lives.

Finally, Elkin discourages critics' calling him a "comic" novelist. He does not wish for his fiction to be equated with the routines of stand-up comics like Lenny Bruce or George Carlin, neither of whose brand of humor he likes. He is not just a one-liner comic, and as he told me, he rejects the label because he feels that there is more to his fiction than humor. Rhetorical intensity and philosophic richness are at the heart of his fiction, but this is nonetheless one very funny novelist. His hyperbolic characters, the madcap situations their obsessions impose upon them, and the verbal humor with which the novelist comments on both yield the full, rich, cleansing laugh provided by delight in incongruity, an outrageous pun, or an unexpected allusion. Readers who delight in humor put to serious purposes should read Elkin for the pure joy of laughing out loud in a world where occasions for uninhibited laughter are increasingly hard to come by.

Rhetoric, theme, humor: they unite in mystery, the core of Elkin's artistic vision. His advice to writers applies to anyone who wants to connect with the universe through that uniquely human medium, language: "Let men make good sentences. Let them learn to spell the sound of the waterfall and the noise of the bathwater. Let us get down the colors of the baseball gloves—the difference in shade between the centerfielder's deep pocket and the discreet indentation of the catcher's mitt. And let us refine tense so that men may set their watches by it. . . . Let us enlist in Vocabulary, Syntax, the high grammar of the mysterious world."[1] This magnificently defines the novelist's purpose: to reveal for us through language the richness of nature (waterfalls) and of pedestrian uses human beings make of matter (bathwater); to differentiate subtly among the things we make and use (baseball gloves); to give us what Ezra Pound called "our address in time"[2] by refining tense; and all the while to reveal the mystery that exists constantly in the world around us.

The "high grammar of the mysterious world" is what Elkin has been writing about since *Boswell*, and it is probably what *The MacGuffin* is about as well. With a recruitment officer like Stanley Elkin, only a fool would wait to be drafted into that high grammar.

Notes and References

Chapter One

1. Three critics use *midfiction* to describe Elkin's middle ground. See Alan Wilde, "'Strange Displacements of the Ordinary': Apple, Elkin, Barthelme and the Problem of the Excluded Middle," *Boundary 2* 10 (1981):182; Charles Molesworth, "Stanley Elkin and 'Everything': The Problem of Surfaces and Fullness in the Novels," *Delta* 20 (February 1985):93–109; and Peter Bailey, *Reading Stanley Elkin* (Urbana: University of Illinois Press, 1985), 190–92.

2. Scott Sanders, "An Interview with Stanley Elkin," *Contemporary Literature* 16 (1975):132–33. In another interview that year, Elkin says his style is artificial but adds, "All style, all style, is artificial," and "I sincerely believe that the sentence is its own excuse for being." Phyllis Bernt and Joseph Bernt, "Stanley Elkin on Fiction: An Interview," *Prairie Schooner* 50 (1975):16.

3. Stanley Elkin, "Three Meetings," *Tri-Quarterly* 63 (Spring–Summer 1985):155–59. Reprinted from *Tri-Quarterly* 17 (Winter 1970). In 1989 Elkin told me he does not consider Nabokov an important influence on him; he could recall reading only three Nabokov books.

4. Doris R. Bargen, "Appendix: An Interview with Stanley Elkin," in *The Fiction of Stanley Elkin* (Frankfurt: Peter D. Lang, 1980), 224; Stanley Elkin and Shannon Ravenel, eds., *The Best American Short Stories 1980* (Boston: Houghton Mifflin, 1980), xiii; Stanley Elkin, "My Father's Life," *Chicago* 36 (June 1987):186. Elkin fondly remembers his father in several interviews, most notably Thomas LeClair, "Stanley Elkin: The Art of Fiction LXI," *Paris Review* 17 (1976):68, and Richard B. Sale, "An Interview with Stanley Elkin in St. Louis," *Studies in the Novel* 16 (1984):324. Contrast Jay Clayton, "An Interview with Stanley Elkin," *Contemporary Literature* 24 (1983):10: "Quite the most interesting man I've ever known. . . . But he was so special that he scared me. I tried to *be* him."

5. LeClair, "Art of Fiction," 57. Elkin also treats the bungalow in his introduction to *Best American Short Stories 1980*, xii–xiii.

6. Sale, "Interview," 322–23. Elkin tells the same story in Bargen, *Fiction*, 221–22, concluding, "I guess that's what made me a writer. Otherwise, I would have been a kind of Sunday writer."

7. "An Interview with Stanley Elkin," *AWP Newsletter* (February–March 1988):12. See also Bargen, *Fiction*, 245.

8. Stanley Elkin, "Why I Live Where I Live," *Esquire* 94 (November 1980):108.

9. "Interview," *AWP Newsletter*, 1.

10. Bernt and Bernt, "Elkin on Fiction," 22–23. Bargen, *Fiction*, makes a de-

tailed case for the kind of Jewish-American writer Elkin is in her first chapter. She also discusses this issue in *Dictionary of Literary Biography*, vol. 28: *Twentieth-Century American-Jewish Writers*, ed. David Walden (Detroit: Gale Research/ Bruccoli, 1984), 47–50, proposing, "In the course of Elkin's career, Jewishness has become increasingly vestigial" and "One might, from the biographical facts, have expected stronger ties."

11. Sanders, "Interview," 140; "Interview," *AWP Newsletter*, 12.

12. Melvin Raff, "Wyndham Lewis and Stanley Elkin: Salvation, Satire, and Hell," *Studies in Contemporary Satire* 8 (Spring 1981):1–8.

13. Sanders, "Interview," 135. In 1989 Elkin told me he dislikes satire because it places the author in an unearned moral position. He agreed, however, that certain minor characters or situations in his books may have satiric implications.

14. LeClair, "Art of Fiction," 70, and "Interview," *AWP Newsletter*, 13. Elkin rejects this label often; he "resents" the term in Sanders, "Interview," 142, and hopes he has "kicked away" the label in Sale, "Interview," 316.

15. Philip Roth, "Writing American Fiction," *Commentary* 31 (March 1961): 223–33, and Bruce Jay Friedman, "Black Humor," in *Black Humor* (New York: Bantam Books, 1965). Both are reprinted in Edward Quinn and Paul J. Dolan, eds., *The Sense of the Sixties* (New York: Free Press, 1968), 445–61, 435–39. Alfred Kazin analyzes "The Guest" as black humor in *Bright Book of Life: American Novelists and Story-tellers from Hemingway to Mailer* (New York: Delta, 1974), 258–59.

16. Robert Scholes, "Metafiction," *Iowa Review* 1 (1970):100; Larry McCaffrey, "The Art of Metafiction: William Gass's *Willie Masters' Lonesome Wife*," *Critique* 18 (1976):22; Bargen, *Fiction*, 36–37. A seminal discussion is William Gass, *Fiction and the Figures of Life* (New York: Vintage, 1970, 1972), especially the title essay and "Philosophy and the Form of Fiction."

17. Marc Chénetier, "An Interview with Stanley Elkin," *Delta* 20 (February 1985):16.

Chapter Two

1. Reviewers judging *Mills* Elkin's best novel to date include: Jeff Clark, *Library Journal*, 1 September 1982, 1676; Thomas LeClair, *New Republic*, 27 December 1982, 38; William Plummer, *Newsweek*, 25 October 1982, 118; and R. Z. Sheppard, *Time*, 1 November 1982, 79. Representing those disappointed with *Mills*: Leslie Epstein, *New York Times Book Review*, 11 October 1982, 11, 30; Josh Rubins, *New York Review of Books*, 16 December 1982, 47; and Frances Taliaferro, *Harper's Magazine* 265 (November 1982):75, who recognizes a major breakthrough but prefers the "'pre-breakthrough' novels of this eccentric virtuoso."

2. See Clayton, "Interview," 11–12 and Robert Earlywine, "An Interview with Stanley Elkin," *Webster Review* 8 (1983):16. In one interview, *Boswell* is his only novel then in print (1975) which Elkin does not consider a candidate for his best work to date: Bargen, *Fiction*, 222–23. In a 1989 conversation, he reiterated that *Mills*, his "story factory," remains his favorite.

3. Stanley Elkin, *George Mills* (New York: Dutton, 1983), 6; hereafter cited in the text as *GM*.

4. The Janissaries were defeated in 1826 after a lengthy campaign by Emperor Mahmud II, whom Mills visits. Realizing they had overthrown five sultans between 1622 and 1807 and executed three, including his father, Mahmud recruited a core of Western troops. The Janissaries rose in 1826 to oppose these troops but were defeated and a "corps, which for over four centuries had been the terror of Europe—and of its own masters—ceased to exist. *Encyclopaedia Britannica* (Chicago: William Benton, 1971), 12:872–73. Elkin's description of *devshirme*, or recruiting captive children (*GM*, 370), is accurate, but the practice ended about a century before George's captivity. Designating Janissary officers as "Meat Cut" or "Soup Man" is also historical. Elkin was inspired to write about the Janissaries while reading Michael Arlen's autobiographical *Passage to Ararat* (New York: Farrar, Straus & Giroux, 1975).

5. Stanley Elkin, *Boswell: A Modern Comedy* (1964; New York: Dutton Obelisk, 1986), 172; hereafter cited in the text as *B*.

6. Compare Robert Morace, "*George Mills*," in *Magill's Literary Annual 1983*, ed. Frank Magill (Englewood Cliffs, N.J.: Salem, 1983), 1:275: "the Mills history has no status other than as fiction, as family myth."

7. See Michael Connaughton, "Stanley Elkin," in *Critical Survey of Long Fiction*, ed. Frank Magill (Englewood Cliffs, N.J.: Salem Press, 1983), 8:889; Doris Bargen, "Stanley Elkin," in *Dictionary of Literary Biography*, vol. 2: *American Novelists since World War II*, ed. Jeffrey Helterman and Richard Layman (Detroit: Gale Research/Bruccoli, 1978), 132–33; and Francine O. Hardaway, "The Power of the Guest: Stanley Elkin's Fiction," *Rocky Mountain Review* 32 (1978):237. Chapter 1 discusses Elkin's rejecting the satirist label.

8. LeClair, "Art of Fiction," 76, 78–79. A shorter version appears in Sanders, "Interview," 145.

9. D. B. Wyndham Lewis, *James Boswell: A Short Life* (London: Eyre and Spottswoode, 1952), 25; Frederick A. Pottle, *James Boswell: The Earlier Years 1740–1769* (New York: McGraw-Hill, 1966), 134, 183.

10. James Boswell, *The Life of Samuel Johnson, L.L.D.*, intro. Herbert Askith, based on Malone's 6th ed. (New York: Modern Library, n.d.), 357.

11. LeClair, "Art of Fiction," 77.

12. Ibid., 58: "When I was about a hundred pages into *Boswell*, I suddenly discovered that I had . . . a lot of elevators, and because I had been trained in the New Criticism I decided, hey, this is pretty neat!"

13. Elkin calls James's attitude "phony allegory. Boswell . . . sees death absolutely everywhere, even in this kind of theatrical Broadway character named John Sallow. . . . It's a parody of Boswell's obsession with death. John Sallow is just another pretty face." Bargen, *Fiction*, 233. This implies that Sallow has not accepted the metaphor; the text is less definitive on this point.

14. LeClair, "Art of Fiction," 78.

15. Bailey, *Reading Elkin*, 201–2, suggests that each Mills represents a division of the cultural enterprise. Greatest Grandfather is *"homo religiousus"*; nineteenth-century Mills is*" "homo politicus"*; contemporary George is *"homo psychologicus."*

16. Elkin told me an inspiration for *Mills* was his learning about Wieliczka from the documentary *The Ascent of Man.*

17. As in the Janissary episodes, Elkin draws loosely on recorded history. King George's secret 1785 marriage with Lady Fitzherbert, a Catholic, was disallowed because of the Settlement Act (1701) and the Royal Marriage Act (1772), both of which Elkin mentions. The Dickensian solicitor and the king's "faithfulness" to Maria are Elkin's inventions. See Sir Charles Petrie's entry in *Encyclopedia Americana*, international ed. (Danbury: Grolier, 1988), 12:511–12.

18. Epstein, *New York Times Book Review*, 11, 30, complains that Elkin fails to emphasize sufficiently Judith's heroic struggle. Quite the contrary: he treats her struggle as very heroic but does not minimize her nastiness to do so. Epstein seems to miss the point; Judith's being a difficult person forces Mills to test his potential.

19. Bailey, *Reading Elkin*, 201, suspects that she means to tempt Mills to kill her by leaving money in the hotel room.

20. Compare Morace, *"George Mills,"* 276: "These understated signs of affection and compassion contrast with the reader's earlier view of Mills as a man unwilling or unable to love." Elkin, however, resisted attributing heroism to Mills's action when we discussed the book: "I found a lot of it touching too, but I wouldn't say that that makes him a person who's lived long enough to know something or do something well."

21. Stanley Elkin, "Religious Themes and Symbolism in the Novels of William Faulkner" (Ph.D. diss., University of Illinois, 1961), 300. The sentence describes Elkin's mature technique perfectly: treating character hyperbolically, he manages to stay clear of parody. Two reviewers noted Faulkner echoes in *Mills*: Clark, 1676: "writing like some stand-up Faulkner," and LeClair, *New Republic*, 38: "the means are no less than Faulknerian." Bailey, *Reading Elkin*, 194, 200, obliquely notes Faulkner echoes in *Mills*.

22. Elkin confirmed this when we discussed the novel and acknowledged extensive debts to eighteenth-century styles and, especially, Faulkner: "You're thinking of the *Absalom, Absalom!* business. And so was I."

23. Bailey, *Reading Elkin*, 211, sees this differently: belief in a sister is an illusion, or "padding" like what Mills used to move furniture, protecting him against acknowledging that "the fate will never be lifted."

24. William H. Gass, "Adventures in the Writing Life," *Washington Post Book World*, 10 October 1982, 10. Elkin tells Gass he too feels this kind of grace. Other instances from the novel include "in grace, out of harm's way" (220); to Judith's daughter (286); in the story of his meeting Louise (291); he caught grace "like a cold" (294); and "he was stuck in his grace like a ship sunk in the sea" (506). Elkin told me, however, that George invented the state of grace whimsically to resist Louise's sexual advances, then began to believe in it.

Chapter Three

1. See William H. Gass, Foreword to *The Franchiser* (Boston: Nonpareil, 1980), vii–ix; also published as "Stanley Elkin's *The Franchiser*," *New Republic*, 28 June 1980, 29–32. Other thoughtful discussions of vocation include Thomas LeClair, "The Obsessional Fiction of Stanley Elkin," *Contemporary Literature* 16 (1974):146–62, and Robert Edward Colbert, "The American Salesman as Pitchman and Poet in the Fiction of Stanley Elkin," *Critique* 21 (1980):52–58.

2. Emily Stipes Watts, *The Businessman in American Literature* (Athens: University of Georgia Press, 1982), 142.

3. Chapter 1 discusses Elkin's dismissing the label satirist. One critic, aware of his comments about satire, argues that in *The Franchiser*, "What sounds like the enthusiastic celebration of a modern consumer culture and the franchiser's glorious quest to homogenize and democratize America . . . may actually be an American dream cast in irony and gone astray." Doris G. Bargen, "The Orphan Adopted: Stanley Elkin's *The Franchiser*," *Studies in American Jewish Literature* 2 (1982): 132. Colbert, "American Salesman," 54, however, sees Elkin's catalogs of consumer culture as celebrations: *The Franchiser* and *The Dick Gibson Show* "present from time to time a Whitmanesque celebration of American scope and greatness, a loving embrace of the range of our life and culture, but . . . these panegyrics and apostrophes, catalogs and apotheoses, are all broadcast on a comic frequency."

4. Stanley Elkin, *A Bad Man* (1967; New York: Dutton Obelisk, 1985), 226; hereafter cited in the text as *ABM*.

5. Stanley Elkin, *The Franchiser* (1976; Boston: Nonpareil, 1980), 164; hereafter cited in the text as *TF.*

6. Bernt and Bernt, "Elkin on Fiction," 25; Clayton, "Interview," 9; Sanders, "Interview," 139.

7. Clayton, "Interview," 3. See also Bernt and Bernt, "Elkin on Fiction," 14: "I don't think that my characters are lost at all. I think they have very specific goals, and whether those goals mesh with my goals or yours is not really material. They know what they want. They are driven men."

8. See Raymond M. Olderman, *Beyond the Waste Land: American Fiction in the Nineteen-Sixties* (New Haven: Yale University Press, 1973), 52–71: in *Cuckoo's Nest*, we can tell good from evil, but in *A Bad Man* "the world is an inverted mad waste land where only radical and violent responses can prove a man's humanity, but also an intensified fear that there are no distinctions . . . between good and evil." Compare Naomi Lebowitz, *Humanism and the Absurd in the Modern Novel* (Evanston: Northwestern University Press, 1971), 126: Feldman is "conceived as a cluster of rhetorical attributes and actually a parody of a bad man (the moral competition between good and evil is simply the deck of cards)." Bargen, *Fiction*, 113, compares Nurse Ratched and the Warden as figures of oppression, hostile to the imagination and the spirit of adventure.

9. Bargen, *Fiction*, 117. Despite objecting to Olderman's reading, Bargen approximates his thesis—that Feldman is a "modern version of the Grail Knight," a

traditional Christ substitute. See Olderman, *Beyond the Waste Land*, 61–63, 67. Connaughton, "Stanley Elkin," 889, notes the "heavily allegorical" nature of the prison and conflict. In an interview, Elkin regrets the allegorical names Freedman, Victman, and Dedman and wishes he could change them but stands by Feldman ("the felled man") and Fisher ("the fisher of bad men, as Christ was the fisher of good men"). Bargen, *Fiction*, 234. Feldman, the central character's name in several early stories, is Elkin's mother's maiden name, but these facts do not inhibit its allegorical significance in *A Bad Man*.

10. John Ditsky, "'Death Grotesque as Life': The Fiction of Stanley Elkin," *Hollins Critic* 19 (June 1982):6. LeClair, "Obsessional Fiction," 152, makes the excellent points that Fisher's prison resembles Feldman's store, that each runs his province by "compulsive fiat, personal harangue, irrational definitions of policy," and that both treat others, associates or inmates, as clowns or pawns. In an interview, Elkin, perhaps plying double entendre more conspicuously than in the novel, says Fisher, not Feldman, is the "bad man" of the title. He admires Feldman as "a cruel man with style." Bargen, *Fiction*, 240.

11. This scene, combined with the emphasis on the Warden's inability to grow facial hair, lends credibility to Olderman's thesis that the Warden is a "Fisher King" from the grail legends, an impotent ruler in need of a cure, and that Feldman is a "grail knight" with restoring powers. See Olderman, *Beyond the Waste Land*, 52–71. My emphasizing similarities between Fisher and Feldman should indicate that I disagree with Olderman's main thesis.

12. Contrast Bargen, *Fiction*, 115, who sees the episode as analogous to Boswell's wrestling with John Sallow, in that although Feldman cannot read the instructions on the chair, he deludes himself into thinking he can kill himself by manipulating them.

13. The novel was inspired when Elkin's friend Al Lebowitz told him "a sad story about a lawyer pal of his who was about to be put away for a year. . . . And I thought, gee, what would it be like for a middle-class guy to spend a year in a penitentiary?" Sanders, "Interview," 145. In another interview Elkin adds, "So I upped the ante philosophically and asked what would it be like for a man to be sentenced for his character?" LeClair, "Art of Fiction," 79. One critic explains Feldman's calm "anticipation of prison life" as "curiosity to see if he is different from the others, all clearly stripped of families and social cares." Lebowitz, *Humanism and the Absurd*, 128.

14. These episodes confirm Bargen's interpretation that the homunculus is a "vestigial social conscience," but this does not inevitably lead to the conclusion that these episodes mean "that guilt can kill." See Bargen, *Fiction*, 115.

15. Bargen, "Orphan Adopted," 133.

16. This is a disease from which Elkin suffers, a point noted by every serious commentator. He did not originally plan to introduce MS in the book, but "it occurred to me that the breakdown of the nerve impulses, this demyelination, corresponds to the energy crisis in America and the energy crisis in the hero. After I was

about three chapters into the book it suddenly occurred to me to give the guy multiple sclerosis." Bargen, *Fiction*, 223. See also Clayton, "Interview," 9. See Bargen, *Fiction*, 251–52, for further comments associating the disease with the national energy crisis. Discussing this novel, Bargen (124) associates Ben's disease, the mysterious diseases of the Finsbergs, and the national energy crisis.

17. Sale, "Interview," 320. Elkin identifies the Insight Lady in "Why I Live Where I Live," 108. Howard Nemerov credits her with the epigraph for his poem "The Author to His Body on Their Fifteenth Birthday, 29 ii 1980."

18. "The Franchiser," *Fiction* 4 (1975):32–35.

19. Clayton, "Interview," 9–10; Sale, "Interview," 315–16.

20. Bargen, "Orphan Adopted," 133–34.

21. Jeffrey L. Duncan, "A Conversation with Stanley Elkin and William H. Gass," *Iowa Review* 7 (Winter 1976):56.

22. Bargen, "Orphan Adopted," 141.

Chapter Four

1. On Elkin's fascination with radio, see LeClair, "Art of Fiction," 79–82, and Bargen, *Fiction*, 246. On *Gibson*'s origins, see Bargen, *Fiction*, 247.

2. Stanley Elkin, *The Dick Gibson Show* (1970; New York: Dutton, 1983), 11; hereafter cited in the text as *DGS*.

3. Many commentators discuss myth. Raymond M. Olderman, "The Six Crises of Dick Gibson," *Iowa Review* 7 (Winter 1976):127–39, says the implications of Dick's growth are those of America's evolution from the Great Depression through the Vietnam era. Bailey, *Reading Elkin*, 53–98, applies Joseph Campbell's "myth of the hero" and treats the myth of the self-made man, offering the splendid insight that Dick's referring to himself as "poor Dick Gibson" alludes to a truly mythic American figure, Ben Franklin's fictionalizing himself for public consumption as "poor Richard." LeClair, "Obsessional Fiction," 153–55, agrees: "The order is myth, the American myth of success with traces of archetypal themes—humble origin, separation and preparation, obscurity . . . , testing, conquering the enemy, and the final offer of the boon of self to others." Bargen, *Fiction*, 143–62, treats two myths: the American dream and the quest for family bonds and substitutes.

4. Compare the metaphor the "tapestry condition" in *George Mills*, discussed in chapter 2.

5. The scene parallels Feldman's confrontation with the electric chair in *A Bad Man*, discussed in chapter 3. Elkin confirmed privately that all Dick's actions are absurdly dramatized to persuade him he is on the track of greatness. See also his comments on Dick's desire for a mythic life: Sale, "Interview," 317.

6. Critics interpret the Morristown episode variously. Bargen, *Fiction*, 150, emphasizing Miriam's protecting her father from bad news, suggests that Gibson learns from her story ways to deal with his family. Bailey, *Reading Elkin*, 59–63, associates Miriam with the "spiritual helper" of Campbell's monomyth, who by arousing his lust and ministering to his lethargy offers Maine an excuse to avoid the world

after the Nebraska failure. Olderman, "Six Crises," 131–32, compares the Morristown retreat with the "Big Lay-Off," or late depression.

7. Olderman, "Six Crises," 132–35; Bailey, *Reading Elkin*, 66–74; Bargen, *Fiction*, 152.

8. Elkin, however, does not agree that Gibson invented the story. Discussing the dodo episode, he says, "His broadcast attracts the presence of the Japanese, and lots of people are killed. He does, in some way, lead a mythic life." Sale, "Interview," 317. When I hinted at the interpretation that follows, Elkin insisted that the episode, although entirely fictional, did happen. In his view, Dick did not make this up.

9. Bailey, *Reading Elkin*, 69, associates Dick's choice with the Hollywood war movie cliché in which the hero faces court-martial or hazardous assignment.

10. Edwin O. Reischauer, *Japan: The Story of a Nation* (New York: Knopf, 1970), 51. For Mauritius's history, see *Encyclopaedia Britannica* (Chicago, 1972), 14:1129–31. Elkin told me the idea for this section came from a television documentary about the dodos of Mauritius.

11. Bargen, *Fiction*, 246, 259. Elkin reiterated to me his conviction that no magic exists in the episode. He emphasized that when Behr-Bleibtreau claims to be stealing Dick's voice, he is merely choking him.

12. LeClair, "Art of Fiction," 83. Streep's tale appeared as "The Memory Expert," *Esquire* 73 (May 1970):152–54, 175–80.

13. LeClair, "Art of Fiction," 81; see also p. 82: "And he is a hypnotist, exactly the kind of guy Gibson sees as out to get him." The Behr-Bleibtreau episodes are variations on Boswell's investing John Sallow with the attributes of his epithet "The Grim Reaper," discussed in chapter 2. Each invests an adversary with what he most dreads (Boswell, death; Gibson, loss of voice).

14. Olderman, "Six Crises," 130; LeClair, "Obsessional Fiction," 155. Elkin told me he introduced Nixon's call after the novel had been sent to the publisher. The closure was not in his original draft, and he insists that no political motive was intended.

Chapter Five

1. Conversation with Joseph Barger, *New York Times Book Review*, 24 March 1985, 34. An extended version appears in Chénetier, "Interview," 32–33. Elkin reiterated this hesitancy in 1989.

2. Stanley Elkin, *The Magic Kingdom* (New York: E. P. Dutton, 1985), 19; hereafter cited in the text as *MK*. In our conversation, Elkin said, "Since he is England's most famous beggar, he decides to use his power for good. It is a very grotesque good. If I were Eddy Bale, I wouldn't have done it in a million years."

3. After choosing this chapter's title, I discovered these sentences: "Life is precious, even in the bleakest circumstances. So what can you do for dying children?" Lee Lescaze, "Voyage to the End at Disney World," *Wall Street Journal*, 12 April 1985, 26.

4. The phrase, explicitly associated with Matthew Gale, is vintage Elkin. See

DGS, 274, and "Representation and Performance," in *Representation and Performance in Postmodern Fiction*, Proceedings of the 1982 Nice Conference on Postmodern Fiction, ed. Maurice Couturier (Montpelier: Delta, 1982), 188. Because of its frequency in Elkin's writing, and its aptness to this issue, I feel justified in taking it out of context to describe the whole misadventure of *The Magic Kingdom*.

5. Elkin resisted my associating Morehead's theory and Flesh's discovery: "No. He is a superb diagnostician. He's also a loony tune."

6. See Lescaze, "Voyage to the End," 26: "In the end, Mr. Elkin's riposte to the blows of disease and death is procreation. A child dies, have another." See also James Wolcott, "Final Fling," *Vanity Fair* (April 1985):95.

7. Elkin confirmed this intention in conversation: "Well, [Colin's] doing this to show the kids, hey, you're bad off, but who ain't?" The inspiration for this key scene was not his trip to Disney World, as I had supposed, but his long-standing admiration for Diane Arbus's photographs.

8. Elkin may have changed his mind on this point since the time he was writing *The Magic Kingdom*. While composing it, he said, "I hope that by the time I'm through with the book the readers will want those kids to die. Because they're essentially vicious children." Chénetier, "Interview," 32. In 1989, when I said I find Bible the most admirable character in the book, Elkin challenged, "Adult character, you mean?" I took this to mean that he now considers some, if not all, of the children at least as admirable as Bible.

Chapter Six

1. Stanley Elkin, *The Rabbi of Lud* (New York: Charles Scribner's, 1987), 90; hereafter cited in the text as *RL*.

2. Chapter 1 discusses the genesis of *The Rabbi*.

3. Elkin told me, however, that Connie's account of her Chicago adventure is intended to be substantively true, if exaggerated.

4. The first and last points were confirmed by Elkin in conversation. Portions of *The Rabbi* were included in a performance of Mid America Dance Company, with Elkin reading "Notes toward a Eulogy for Joan Cohen" while dancers interpreted this text visually. See "The Muses Are Heard: Dancing in the Heart of the Regional Arts," *Harper's* 277 (December 1988):64, 70.

Chapter Seven

1. Preface to Stanley Elkin, *Searches and Seizures* (Boston: David R. Godine, 1980 [c. 1973]); hereafter cited in the text as *SS*.

2. LeClair, "Art of Fiction," 84; LeClair, "Obsessional Fiction," 161.

3. LeClair, "Art of Fiction," 86. Bailey, *Reading Elkin*, 154, offers the excellent insight that these teeth remind Main of "untempered ferocity" he finds missing in the modern world, while other bondsmen, at lunch, devise strategies to deal with Bail Reform Act "leniency" and "compassion."

4. These odd names were suggested by automobile license plates. That assigned Elkin's auto was either OYP or GLYP. He saw the other on a British car. Conversation, 1989. Bargen, *Fiction*, 171, 298n, heard a similar story and notes that the names "resemble those of cavemen in popular literature."

5. Compare Wilde, *Horizons*, 130–31, who sees this pursuit as "another symbolic gesture" that will provide Main with "wonder and delight" as the "zestful detective at a new boundary."

6. This concept is treated more fully, as it applies to *The Franchiser* and *A Bad Man*, in chapter 3.

7. E. E. Cummings, *Poems 1923–1954* (New York: Harcourt, Brace, and World, 1954), 195.

8. Compare Harry C. Erdinger, "Bears in Three Contemporary Fictions," *Humanities Association Review* 28 (1976):143–44, 150: "Marriage with Jane would plunge Brewster into a pit of complete self-absorption." See also Bailey, *Reading Elkin*, 141–42, who sees marriage with Jane as "solipsistic . . . self-extinction."

9. Bargen, *Fiction*, 177–84, uses *rape* and *rapist* to describe Ashenden's encounter with the bear. If *rape* applies here, Ashenden is the one being raped. He believes that satisfying the bear is the only way to save his life. His subsequent pleasure does not make him a rapist.

10. Erdinger, "Bears in Fictions," 144; LeClair, "Obsessional Fiction," 161.

11. Bargen, *Fiction*, 236–37. On the genesis, see also Sanders, "Interview," 145. Discussing the novella, Bargen concludes that resemblances between "The Making of Ashenden" and "The Bear" are broadly thematic and that Ashenden resembles Bellow's Henderson more than Faulkner's Ike McCaslin.

12. Stanley Elkin, *The Living End* (New York: E. P. Dutton, 1979), 54; hereafter cited in the text as *LE*.

13. Raff, "Lewis and Elkin," 1–8. Chapter 1 discusses Raff's position and Elkin's rejection of the label "satirist."

14. Northrop Frye, *Anatomy of Criticism: Four Essays* (New York: Atheneum, 1969), 223; Raff, "Lewis and Elkin," 7.

15. Raff, "Lewis and Elkin," 6. Raff sees Quiz as the only "sensible" character, or "obsessive intelligence" (a term from *Boswell*), who can operate in a random universe.

16. Connaughton, "Stanley Elkin," 892: "he created the universe and controls human destinies for the same reasons a novelist creates a story." Wilde, *Horizons*, 158: "less artist than aesthete, the reflexive Creator whose murky design exposes in himself and in the world the absence of any moral center," a "prototypical exponent of art for art's sake." Heide Ziegler, "Postromantic Irony in Postmodernist Times," in *Representation and Performance in Postmodern Fiction*, ed. Maurice Couturier (Montpelier: Delta, 1982), 97: "God Himself assumes the role of ultimate artist, creating the world as a place of hope and despair because it would make for a better story." Bailey, *Reading Elkin*, 185: "the value that underlies all of Elkin's God's creation" is one that "underlies all of Elkin's own creations as well."

Chapter Eight

1. Stanley Elkin, *Criers and Kibitzers, Kibitzers and Criers* (New York: Random House, 1966); hereafter cited in the text as *CK*. Stanley Elkin, "The Graduate Seminar," *Fiction* 1 (1972):10–11, expanded in *Early Elkin*; Stanley Elkin, *Early Elkin* (Flint, Mich.: Bamberger Books, 1985); Stanley Elkin, "Corporate Life," *Chicago* 34 (March 1985):157–59. Stanley Elkin, "What's in a Name? The 1987 Elizabeth and Stewart Credence Memorial Lecture," *Denver Quarterly* 21 (1985): 109–26, like Elkin's account of his meetings with Nabokov, takes the form of autobiographical reminiscence, but is entirely fictional.

2. David Galloway, who considers this "one of the most important collections of short stories published in recent years," argues that the first story, "Criers and Kibitzers," sounds a "note of unrelieved despair," whereas the last, "Perlmutter at the East Pole," "echoes with a moving shout for the human spirit." "Visions of Life in Recent Fiction," *Southern Review* 4 (1968):860.

3. See Bargen, *Dictionary of Literary Biography*, 2:131: "Most of Elkin's fiction is dominated by orphaned protagonists who are obsessed with a professional life they cherish in lieu of a family life." See also Bargen, "Orphan Adopted" and *Fiction*. Chapter 3 mentions my reservations about applying this concept too liberally, but the key point is that the orphan represents an extreme synecdoche for alienation.

4. See Ditsky, "'Death as Grotesque as Life,'" 5: "Allying himself, dangerously, with those he considers archetypal outsiders, . . . he courts some sort of ritual, self-sacrificial death."

5. Hardaway, "The Power of the Guest," 240.

6. Bargen, *Fiction*, 261–62.

Conclusion

1. Duncan, "Conversation with Elkin and Gass," 77.

2. Ezra Pound, *Guide to Kulchur* (1930; New York: New Directions, 1968), 83.

Selected Bibliography

PRIMARY WORKS

Novels and Stories

Boswell: A Modern Comedy. New York: Random House, 1964. Novel.
Criers and Kibitzers, Kibitzers and Criers. New York: Random House, 1966. Stories.
A Bad Man. New York: Random House, 1967. Novel.
The Dick Gibson Show. New York: Random House, 1971. Novel.
Searches and Seizures. New York: Random House, 1973. Novellas. British edition, *Eligible Men.* London: Gollancz, 1974.
The Franchiser. New York: Farrar, Straus & Giroux, 1976. Novel.
The Living End. New York: E. P. Dutton, 1979. Novellas.
Stanley Elkin's Greatest Hits. New York: E. P. Dutton, 1980. Stories and Novellas.
The First George Mills. Dallas, Texas: Pressworks, 1980. Part I of *George Mills.* Illustrations by Jane E. Hughes. Limited Edition, 350 signed copies.
George Mills. New York: E. P. Dutton, 1982. Novel.
Early Elkin. Flint, Mich.: Bamberger Books, 1985. Stories and a "reading memoir."
Stanley Elkin's The Magic Kingdom. New York: E. P. Dutton, 1985. Novel.
"Corporate Life." *Chicago* 34 (March 1985):157–59. Story.
The Rabbi of Lud. New York: Charles Scribner's Sons, 1987. Novel.
The Six-Year-Old Man. Flint, Mich.: Bamberger Books, 1987. Screenplay.
The MacGuffin. Novel in progress.

Nonfiction

"Religious Themes and Symbolism in the Novels of William Faulkner." Ph.D. dissertation, University of Illinois, 1961.
"Miss Taylor and Family: An Outside View." *Esquire* 62 (November 1964):43, 44, 46, 118, 120.
"The Six-Year Old Man: A Screenplay." *Esquire* 70 (December 1968):142–45, 226, 228, 232–33, 236–37, 240, 244, 246–47, 251–53.
"Three Meetings." *Tri-Quarterly* 17 (Winter 1970):261–65. Reprinted in *Tri-Quarterly* 63 (Winter 1985):155–59 and in *Nabokov.* Edited by Alfred Appel and Charles Newman. Evanston: Northwestern University Press, 1970.
Introduction to *Stories from the Sixties.* Edited by Stanley Elkin. Garden City, N.Y.: Doubleday, 1971.

"The World on $5 a Day." *Harper's Magazine* 245 (July 1972):41–46.
"Inside Jean-Louis Trintigant." *Oui* 2 (January 1973):84–86, 166, 168–69, 172–74.
"A La Recherche du Whoopee Cushions." *Esquire* 82 (July 1974):126–29.
"Plot." *SubStance* 27 (1980):70–74.
"Why I Live Where I Live." *Esquire* 94 (November 1980):108–11.
Introduction to *The Best American Short Stories 1980*. Edited by Stanley Elkin and Shannon Ravenel. Boston: Houghton Mifflin, 1980.
"Representation and Performance." In *Representation and Performance in Postmodern Fiction*. Edited by Maurice Couturier, pp. 181–91. Proceedings of the Nice Conference on Postmodern Fiction, April 1982. Montpelier: Delta, 1983.
"Performance and Reality." *Grand Street* 2 (Summer 1983):110–22.
"My Tuxedo: A Meditation." *Chicago* 34 (May 1985):154–57. Excerpted as "In Praise of Tuxedos." *Harper's* 271 (November 1985):32–35.
"Alfred Kinsey: The Patron Saint of Sex." *Esquire* 100 (December 1986):48, 50, 53, 55.
"Summer: A True Confession." *Chicago* 35 (June 1986):161–64.
"What's in a Name? The 1987 Elizabeth and Stewart Credence Memorial Lecture." *Denver Quarterly* 21 (Spring 1987):109–26. Excerpted as "Stanley Elkin on Stanleyness." *Harper's* 276 (May 1988):36–37.
"My Father's Life." *Chicago* 36 (June 1987):185–94.
"Acts of Scholarship." *Chicago* 36 (September 1987):168–73.
"The Muses Are Heard: Dancing in the Heart of Regional Arts." *Harper's* 277 (December 1988):62–71.
"Talk Up! The First Amendment as Art Form." *Grand Street* 8 (Winter 1989):94–107.

SECONDARY WORKS

Interviews

"An Interview with Stanley Elkin." *AWP Newsletter* (February–March 1988):1, 10–14.
Bargen, Doris. "An Interview with Stanley Elkin." In her *The Fiction of Stanley Elkin*, 213–65. Frankfurt: Peter D. Lang, 1980.
Bernt, Phyllis, and **Bernt, Joseph.** "Stanley Elkin on Fiction: An Interview." *Prairie Schooner* 50 (1975):14–25.
Chénetier, Marc. "An Interview with Stanley Elkin." *Delta 20* (February 1985):15–25.
Clayton, Jay. "An Interview with Stanley Elkin." *Contemporary Literature* 24 (1983):1–11.

Dougherty, David C. "A Conversation with Stanley Elkin." *Literary Review* (Winter 1991).

Duncan, Jeffrey. "A Conversation with Stanley Elkin and William H. Gass." *Iowa Review* 7 (1975):48–77.

Earlywine, Robert. "An Interview with Stanley Elkin." *Webster Review* 8 (1983):5–16.

Gass, William H. "Adventures in the Writing Life." *Washington Post Book World*, 10 October 1982, 1, 10.

LeClair, Thomas. "Stanley Elkin: The Art of Fiction LXI." *Paris Review* 17 (Summer 1976):53–86. Reprinted in Thomas LeClair and Larry McCaffrey, eds., *Anything Can Happen: Interviews with Contemporary American Novelists.* Urbana: University of Illinois Press, 1983, 1988.

Renwick, Joyce. "Stanley Elkin: An Interview." *Mid-American Review* 5 (1985):61–67.

Sale, Richard B. "An Interview with Stanley Elkin in Saint Louis." *Studies in the Novel* 16 (1984):314–25.

Sanders, Scott R. "An Interview with Stanley Elkin." *Contemporary Literature* 16 (1974):131–45.

Strausbaugh, John. "Elkin Magic." *Baltimore City Paper* 12 May 1989, 26–28.

Bibliographies

Chénetier, Marc. "Stanley Elkin: Bibliographie Selective." *Delta* 20 (February 1985):207–14.

McCaffrey, Larry. "Stanley Elkin: A Bibliography 1957–1977." *Bulletin of Bibliography* 34 (1977):73–76.

Robbins, William M. "A Bibliography of Stanley Elkin." *Critique* 26 (1985): 169–84. Includes reviews and nonprint material.

Special Issues

Delta (Elkin Special issue) 20 (February 1985).

"Stanley Elkin and William H. Gass: A Special Feature." *Iowa Review* 7 (1975). Work in progress by each, a conversation with both, criticism.

Critical and Biographical Studies

Abrioux, Yves. "Animal et être parlant: 'The Making of Ashenden.'" *Delta* 20 (February 1985):149–80.

Bailey, Peter Joseph. "M.S. as Metaphor." *Delta* 20 (February 1985):57–71. Disease as metaphor in Elkin and Joan Didion.

————. "Pattern and Perception in the Fiction of Stanley Elkin." *Dissertation Abstracts International* 41 (1179):1585A.

————. *Reading Stanley Elkin.* Urbana: University of Illinois Press, 1985. Expanded version of thesis, includes new material on *Mills* and *End*.

—————. "Stanley Elkin's Tales of Last Resorts." *Mid-American Review* 5 (1985): 73–80. "The Condominium" and "Among the Witnesses."

Bargen, Doris. *The Fiction of Stanley Elkin.* Frankfurt: Lang, 1980. Discusses family theme in early fiction. Includes an important interview.

—————. "The Orphan Adopted: Stanley Elkin's *The Franchiser.*" *Studies in American Jewish Literature* 2 (1982):132–43.

—————. "Stanley Elkin." In *Dictionary of Literary Biography*, vol. 2: *American Novelists since World War II*, 131–36. Edited by Jeffrey Helterman and Richard Layman. Detroit: Gale Research/Bruccoli, 1974. Introductory.

—————. "Stanley Elkin." In *Dictionary of Literary Biography*, vol. 28: *Twentieth-Century Jewish-American Writers*, 47–50. Edited by David Walden. Detroit: Gale Research/Bruccoli, 1984. Elkin as a Jewish-American writer.

—————. "Stanley Elkin." In *Dictionary of Literary Biography Yearbook: 1980*, 36–40. Edited by Karen L. Rood, Jean W. Ross, and Richard Ziegfield. Detroit: Gale Research/Bruccoli, 1981.

Chénetier, Marc. "Organisme, organicisme et ecriture dans *Searches and Seizures.* *Delta* 20 (February 1985):181–206.

Colbert, Robert Edward. "The American Salesman as Pitchman and Poet in the Fiction of Stanley Elkin." *Critique* 21 (1978):52–58. Excellent discussion of Elkin's language.

Connaughton, Michael. "Stanley Elkin." In *Critical Survey of Long Fiction*, 8:884–93. Edited by Frank Magill. Englewood Cliffs, N.J.: Salem Press, 1983. Solid introduction.

Coover, Robert. Preface to *Stanley Elkin's Greatest Hits.* New York: E. P. Dutton, 1980, ix–xii. Appreciation by fellow novelist.

Couturier, Maurice. "Elkin's *George Mills*; or How to Make an Ectoplasm Schmooze." *Delta* 20 (February 1985):73–91. Poststructuralist analysis.

Danon-Boileau, Laurent. "Declinasion du non." *Delta* 20 (February 1985): 111–26. "The Condominium."

Ditsky, John. "'Death as Grotesque as Life': The Fiction of Stanley Elkin." *Hollins Critic* 19 (June 1982):1–11. Excellent survey of the early fiction.

Dittmar, Kurt. "Stanley Elkin, 'I Look Out for Ed Wolfe.'" In Peter Freese, ed., *Die Amerikanische Short Story der gegenwart: Interpretation*, 252–61. Berlin: Schmidt, 1975. In German.

Edinger, Harry G. "Bears in Three Contemporary Fictions." *Humanities Association Review* 28 (1976):141–50. Fascinating analysis of "Ashenden."

Gass, William. "Stanley Elkin's *The Franchiser.*" *New Republic* 28 (June 1980): 29–32. Reprinted as Foreword to *The Franchiser.* Boston: Godine, 1980. Brilliant account of vocation.

Guttmann, Allen. "The Black Humorists." In *The Jewish Writer in America: Assimilation and the Crisis of Identity*, 76–85. New York: Oxford University Press, 1971. Elkin as Jewish-American novelist.

Hardaway, Francine O. "The Power of the Guest: Stanley Elkin's Fiction." *Rocky*

Mountain Review of Language and Literature 32 (1977):234–45. A solid survey.

Lebowitz, Naomi. "The Twentieth-Century Novel: Old Wine in New Bottles." In *Humanism and the Absurd in the Modern Novel,* 125–28. Evanston: Northwestern University Press, 1979. Absurd and black humor.

LeClair, Thomas. "The Obsessional Fiction of Stanley Elkin." *Contemporary Literature* 16 (1974):146–62. Fine study of obsession in the early novels.

Lee, L. L. "The Anonymous American As Historian: Stanley Elkin's *Boswell.*" *Critique* 26 (1985):185–91. Novel as historical allegory.

McCaffrey, Larry. "Stanley Elkin's Recovery of the Ordinary." *Critique* 21 (1978): 39–51. Important study of language in *Franchiser.*

Molesworth, Charles. "Stanley Elkin and 'Everything': The Problem of Surfaces and Fullness in the Novels." *Delta* 20 (February 1985):93–100. Elkin as "mid-fictionist."

Morace, Robert. "George Mills." In *Magill's Literary Annual 1983,* 1:273–77. Edited by Frank Magill: Englewood Cliffs, N.J.: Salem Press, 1983. Good overview.

Olderman, Raymond M. "The Fisher King Turns Warden." In *Beyond the Waste Land: A Study of the American Fiction of the Nineteen-Sixties,* 52–71. New Haven: Yale University Press, 1972. *Bad Man* as grail quest; provocative.

_____. "The Six Crises of Dick Gibson." *Iowa Review* 7 (1975):127–40. Historical allegory; provocative but unconvincing.

Raff, Melvin. "Wyndham Lewis and Stanley Elkin: Salvation, Satire, and Hell." *Studies in Contemporary Satire* 8 (Spring 1981):1–8. *Living End* as satire.

Sadkin, David. "Stanley Elkin." In *Critical Survey of Short Fiction,* 4:1338–43. Edited by Frank Magill. Englewood Cliffs: Salem Press, 1981. Thin on stories, surveys novellas.

Sammarcelli, Françoise. "Comparision et interiorité dans *Searches and Seizures* de Stanley Elkin." *Delta* 20 (February 1985):127—47.

Saltzman, Arthur M. "Ego and Appetite in Stanley Elkin's Fiction." *Literary Review* 32 (1988):111–18. Excellent discussion of integration of plot and rhetoric in the fiction.

Tanner, Tony. *City of Words: American Fiction, 1950–1970.* New York: Harper & Row, 1971.

Watts, Emily Stipes. "The Businessman as Hero." In *The Businessman in American Literature,* 137–43. Athens: University of Georgia Press, 1982. *Bad Man* and *Franchiser* as positive images of the businessman.

Wilde, Alan. "A Map of Supersensiveness: Irony in the Postmodern Age." In *Horizons of Assent: Modernism, Postmodernism, and the Ironic Imagination,* 127–65. Baltimore: Johns Hopkins University Press, 1981. "Bailbondsman" and *Living End* as "postmodern irony."

Index